ECONOMIC SANITY
or COLLAPSE

ECONOMIC SANITY or COLLAPSE

Including the Roman-Loebl Approach to Economics

Gerald R. Zoffer

McGraw-Hill Book Company

NEW YORK
ST. LOUIS
SAN FRANCISCO
TORONTO
DÜSSELDORF
MEXICO
LONDON
SYDNEY

1 2 3 4 5 6 7 8 9 0   D O D O   8 7 6 5 4 3 2 1 0

LIBRARY OF CONGRESS CATALOGING IN PUBLICATION DATA
Zoffer, Gerald R.
   Economic sanity or collapse.

   Includes index.
   1. Economic history—1945–   2. United
States—Economic policy—1971–   I. Title.
HC59.Z63   330.9'04   79-21091
ISBN 0-07-072860-7

Book design by ROBERTA REZK.

SPECIAL ACKNOWLEDGMENT

In writing a book as iconoclastic and trail-blazing as this one, it was first necessary to rid oneself of many preconceived notions about the nature of economics. It fell to Dr. Eugen Loebl to spend many patient hours with me accomplishing that end. Beyond that lay the new ideas incorporated in the Roman-Loebl approach to economics, ideas which, if applied, could very well spell the difference between a viable American economy and a collapsing one.

Without Dr. Loebl's aid in shedding new light on the economic past, and making recommendations for new approaches to such pressing problems as inflation, taxation and the role of government in the economy, this book could not have been written.

Gerald R. Zoffer

CONTENTS

INTRODUCTION

The United States has come to a point in its history where it is faced with the choice of economic sanity or collapse.

The crisis has been brought on by the application of fallacious concepts, and increasing government interference in the economy, which have given us inflation, high involuntary unemployment, and falling productivity. We are being taken down the same road to the welfare state traveled by Britain under the former Labour government, and Sweden.

The economic catastrophe staring us in the face involves no less than runaway inflation leading to the total collapse of the American dollar. Some experts already aver that we have passed the point of no return, that the debasement of the American dollar, despite respites, will continue until there is some final appalling blowup.

When we look to conventional economists for a way out of our dilemma, we find their thinking to be bankrupt. When we look to government for corrective change, we encounter massive bureaucratic inertia. *Economic Sanity or Collapse* will address these problems, outline them, locate their roots and antecedents in history, and offer a way out.

Economic Sanity—or Collapse is iconoclastic in two major respects. To begin with, it doesn't accept textbook explanations of economics. It tries to show that for the 200 years since the Industrial Revolution, tacitly accepted economic approaches and concepts have for the most part been fallacious, misleading, or inadequate. Second, it promulgates a different approach to economic problems, one designed to swing us away from possible collapse and toward economic stability.

This new approach was developed by Stephen Roman, a prominent Canadian industrialist, and Professor Eugen Loebl, former Marxist and world-renowned economist, and is embodied in a book on which they collaborated, *The Responsible Society* (Regina Ryan, Two Continents Publishing Group, Ltd., New York, 1977).

Stephen Roman, a Slovak, emigrated to Canada from Czechoslovakia at an early age. Starting out as a laborer, he rose to become the owner of a multi-billion-dollar empire comprised of uranium and coal mines, oil and gas deposits, and building and insurance companies. He is a practical, no-nonsense businessman who knows what is feasible and what isn't.

Dr. Loebl is also a Slovak who was born and grew up in Czechoslovakia. He became a Marxist and in the 1940s was appointed first Deputy Minister of Foreign Trade for his country. In 1949 he was ordered by the Russians to stop trading with the West. Placing the needs of his country above ideology, he refused, and was sentenced to life imprisonment. He remained in prison for eleven years, five of them in solitary confinement. It was during those years that he pondered the essence of Marxism and capitalism and developed the ideas to be found in this book. Dr. Loebl was released through friendly intervention in 1960, rehabilitated, and appointed Director of the Czechoslovak State Bank. He was picked to join the ill-fated Dubcek government when, in 1968, the Russians and their minions invaded Czechoslovakia. Loebl fled the country, eventually reaching the United States, where he now resides.

Loebl and Roman first met in New York in 1974 and discovered, to their surprise, that their criticisms and remedies for economic and social problems coincided.

L'Osservatore Romano, the official newspaper of the Vactican, has praised the Roman-Loebl approach to economics, the first time in history that the Vatican has openly espoused a particular economic outlook.

Morarji Desai, Prime Minister of India, personally invited Dr. Loebl to visit him to expound on his concepts. A special chapter in this book, "Third World Economics," deals with the Roman–Loebl approach as applicable to India.

Conventional economics denies the human element, isolating itself from the real world of human interactions, treating itself as a "hard" science, like physics. By such an approach economics is reduced to mere equations.

Conversely, the Roman–Loebl approach begins by affirming economics as the sum total of human beings living and working with each other. It applies the Judeo-Christian philosophy, with its regard for the human being, to the economic sphere; and it sets forth solutions to economic problems within those parameters.

This approach is the most dramatic breakthrough in economic thinking since Adam Smith and Karl Marx. It is the only way out of the economic impasse in which we find ourselves.

PART ONE

An Economy in Disarray

The problems that face the United States today are a high unemployment rate, a huge balance-of-trade deficit, lagging productivity, rising labor costs, inadequate investment and a continuing inflation.

—Council of Economic Advisers

A sense of alienation from government has been growing among the American people.

—Mobil Oil Company advertisement

The expanding role of government in managing national income and wealth is perhaps the most powerful economic fact of the twentieth century.

—George and Joan Melloan
The Carter Economy(1978)

Unfortunately, all the rhetoric about deficits and balanced budgets obscures the real danger that confronts us: the gradual disintegration of our free society.

You asked, Mr. Chairman, about the consequences of deficits. But we all know what they are. We all know that neither man nor business nor government can spend more than is taken in for very long. If it continues, the results must be bankruptcy.

In the case of the federal government, we can print money to pay for our folly for a time. But we will continue to debase our currency, and then we'll have financial collapse. That is the road we are on today. That is the direction in which the "humanitarians" are leading us.

That is why we must be concerned about the cancerous growth of government and its steady devouring of our citizens' productive energies. That is why we must be concerned about deficits and balancing the budget. The issue is not bookkeeping. It is not accounting. The issue is the liberty of the American people.

—William E. Simon, former Secretary of the Treasury,
testifying before a House Subcommittee on Democratic
Research Organization, April 30, 1976

Our economy is out of control, our currency is in danger, our institutions of government are unresponsive or inept . . . We are at war today. With inflation, with unemployment, with lack of education, with racial discrimination. We are,

further, not winning. If we lose, our system of government may not survive. . . . *America's problems are increasing deficits papered over by accounting gimmicks, increasing reliance on borrowed money to finance those deficits, large hidden liabilities in the form of unfunded pensions and Social Security and the loss of private sector jobs because of high taxes and low productivity.*
—Felix Rohatyn, former chairman of the Municipal Assistance
Corporation and senior partner in Lazard Freres and Company

The fiscal posture of the government is excessive and virtually without historical precedent.
—Henry Kaufman, General Partner,
Solomon Brothers, Summer, 1978

Carter's fiscal follies will drag us down to perdition.
—French President Giscard d'Estaing, at Copenhagen
summit meeting of European leaders, April 1978

The primary source of inflationary pressures has been the federal budget and the programs it finances.
Business Week editorial, April 30, 1979

RAGING INFLATION IN THE SEVENTIES

1

With an inexorable month by month rise in prices and with wages playing catch-up, it is no surprise that Americans consider inflation the single most pressing problem of the 1970s. It may, however, come as a shock to many that neither the Carter administration nor the previous administrations dating all the way back to the days of Franklin Delano Roosevelt have come up with any effective way of curbing inflation, let alone eliminating it from the economic picture.

In 1979 the American economy was in its fourth year of growth and expansion, yet federal deficits remained awesomely large. They have risen steadily since 1965, moved up sharply into the $60 billion per annum range when Carter became president in 1976, and have dropped only moderately, with even that drop attributed to the move by Congress to simply postpone certain 1979 spendings to 1980. Counting off-budget spending, the 1979 federal deficit is expected to reach $61.4 billion.

Average Americans are hard-pressed to understand how an economy that has hitherto provided them with the highest standard of living in history suddenly seems to be out of control. Prices rise without letup, taxes increase beyond endurance, and actual take-home pay decreases for workers. Inflation is literally destroying the middle class of the United States, driving it into the ranks of those who rely, wholly or in part, on the beneficence of the federal government. Life for those on fixed incomes, like senior citizens and the indigent, has become unendurable. Meanwhile, the federal government goes its merry way, spending prodigiously, oblivious to the cries of anguish and frustration from the electorate.

Such a pattern has taken on a life of its own, with all protests countered by the assertion that "the people" won't stand for large cutbacks in federal spending. On close examination, "the people" turn out to be special interests benefiting from the federal programs subject to criticism.

We know how President Franklin Delano Roosevelt applied Keynesian thinking to the United States economy back in the 1930s. His deficit spending programs did stimulate the economy but never cured unemployment; indeed, it took the Second World War to pull the country out of its economic doldrums. But politicians, being what they are, recognized the voting appeal of making government a generous "Big Daddy" to the people. Whereas Keynes had advocated government deficit spending only during times of excessive unemployment (for instance, when the economy was in the trough of a business cycle), the politicians saw no reason why deficit spending should not become a permanent feature of the economy, good times and bad. After all, with hardly any effort, one could find hundreds—thousands—of areas where government could dispense funds with the knowledge that the beneficiaries would show their appreciation at the polls.

The Tragedy of Currency Debasement

Washington politicians are notoriously inured to grass-roots complaints, and only when the clamor can no longer be disregarded do they deign to make token reductions in spending, or pass superficial tax cuts. Even then, these actions have a schizophrenic quality. When one examines the bills passed by the Ninety-fifth Congress since January 1977, a humanitarian spirit seems to be present, at first glance. But note: A cut in income taxes was offset by a substantial increase in Social Security tax; tax credits for home insulation and the installment of solar equipment was offset by higher utility bills from the gradual decontrol of natural gas prices. Other important bills unashamedly added to inflation: annual average pay increases of six percent for some 3.5 million white collar employees and military personnel; curbs on strip mining and new restrictions on offshore oil and gas drilling to please the environmentalists; larger pensions for veterans, an increase in the minimum wage, and billions more for welfare.

When prices and wages rise and productivity falls and government nonproductive spending continues unabated, one inexorable result must be the debasement of the currency— precisely what has occurred. If the value of the American dollar in 1939 was 100 percent, by mid-1978 it was worth only 21.2 percent. The dollar lost 10 percent of its value between March 1977 and August 1978. It is estimated that each 5 percent decline in the dollar adds one-half to three-quarters of a percentage point to the U.S. Consumer Price Index after one year. And if inflation maintains its pace of 1978, the 1988 American dollar will be worth less than ten cents.

It was John Maynard Keynes himself who warned against such debasement decades ago. In his *Economic Consequences of Peace* (1920), he wrote:

> *By a continuing process of inflation governments can confiscate secretly and unobserved an important part of the wealth of their citizens. There is no subtler, no surer means of overthrowing the existing basis of society than to debauch the currency. The process engages all the hidden forces of economic law on the side of destruction and does it in a manner which not one man in a million is able to diagnose.*

It has taken some forty years, but it has finally sunk into the consciousness of the American people that the Keynesian concept of government spending as a remedy for investment shortages is one of the basic causes of inflation and the unhealthy performance of the American economic system. It has dawned upon Americans that they are, in the words of *Business Week* magazine, the victims of "the Great Government Inflation Machine."

An Economic "General" Reviews Inflation Data

A good general, assuming command of an army during wartime, will immediately ask to be apprised of the overall situation. What is the strength of the enemy? Where and how are they deployed? What back-up resources exist on either side? Is the military situation in hand or has it been deteriorating? What is the enemy's state of morale? Our own?

An economic "general" asked to take charge of the American economy in 1979 and come up with a "battle plan" to combat inflation, the economy's greatest enemy, will first go through all available information to form an overall picture of the situation.

He will find an economy in disarray, the end result of some forty years of politically motivated economic policies. And he'll discover an antiquated tax system designed to encourage federal profligacies.

Before becoming involved in detail, the general will take note of these salient facts:

—Until 1928, total government spending in the United States never exceeded 10 percent of the national income. Total federal spending never exceeded 3 percent of the national income, and most of that was for the army and navy.

—In 1929 government expenditures—federal, state, and local—were 11 percent in proportion to the Gross National Product; in 1978 they were 37 percent.

—Consumer prices have risen an astounding 373 percent since 1939. Incredibly, from 1973 to 1975, the years of the worst recession since the depression of the 1930s, prices rose by 21 percent. Prices have climbed 11.4 percent during the time Carter has been president. Food costs rose 10 percent in 1978 and rose even faster in 1979—an estimated 18 percent!

—The federal budget has been in balance for only five of the twenty-nine years since 1950.

—Runaway federal spending has fueled inflation more than any other single factor. Total federal deficits from 1970 through 1978 were $289 billion, and the 1979 deficit, contrary to government expectations, is anticipated at over $50 billion, including off-budget spending.

—The minimum wage went from $2.30 to $2.65 per hour in January 1979 and is scheduled to go to $3.10 in January 1980 and $3.35 in 1981. The full impact on business costs of these increases will push prices higher and add to inflation.

—At the beginning of 1977 there was a $4.6 billion increase in the Social Security payroll tax, the first in a series of such tax increases that will total some $227 billion over the next ten years. The extent to which both prices and wages will increase to make up for these Social Security taxes can only be conjectured.

—United States productivity is down. The growth in output per man-hour has fallen off from better than 3 percent a year in the 1960s to only half that much in the mid-1970s. Figures show that 1976 and 1977 quarterly gains in output per man (annualized) averaged 1.6 percent. In 1978 productivity in the nonfarm private sector rose at the rate of .6 percent; yet labor costs have risen steadily. Hourly compensation (including wages, fringes, and the employer's share of Social Security taxes) increased about 8.5 percent a year from early 1975 through 1977. In 1978 it went above 9 percent, and now is running at the rate of 10 percent in 1979.

—Thanks to inflation and higher taxes, it now takes $25,000 a year to give a family of four the buying power it had with $13,200 in 1970.

—In 1930 transfer payments—benefits moved from one economic class to another through government action (i.e., insurance, pensions, food stamps, etc.)—were equal to 3 percent of America's total wage-salary bill. In 1978 they were

21 percent, a matter of some $250 billion. According to a detailed study made by the Institute for Socioeconomic Studies in White Plains, New York, funds appropriated for transfer programs in 1977 came to 70 percent of all federal tax receipts, 29 percent of personal consumption expenditures, and 19 percent of the Gross National Product.

—Over the past decade, spending for research and development in the United States has increased in real terms at an annual rate of only 2.5 percent. Says *Business Week*, "Far too many Research and Development dollars are being spent by companies to meet federal safety, health and environmental regulations, rather than to develop new products and processes." This development is all the more sad when one considers that technological innovation generated almost half of the nation's growth from 1929 to 1969.

—Although reported corporate profits in 1979 were double those of a decade ago and have increased almost 50 percent in the five-year period between 1973 and 1978, a different picture emerges with proper accounting for inflation. It shows that true profits after taxes are up only one-third from those a decade ago, which means that in real terms they are down.

—*Business Week*, March 19, 1979, reported that, on paper, U.S. business earned a record $202 billion before taxes in 1978 and $118 billion after. In each case that was 16 percent more than was earned in 1977 and 68 percent more than was earned in 1975. However, more than $42 billion of 1978's after-tax earnings "simply vanish after phantom inventory gains are extracted and depreciation expense is raised to reflect more accurately the true cost of replacing aging assets at a time when inflation is raging unchecked."

—In 1978 business incurred an $84 billion tax bill, which is $17 billion more than it would have been had the assessment been based on adjusted rather than illusory profits. Also, business set aside $69 billion in retained earnings, which should be enough to finance future growth. "But," points out *Business Week*, "when retained earnings are adjusted for inflation and underdepreciation, the amount kept by business shrinks to an effective $27 billion. That is less than companies retained in 1977 and no better than companies did in the mid-1960s."

—Because of inflation, companies are understating depreciation allowances because the cost of replacing assets is far below what companies are allowed to recover. The Commerce Department has admitted that if the replacement cost of aging assets had been more accurately measured, reported corporate profits in 1978 alone would have been $18 billion lower. In effect, companies are unwittingly decapitalizing themselves.

—Because of inflation at home, the American dollar's value has been declining abroad. As a result, many imports, including steel; foreign cars; machinery; radios and TV sets, have become more expensive, making it easier for U.S. producers to boost prices at home.

—United States-produced crude oil now costs more than twice what it did in 1973. The price of OPEC oil is nearly five times what it was.

—The cost of federal regulatory demands to industry is staggering. Next to nonproductive federal programs, there is nothing that has fueled inflation so much as added costs, passed along to consumers, mandated by regulatory agency decrees.

THE FEDERAL REGULATORY AGENCIES:

MODERN-DAY DINOSAURS

2

The statistics quoted in the previous chapter reveal only a small part of the American economic story. They are part of more ponderous forms representing huge government outlays, actual and potential. The "general" we have placed in charge of the economy will have no trouble identifying some of the major "bodies" in the economic continuum: regulatory agencies, social services, income transfer programs, and potential monsters like a national health plan. The continuum itself is ruled by a philosophy rooted in the politician's love of spending in good times and bad. When President Carter was elected, it was partially on the basis of his promise to reduce the bloated federal budget. Instead, he substantially increased the budget that President Ford left behind. Added were $7 billion for income security; $3 billion for health; $12 billion for education, job programs, and social services; $1.7 billion for community and regional development; and $3.5 billion for agriculture. Total additions: $27.2 billion. The sole decrease was for national defense—$5.5 billion.

To understand a little of what has happened and is continuing to happen in the United States economy (a detailed picture is beyond the purview of a single book), one must educate oneself in a few major areas of government spending; in particular, federal regulatory agencies. Consider the possibilities if these agencies had existed at the turn of the century.

How the United States Never Entered the Automobile Age

In 1908 an American inventive genius named Henry Ford began production of an automobile he called the Model T, and announced plans for a mass-produced, inexpensive automobile that would put America on wheels and change the face of the nation. The Model T was offered at $850, roughly half the cost of automobiles being sold at the time.

Ford was self-schooled, the homespun, self-reliant type of American still celebrated in folklore. In one sense that was good, because Ford didn't have to unlearn what the educated experts knew couldn't be done; but in another sense Ford was at a great disadvantage: He had never bothered to acquaint himself with the function of federal regulatory agencies. To him, the Environmental Protection Agency (EPA), Federal Trade Commission (FTC), Occupational Safety and Health Administration (OSHA), Equal Employment Opportunity Commission (EEOC), and Securities and Exchange Commission (SEC) were just so many bureaucratic names. Also, he had never taken notice of self-styled consumer protection groups, particularly one headed by an egalitarian attorney named Rafe Crowder.

Had Ford known at the beginning of his ordeal what awaited him, it is doubtful whether he would have followed through with his imaginative plan to bring out a serviceable automobile at an affordable price.

The automobile originated in France. During the first years of the twentieth century the American car was nothing more than an imported toy for the wealthy. A typical auto sold for about fifteen hundred dollars, which effectively put it beyond the reach of the masses. In 1907, Woodrow Wilson, president of Princeton University, cautioned students against the automobile, terming it a "picture of the arrogance of wealth." It hardly seemed worthwhile to issue a warning because no more than eight thousand automobiles, or "horseless carriages" as they were called, were in use in the United States in 1900. This small number did not merit the attention or concern of the federal regulatory agencies or consumer protection groups.

The picture changed when word spread that Henry Ford was out to build millions of automobiles. Regulators and zealous consumer groups descended on Ford like a swarm of bees.

Ford was a reticent man by nature, and the thought of subjecting himself to federal interrogation appalled him. However, his advisers told him that there was no other way if he wanted to build automobiles. They pointed out to him that a veritable mountain of products—drugs, toys, household appliances, foods, furniture, etcetera, had either never been marketed or had been driven from the market by the regulatory agencies, and it was therefore best to try to meet their arguments and demands.

"What do they want?" asked Ford.

"We won't know until we give them information, and lots of it," was the answer.

Ford had forebodings as he morosely contemplated the situation. Automobiles were his whole life. Take away his dream of building a "universal car" as he fondly called his Model T, and there was nothing worth living for. "I'll face them," he said.

As a starter, Ford was inundated by a Niagara of forms that had to be filled out. There were thousands of them asking detailed questions about every aspect of his operation, from manufacturing to hiring practices. "I'm going to need an army of clerks sitting around doing nothing but filling out forms," wailed Ford. "I can't afford it."

"Raise the price of your automobile to cover the cost," his advisers told him.

"But I was planning to reduce the cost to $360 in a few years, if I sell enough Model Ts," Ford said.

"Then you'll go broke," he was cautioned. "Bureaucrats need information like a thirsty man needs water. Tons of paper work is the only thing they can show to justify their existence. If you don't give them their forms, they'll put you right out of business."

Shortly thereafter, it was announced that the price of the Model T was being raised to one thousand dollars.

When inspectors from the Environmental Protection Agency tested the Model T they were appalled. The head of the EPA personally announced that millions of Model T automobiles would create massive air pollution. "It's a foul smelling contraption," he said.

A federal subcommittee closely questioned Ford:

"Isn't it true, Mr. Ford," a spokesman for the committee said, "that automobile drivers have to wear linen dusters, goggles, and a veil for protection from the clouds of dust raised by automobiles in motion?"

"That's because roads are bad. Dirt roads raise dust," Ford replied.

"I suppose you read Arthur J. Eddy's book *Two Thousand Miles in an Automobile* that came out in 1902. He went twenty miles an hour on rutty roads, with a puncture and a tire change every hundred miles."

"No, sir," Ford said. "I didn't read it. I'm not much of a reader."

"Well, I read it. Bad roads means expensive automobile upkeep for Americans. Are you going to spend your own money building better roads for your automobiles to drive on?"

"No, sir. I build automobiles, nothing but."

"Then it's a matter of indifference to you if millions of your automobiles raise huge clouds of dust that get into people's eyes, noses, and throats?"

"No, I care, but there's nothing I can do about that. If people want to drive automobiles, they have to put up with inconveniences," Ford said.

"And what about the foul smell the EPA says the Model T gives off?" the spokesman persisted.

"That's from oil and fumes."

"Health hazards, wouldn't you agree, Mr. Ford?"

"Like I said, people want to drive, they have to put up with inconveniences."

Of course, the EPA didn't see it that way at all. The agency demanded changes in the Model-T design to eliminate fumes and to reduce health hazards from dust clouds raised by the moving vehicles. For good measure, they also demanded changes to reduce the noise level of the Model T as it chugged along. "People can't hear themselves talk," was the complaint.

"I'm not sure I can do all that," said Ford. "And if I could, it would take a lot of money."

"Raise the price of your automobile to cover the cost," said his advisers.

But Ford decided to see what else was expected of him before making any decision.

The Occupational Safety and Health Administration (OSHA) sent inspectors to Ford's factory and came away with a long list of infractions. They included such things as untidy washrooms, inadequate lighting, unsafe working conditions, and excessive noise. The cost of meeting OSHA demands was hopelessly beyond Ford.

"Raise the price of your automobile," said his advisers.

The Equal Employment Opportunity Commission (EEOC) was hostile to Ford from the beginning. "Ford makes no allowance for women and minorities," said the agency. It demanded comprehensive programs from Ford to train and employ women, blacks, Hispanics, Eskimos, and the handicapped. "We're not going to let you operate like some medieval lord," the EEOC told Ford. "We want regular submissions from you on your hiring practices, and we'll prosecute vigorously if you don't comply with agency regulations."

"You mean, I can't hire who I want to hire?" asked Ford.

"Yes, you can, as long as you stay within our guidelines," was the answer. "Your workers must include a certain percentage of women, minorities, and so forth. And don't forget the training programs."

The Federal Trade Commission (FTC), responsible for protecting businesses from unfair competition, was concerned with Ford's plan for mass production of automobiles.

"How much is your Model T selling for?" asked the agency.

"It was selling for $850," replied Ford, "but it's been upped to $1,000, just hiring people to fill out federal forms." He thought to himself: And it's going to go a hell of a lot higher if I give in to these leeches.

"That's a much lower price than your competition," said the FTC. It sounded like an accusation.

"I was planning for it to come way down from that," said Ford.

"Like what?"

"Like $360," said Ford.

"That would destroy all competition," said the FTC. "You could very well become the only automobile manufacturer in the United States."

"I hope so," Ford said.

"No, Mr. Ford," the FTC said. "We couldn't allow that. That's monopoly."

"I thought building a better mousetrap is the American way," said Ford.

"Not when it leads to monopoly," said the FTC.

Ford was incredulous. "Do you expect me to make the price

of my automobile artificially high just to keep some inefficient, overpriced automobile makers in business?" he asked.

"It's not in our jurisdiction to tell you how to price your automobile," snapped the FTC. "We're concerned only with the danger of monopoly."

It was a Catch-22 situation decades before the phrase became known.

Rafe Crowder, self-styled consumer protectionist, came along to get in his licks.

"Your Model T is built to go thirty, maybe forty miles an hour, isn't that right?" he asked.

"That's right," said Ford.

"Have you thought of the danger to pedestrians of millions of automobiles traveling at those speeds?"

"People have to get used to automobiles."

Crowder pounced. "Get used to putting their lives in jeopardy every time there's an automobile around? What if a tire punctures? What if the driver falls ill and loses control of the wheel? What if some pedestrian can't move fast enough to get out of the way of a moving automobile?" Without waiting for answers he plowed on: "Your Model T doesn't even have windshield wipers or a rearview mirror, is that right?"

"That's right. Anyone can put them on, if they want to. I'm trying to keep my prices down."

"At the expense of safety to the people," shouted Crowder. "Did you know that the fenders on your automobile tend to soften and wrinkle?"

"I've heard tell," said Ford.

"That's dangerous in a collision," accused Crowder. "And your head lights, how far will the beams shine at night?"

"Far enough."

"That's not a good enough answer, Mr. Ford. You need tests, lots of tests. Also, your automobile horn. Do you know that the sound frightens people and horses?"

"Have to have a horn," retorted Ford.

"But have you thought of experimenting with different types of sound?" asked Crowder. "Maybe something less jarring, more pleasant."

"Horses scare, no matter what," said Ford.

"There are a lot of horses on the roads of America," said Crowder. "The horn is a menace to them, especially when they're pulling buggies. By the way, your automobile body is made of wood, isn't it?"

"That's right."

"Don't you know what happens to wood in bad weather?"

"I plan to switch to metal, once I sell enough automobiles," said Ford.

"That's the future, Mr. Ford. We're talking about now. Do you really think an automobile is safe that has a gasoline engine geared to the rear axle by a bicycle chain?" Crowder didn't wait for an answer. "And the gasoline tank is under the front seat. What if it should explode in an accident?"

"People might get hurt," admitted Ford.

"My organization is going to press Congress for new, strict laws on automobiles," said Crowder. "We are not going to stand idly by while your tin lizzies, as they're aptly named, endanger life and limb and pollute our air. As far as I'm concerned, the Model T is unsafe at any speed."

Crowder was true to his word. He was adept at organization and his group was too strong for Congress not to pay attention. The Model T was attacked as a dangerous vehicle. It was also argued with great success that to allow the automobile to become a major means of transportation would mean the elimination of thousands of jobs. As one congressman put it, "We have livery stables, carriage and wagon factories, harness makers, granaries, and so forth. Are we going to stand by and allow Ford's contraption to put hundreds of companies out of business and throw thousands of people out of work—all just to feed the monstrous ego of a crude, uneducated man? I say to you, the automobile is not that important to us. I'm happy with the horse and buggy, and so are millions of decent, law-abiding Americans."

As for the federal regulatory agencies, they knew what they wanted and wouldn't settle for anything else.

Between everything, Henry Ford did some mental calculations and came to the conclusion that he would have to sell his Model T for somewhere in the neighborhood of five thousand dollars to satisfy all regulatory demands for product and factory changes, and to meet the cost of federally demanded paper work. Beyond that would be the cost of high legal fees fighting continuous government investigations.

Ford quietly closed up shop, and the automobile remained what it was before he came along—an imported toy for the wealthy.

And that's the story of how the United States never entered the automobile age.

The Cost of Regulation

In the past fifteen years, almost 250 agencies, departments, bureaus, and commissions were created to help the federal government function. When Jimmy Carter was running for president he singled out the "wasteful, inefficient, and duplicative" regulatory agencies and vowed that the 1,900 federal agencies would be cut to around 200 if he were elected. He did abolish 760 federal units in two years, but created 350 more.

In 1979 some forty-one government agencies were busy "regulating" some part of the American economy. As a matter of fact, one should really say "most" of the economy instead of just "some part" because there was hardly an area left untouched by the regulators. They were regulating product safety; food package labels; advertising; drugs and transportation; hiring, firing, and working conditions; speed limits and community relations; and factory changes to meet stringent environmental rules. The zealousness of the regulators was admirably summed up in a cartoon by Don Hesse of the St. Louis *Globe-Democrat* which showed an individual labeled "Government Overregulation" hammering away at a small, shapeless victim marked "The Problem" with an oversized bag inscribed "The Cost."

Willard C. Butcher, president of the Chase Manhattan Bank, stated in *Business Week* (November 6, 1978) that according to the bank's research, in 1977 government regulation cost the country more than $100 billion. "More than $5 billion was for administrative costs—including federal, state and local. On the federal level alone, more than $3 billion covered the salaries and supplies of the army of 100,000 workers who staff the 41 regulatory agencies. Outlays of these agencies have increased by 100 percent over the past five years. The largest part of the $100 billion regulatory budget, about $85 billion, was in compliance costs—the price businesses and individuals paid to respond to regulation. The private sector is forced to fill out more than 4,000 different federal forms each year, an activity that last year took upwards of 143 million man-hours at a cost—including legal fees, salaries, benefits and overhead—of $25 billion. The steel industry alone has to comply with some 5,600 regulations administered by 26 different federal agencies. General Motors Corp. spends more than $1 billion per year—equal to 2 percent of its sales and one-third of its net profits—to comply with regulations imposed by all levels of government.

"The bulk of 1977 compliance costs—a huge $32 billion—went to the area of pollution, abatement and control."

Butcher estimated the loss of income from having to invest in nonproductive rather than productive projects at $13 billion for 1977.

Murray L. Weidenbaum, former assistant secretary of the Treasury and now director of the Center for the Study of American Business at Washington University in St. Louis, agrees with Butcher that compliance with federal regulations will cost the private sector over $100 billion a year, or twenty percent of the entire federal budget. "Each agency," he says, "is concerned with just its own narrow interest, and it is oblivious to the effects of its actions on the company, an entire industry, or even on society as a whole. For instance, how can passenger-car manufacturers make a car that includes an array of antipollution gadgets, yet still be lighter to save gas and cheap enough for people to afford?"

Attorneys Lloyd N. Cutler and David R. Johnson state in the *Yale Law Journal* that the current regulatory picture is that of "a patchwork of specialized and fiercely independent agencies with different perspectives, whose concerns necessarily overlap and whose actions may contradict one another."

Barry Bosworth, director of the Council on Wage and Price Stability, says that "government regulation adds about three-quarters of a percent annually to the rate of inflation."

To the consumer, mere statistics don't tell the story of the cost of government regulations nearly as well as easily understood examples. In 1978, for example, the price of the average automobile went up by $666 as a result of federally mandated safety and environmental features. Regulatory requirements imposed by federal, state, and local governments in 1979 added between $1,500 and $2,500 to the cost of a typical new house.

If the cost of government regulation to the consumer translates itself into a higher price for a car or a house, then for business enterprises it translates into a marked reduction of capital investment. This is because the annual cost of meeting government regulations forces companies to cut back on the development of new technologies. Instead of being able to allocate funds for research and development, the building of a new plant, the purchase of needed equipment, or the hiring of additional employees, companies find themselves spending profits to satisfy the federal government's insatiable demand for information and compliance with illogical and wasteful regulatory demands.

The amount of paper work that flows into Washington daily

in response to government demands for corporate information is awesome, and it has been conceded that most of it remains unread; indeed, there aren't enough hours in a day for anyone to scan even a fraction of what is forwarded. However, in the world of bureaucracy a bureaucrat is judged—indeed, can only be judged—by the amount of paper work handled by his agency. The more paper work, the greater the need for more bureaucrats to handle it. Thus are bureaucratic empires built and maintained. And beyond the cost to the companies of doing this paper work lies the cost of complying with whatever directives are handed down by federal regulatory agencies eager to display their strength.

Two Types of Regulators

The budgets of the primary regulatory agencies, impressive though they are, don't begin to tell the story of how much the agencies cost the nation in terms of inflation. There is no way to gather the information from millions of business enterprises in this country that would show precisely how much more was added to the cost of doing business (and passed along to the consumer in the form of higher prices) by regulatory agencies intent on justifying their existence. Moreover, there is no way of knowing the amount of capital cutbacks forced upon companies who had to spend money meeting regulatory requirements. But one can speak with confidence in terms of hundreds of millions of dollars.

There are two types of regulatory agencies: those that operate within a cabinet department, like the Food and Drug Administration in the former Department of Health, Education and Welfare; and those agencies that are completely independent, like the Environmental Protection Agency and the Federal Trade Commission.

When a regulatory agency is created by an act of Congress, it is given wide discretionary powers. It can propose and enact rules, carry them out, and enforce them. Fortunately for the American people there are limits to agency powers, or else the bureaucratic tendency to keep expanding would create an impossible climate to operate in for the private sector. The courts can nullify a regulatory action if it is not in accord with the law that the agency is supposed to enforce. And Congress has the power to change the law under which an agency operates, or else deny the agency the funds to carry out a particular program. There is another restraint, of sorts: The Senate can veto the president's choice to run an agency. Despite these limitations, once a regulatory agency is on the move it wields awesome powers.

Environmental Protection Agency

The *Tyrannosaurus rex*, by far, of the regulatory agencies is the Environmental Protection Agency (EPA), founded in 1970 to develop and enforce environmental quality standards for air, water, and noise pollution and for toxic substances and pesticides. The agency has over ten thousand employees and a budget of over $850 million. For sheer ferocity, the EPA has no comparison.

It came out shooting from the hip right from the beginning in 1970, when the Clean Air Act was passed by Congress. The act gave the EPA the authority to set air quality standards at a level necessary to protect the public health and welfare. The EPA subsequently set ozone standards which proved to be unrealistic and were superficially amended when there were industry protests. The Council on Wage and Price Stability estimated that the cost of the EPA rules on ozone standards to industry would run around $19 billion annually, and Congressman David Stockman, a member of the National Commission on Air Quality, called the EPA ozone standard a $100 billion consumer fraud (editorial, *Wall Street Journal*, January 24, 1977).

Another early thrust by the EPA was directed against U.S. copper producers, who were given five years to clean up the sulfur dioxide fumes from their smelters. What happened was that the companies cited had to spend so much money complying with EPA rulings that they denuded themselves of needed capital. Inspiration Consolidated Copper Company spent $62.5 million building a new smelter system, then another $60 million trying to work out the bugs. The company went $25.7 million in debt and merged with another company. Asarco spent $238.6 million on pollution equipment and also became a merger candidate as a result. The Phelps Dodge Corporation spent $330 million to satisfy the EPA. Kennecott Copper Corporation spent $411 million. Copper industry executives estimate that the industry has spent $2 billion since 1970 trying to comply with EPA air-pollution regulations on sulfur dioxide emissions. The industry's debt has soared from $250 million to $3.2 billion. In effect, the EPA has added ten cents a pound to the cost of producing copper.

The EPA has also gone after the steel industry. Although the demand for steel is growing at the rate of two percent a year, steel companies say that the cost of meeting federal regulatory requirements could force them to postpone expansion plans. In May 1979 the Crucible Alloy Division of Colt Industries began making changes in its Midland, Pennsylvania, steel plant to satisfy the EPA. The changes are expected to cost the firm $52 million.

Antipollution standards set by the EPA for coal-fired power plants are expected to add $700 million to annual operating costs. Administration economists estimate that EPA rules to control exposure to smog will cost at least $14 billion a year.

In the spring of 1978 the EPA really ran amok. For one thing, it came up with new regulations which, if allowed by Congress, would eat up all the profits of the oil industry. The agency declared that drilling mud, oil production brine, and crude oil residue are "hazardous wastes." The EPA regulations, said the American Petroleum Institute, would cost the industry $45.5 billion annually. The agency also drew up twenty-four regulations that would each cost some $100 million to industry. Included were detailed lists of tests and reports companies would have to complete before being allowed to market a new chemical, as well as antipollution standards for new coal-fired power plants.

In May 1979 the Council of Economic Advisers circulated a list of thirty-five coming regulatory rules, fourteen of them proposed by the EPA.

A survey in 1979 was conducted for the Business Round-table on the direct cost of federal regulation to forty-eight major companies. The study measured the incremental costs of complying with the rules of six federal agencies and programs in 1977—costs incurred solely because of regulation. The total amount of the costs was $2.6 billion, of which more than $2 billion were attributed to the rules of the EPA.

Certainly the most newsworthy and inflationary action of the EPA is connected with the agency's activities in auto emissions, activities which had much to do with the gasoline shortage that developed in May 1979. The *Wall Street Journal* (May 4, 1979) told the story:

The EPA "has forced rapid conversion to unleaded and low-leaded gasoline without accurately gauging the consequences for petroleum refining. When refiners take the lead out of gasoline, they must use more of the scarce natural elements in crude oil to give gasoline its necessary anti-knock properties. You thus get less gasoline from a barrel of crude when you are making unleaded or low-lead fuel than when you are using lead.

"New catalyst-equipped cars that require unleaded have been selling briskly. . . . Unleaded demand has shot up 70 percent in the last two years and will go up another 22 percent this year, according to a Chase Manhattan Bank estimate.

"While the EPA is forcing unleaded demand upward DOE (Department of Energy) has a ceiling clamped on the price, discouraging expansion of capacity. . . .

"Put all this together and you have motorists wandering around looking for unleaded gasoline, courtesy of their federal government. EPA need not have caused this shortage. Its insistence on catalysts was unnecessary to achievement of acceptable air quality. It has subsequently displayed its arbitrariness by rejecting MTM, a lead substitute which is compatible with catalysts, which would have stretched the gasoline supply and which EPA cannot show to have adverse health effects when emitted with exhaust."

Federal Trade Commission

When *Business Week* used the words "one of the most prolific sources of constricting regulations," it might have been referring to any of the major regulatory agencies. In fact, it was talking about the Federal Trade Commission which, under chairman Michael Pertschuk, has become one of the most interventionist of the regulatory dinosaurs. It was formed in 1914 to enforce some antitrust laws, protect businesses from unfair competition and enforce truth-in-lending and truth-in-labeling laws. By the late 1970s it was operating with a budget of around $65 million and had close to two thousand employees, its time mainly taken up developing harebrained schemes designed to harass business enterprises.

FTC crusades go on for years and are a source of unending income to the legal professionals retained to battle the agency, costs which must be borne by the victimized companies and, inevitably, by consumers. In 1973 the FTC took aim at the major oil companies. Four years later an Exxon vice-president, J. G. Clarke, went before the Senate Antitrust Subcommittee to declare, "I have here the initial subpoena that we received. It is eighteen hundred pages long. It would have required our

United States division to have searched half a billion pages of documents which, we computed, if stacked would reach nine miles high." (*New York Times*, July 17, 1977)

FTC attorneys—there are six hundred of them—generally have no compunction about loading companies down with unnecessary legal and administrative costs. "If you're an antitruster," Mary Gardiner Jones, a former FTC commissioner, says airily, "you're used to seven- to nine-year cases." FTC charges against AT&T are more than five years old; they are more than seven years old against the major cereal manufacturers, whom the FTC has accused of maintaining something called a "shared monopoly"; and they are more than five years old against IBM. In 1966 a case against the Pillsbury Company was halted fourteen years after a FTC complaint was issued. One can imagine the legal and administrative costs to the aforementioned companies over the years.

Is it "bad" for a company to charge low prices for its products? It is as far as the FTC is concerned. Witness the agency's case against the Du Pont Corporation. According to the FTC, Du Pont is guilty of discouraging competitors' expansion plans by charging low prices for titanium dioxide and making early announcements of its own plans to expand capacity. It isn't fair, the FTC maintains, for Du Pont to keep its prices low because of a less costly technique it has developed for making titanium dioxide, a pigment used for whitening plastics. After all, Du Pont might gain a "stranglehold" on new domestic capacity for making the pigment! The courts, showing wisdom, found in favor of Du Pont.

The FTC is not above creating problems even where there is no evidence of corporate wrongdoing. One of its projects was a wide-ranging study of the "economic performance" of the automobile industry. General Motors, two of its dealers, and the Chrysler Corp. and American Motors Corp., sued the FTC to halt the probe. The regulatory attitude, contended General Motors Chairman Thomas A. Murphy, is "an incentive to find something wrong and to punish." As if in agreement with Murphy's characterization of the FTC probe, one FTC lawyer told a judge at a hearing that the FTC "doesn't necessarily know what violation of law it's looking for. It's engaged, if you will, in a fishing expedition, but it's doing so in a good faith effort." (*Wall Street Journal*, January 22, 1979)

The FTC is currently concerned with new regulations dealing with doctors' advertisements, funeral prices, new home warranties, and a bread-and-butter item—corporate mergers. Meanwhile, it has created a brouhaha by publishing a report recommending a federal ban on TV advertising directed at children under eight.

Occupational Safety and Health Administration

The Occupational Safety and Health Administration (OSHA) has jurisdiction over the health and safety of workers in virtually all private places. Unfortunately, it has never been offered guidelines for selecting which places it should inspect. However, OSHA does have a budget of around $140 million and almost three thousand employees, and there is no end to the number of ways the agency can meddle in the economy at considerable cost to industry. For example, there is too much noise in the country, so OSHA set about formulating a policy for controlling workplace noise. What would it cost to lower the decibel count in industry? In 1976 a study was prepared for OSHA on the subject. It showed that enforcing the noise regulations OSHA had in mind, by requiring businesses to buy the necessary engineering controls, would cost companies about $18.5 billion!

OSHA wants rules to control worker exposure to pesticides, and other rules to protect workers from skin disorders. It wants regulations requiring companies to tell workers about potential hazards of chemicals they handle. One OSHA regulation to limit worker exposure to suspected cancer-causing chemicals will, according to the chemical industry, cost $17 to $47 billion for equipment alone. Of course, no one should tolerate chemical and other hazards in the workplace, but business should not suffer severe penalties where the allegations are merely suspicions and have not been established scientifically.

Equal Employment Opportunity Commission

In 1964 the Equal Employment Opportunity Commission (EEOC) was created to investigate and rule on charges of racial and other discrimination by employers and labor unions. At that time the country certainly needed sensitizing to the importance of giving equal job opportunities to Americans regardless of color of skin, or sex. As the years slipped by, barriers broke down not so much because of governmental laws but because of the innate sense of fair play in most employers. Of course, there were pockets of resistance—there always will be, so deeply ingrained is prejudice—but generally progress was very satisfactory, especially in the large companies.

The EEOC, very much in business in the late 1970s, continues to act as though American employers are still basically hostile to the idea of unprejudiced hiring practices. The agency, with its budget of just under $100 million and its roughly twenty-five hundred employees has for years now been embarked on a program it calls "affirmative action." It is no longer enough, in the eyes of the EEOC, for a company to give the same job opportunity to, say, a black as it would to a white. Expertise and quality of work, not to mention productivity, are no longer to be the criteria for hiring. The agency wants companies to search out, hire, train, and promote minorities. Companies are being asked to detail job descriptions, hiring techniques, and complicated validations showing how their personnel tests relate to job performance. There must also be provisions for considering alternative tests that will allow for the hiring of more minority or women job seekers.

The amount of paper work required of business enterprises to comply with the ever-growing demands of the EEOC is simply staggering. A study cited earlier, in which the Business Roundtable, an organization of business leaders, reviewed the direct costs of federal regulations to forty-eight major companies, found that next to the EPA, the rules imposed on the companies by the EEOC were the most costly—a matter of $217 million annually—in administrative and reporting expenses. The EEOC has already made known its plans to increase its record-keeping requirements. It would like a company to keep employment records for two years instead of the currently required six months. The agency also wants guidelines for accommodating employees who want time off for religious holidays. What this has to do with ensuring equal job opportunities is not clear.

There is also a matter of bureaucratic overlapping in EEOC activities. This agency has been operating in the same area as the Labor Department's Office of Federal Contract Compliance, which expanded from two hundred to fourteen hundred employees in 1978 and is setting up a network of sixty to seventy offices around the country in preparation for more active enforcement. This office can cut off government contracts to companies which don't comply with equal employment requirements.

Americans are intelligent, compassionate people. Our large business enterprises are run by individuals, and these individuals are, in the main, no less intelligent and compassionate than others. It is therefore an insult to set up a huge federal bureaucracy instructing employers as to the ratios of the various races, colors, and sexes they must have in their employ. It is no less demeaning when a college is told that it must base its entrance qualifications on race or sex. In industry, there is a further tragedy involved: The loss of gain to the nation, when jobs are not filled according to proven past experience, but on the basis of color of skin or sex. Allen Sloan, a New York attorney specializing in job hiring practices, says that new rules on "employee selection procedures" will "result in the hiring of minimally qualified rather than best qualified employees."

Racial discrimination became illegal with the passage of the Civil Rights Act of 1964, and sex discrimination was outlawed in 1967. There has been broad compliance by American industry with these laws. To allow the EEOC and the Labor Department's OFCC to continue to harass the business sector as they have, and to add to inflation—since in the final analysis all costs imposed by the regulators are passed along to the consumer in higher prices—simply makes no sense.

Securities and Exchange Commission

A regulatory culprit that has wandered far afield from what Congress originally intended its activities to be is the Securities and Exchange Commission (SEC). It was founded in 1934 to protect investors from deceit and manipulation of stock prices, a necessity in view of what helped bring on the stock market crash of 1929. The SEC was also given the authority to supervise stock exchanges and regulate holding and investment companies. These are modest enough goals, but as Homer Kripke, an NYU law professor and former staff member of the SEC, says of the agency, "It's dominated by lawyers with a moralistic approach to securities regulation." The result is that even with a relatively small budget of about $60 million and two thousand employees, the SEC has flexed big muscles. It is attempting to regulate the structure of corporate boards, management compensation, questionable payments by U.S. corporations, and accounting rules. It is also trying to make it more difficult for business mergers.

Banking Regulators

The impulse on the part of federal regulators to dictate to the private sector is also evident in banking. In October 1977 Title

VIII of the Housing and Community Development Act, that is, the Community Reinvestment Act (CRA), was signed into law. The CRA has called upon appropriate federal bank supervisory agencies and the Federal Home Loan Bank Board to assess the lending records of banking institutions. Such action is to make certain that loans are extended by private lenders for social purposes, as determined by bureaucracy. This means, among other things, that loans should be made on the basis of catering to certain groups and areas even when the risk of non-repayment is extremely high.

During the decade 1968 to 1977 private lenders have been swamped with regulatory acts relating to credit practices, as evidenced by the following:

       1968: Consumer Credit Protection Act
       1970: Fair Credit Reporting Act
       1974: Fair Credit Billing Act
       1974: Equal Credit Opportunity Act
       1974: Real Estate Settlement Procedures Act
       1975: Federal Trade Commission Improvement Act
       1975: Home Mortgage Disclosure Act
       1976: Equal Credit Opportunity Amendments
       1976: Consumer Leasing Act
       1976: Debt Collection Practices Act
       1977: Community Reinvestment Act.

Regulatory Confusion

As if the cost of complying with individual government regulatory agencies isn't enough, industry has found itself saddled with an additional problem: trying to comply with the rules of one agency that conflict with another. The EPA, for example, wants steel mill operators to put hoods over coke ovens to help reduce air pollution; but OSHA opposes these devices because they increase the emissions breathed by coke oven workers. The meat-packing plants need stainless steel or tile surfaces to help them comply with the Department of Agriculture's food-handling standards. These surfaces, however, are highly reflective of sound and may cause the plant to exceed OSHA's noise limits.

Not long ago the Carter administration showed signs of concern over the enormous inflationary impact of the regulatory agencies. The White House issued a plan for its own budget and economic officials to monitor regulations and try to control the impact. Predictably, the agencies fought back. They joined forces to protect their authority, and their success or failure in maintaining their power will go a long way in determining to what degree inflation will be fueled by regulatory operations.

A BLOATED FEDERAL BUREAUCRACY

3

With federal government intervention in the economy at an all-time high, it comes as no surprise that a huge, overpaid bureaucracy is required. It is needed to keep track of and enforce whatever the federal government does to keep its fingers in the economic pie.

In 1950 there were 1,960,708 federal civilian workers earning a total of $7 billion; by 1977 there were 2,901,973 federal civilian workers earning $46.5 billion. For those wanting an even more detailed comparison between the past and present, in the early 1930s there was one government worker for every ten in industry. In the late 1940s the ratio was one to six. Since 1970 it has been one to every four.

The *National Journal* (editorial in *Wall Street Journal,* May 10, 1979) following a detailed analysis, has estimated that there are 8 million workers who get all or most of their income from the federal government but who don't show up on federal payrolls. About 3 million of the 8 million, says the *Journal,* provide goods and services to the federal government itself, and the other 5 million work for other employers like state and local governments, with the federal government actually paying their salaries.

It is not generally recognized that the largest single cost of the federal government is employee compensation. Charles J.

Zwick, director of the Office of Management and Budget in the Johnson administration and chairman of the President's Commission on Military Compensation, said in the *New York Times* of March 4, 1979, "In many job markets Federal employees are the highest paid of all. Compensation for Government blue-collar workers sometimes ranges up to twice that of persons performing the same type of work in private industry." Zwick cited a recent study by the Civil Service Commission which estimates that 11.5 percent of Government white-collar workers—roughly 155,000 in number—enjoy status and pay not justified by their responsibilities. The commission sets the cost of this overgrading at $436 million a year.

One president after another—Andrew Jackson in 1867, Woodrow Wilson in 1914, Herbert Hoover in 1928, Harry Truman in 1955, Lyndon Johnson in 1965, Richard Nixon in 1971, and Jimmy Carter in 1976—have all inveighed against the bloated bureaucracy in Washington and striven to reorganize it, to no avail. Every year 10 billion sheets of paper are mailed to business enterprises for completion. This tide of paper that flows from federal offices costs more than $40 billion!

Federal employees are given annual raises that shield them from inflation. These automatic pay hikes have boosted the average federal salary from $6,000 to $16,250 over the fifteen-year period 1963 to 1978. This is double the growth rate for wages in industry. Most attractive, too, for the bureaucracy is that federal retirement benefits are indexed to the cost of living. Any such application to private pension plans would bankrupt them utterly. And the icing on the cake is that most government employees are eligible each year for three percent "merit" raises, on top of annual wage boosts that link their salaries to comparable jobs in private industry. Of course, the way it works out, the employees really need show no merit at all. Most get the satisfactory ratings from their supervisors that automatically lead to these pay increases.

Of course there is waste, inefficiency, and overpayment in

the federal bureaucratic structure. How can it be otherwise? There's no system of rewards or penalties to motivate workers, and it takes years to fire a federal employee under the buffer system of rules that shield even the most blatantly incapable employees from being let go. What makes the situation all the more intolerable is that the bloated bureaucracy is mainly the result of unnecessary government intervention in the economy, the product of Keynesian economic philosophy. What is needed is a change in rules so that discharging the inefficient is permitted. And the number of employees required by the government would be cut drastically if government reduced its role in the economy and permitted the free enterprise system to operate on its own. Time and again books and journals have specified areas where the federal government should not be active. Stopping activity in such areas would result in enormous savings to the American people, savings that would include money paid to bureaucrats. Where inflation enters the picture is that the federal bureaucracy—like state and local—is non-productive, that is, its employment contributes nothing to increasing the real wealth of the nation. The increase is provided by the private sector. However, private sector employees as well as government bureaucracy all vie for available goods and services. If real productivity is down—which it is—and more people keep joining the ranks of the nonproductive, that is, the bureaucratic sector, the end result must be inflationary. Exorbitant salaries and automatic pay increases to millions of individuals who are not only nonproductive but whose activities actually increase immeasurably the cost of doing business for the private sector, can add up to only one thing: inflation.

CETA—A Staggering Boondoggle

The ghost of John Maynard Keynes nodded approvingly when, in 1973, Congress created the Comprehensive Employment and Training Act (CETA). Originally funded at $1.5 billion a year, CETA was intended primarily to provide job skills to the hard-core unemployed. By fiscal 1979 the annual cost for CETA had risen to an estimated $11.4 billion. The intent was good: Who can fault a program that wants to put the poor unemployed to work and provide an alternative to welfare? Like so many government programs, however, things didn't work out as planned. The low skilled and minority workers, in the main, didn't get the jobs CETA was supposed to provide; it turned out that millions of CETA funds have been used to underwrite the payrolls of local governments—financing existing government jobs rather than creating new employment. Beneficiaries of CETA have been political workers, friends, and relatives of local officials. In the city government of Washington, D.C. it was discovered that 56 of 126 employees of the city council have been receiving CETA money. Forty-four of these CETA employees draw between ten thousand and twenty thousand dollars a year. To counteract such monetary abuses, Congress passed an amendment limiting the maximum amount any CETA worker could be paid from combined federal and local funds to ten thousand dollars a year in most parts of the country and twelve thousand dollars in high wage areas. But this is small comfort when one realizes that 14 million Americans are currently working full-time for under eight thousand dollars a year and that the minimum wage is only fifty-five hundred dollars.

Keynes was all for providing employment regardless what, if anything, was produced. In one issue of *Reader's Digest,* Ralph Kinney Bennett illustrated to what ends such a philosophy can lead. His investigations showed CETA funds going to such projects as building a steel-reinforced concrete rock in Oregon to be used for practice by rock climbers, paying for a "nude sculpting workshop" in which naked men and women run their hands over one another's bodies, and funding an avowed Marxist-Leninist in Atlanta to "keep an eye on" local government.

We are talking about an $11 billion-plus budget which adds next to nothing, if anything at all, to the wealth of the nation and yet is fervently supported by such Senate stalwarts as Senator Ed Muskie (Democrat, Maine) and Senator Henry Bellmon (Republican, Oklahoma). In 1978 Congress cut back the number of CETA jobs from 725,000 to 660,000, but still voted to extend the life of this program another four years. If what happened in Florida is any criterion, the cutback is not nearly drastic enough. The *U.S. News & World Report* issue of October 23, 1978, reported that a federal grand jury investigation that year, involving only twenty-nine of about four hundred CETA programs in Dade and Monroe counties in Florida, found that agencies had falsified records and wasted funds. The jury noted that $160 million had been spent in the area since 1974 "without any attempt to distinguish those programs which seem effective from those that clearly are not."

When billions of dollars of taxpayers' money are spent to create jobs for the wrong people, or fund projects and programs that don't even have a transitory value let alone add to the wealth of the nation, the result must be inflationary.

Enormous Federally Guaranteed Loans

Excessive government spending that is visible—that appears in the budget—is certainly open to criticism. But in recent years there has been a far more ominous development: an ongoing explosion in federal credit programs that is "invisible" as far as federal spending is concerned.

When anyone takes note of the federal budget they see allocations totaling about $500 billion. What is not seen are certain types of loans advanced under federal auspices, which include federally guaranteed loans by private lenders and loans by government-sponsored agencies. Two such examples are the Student Loan Marketing Association, which has about $1.3

billion in loans outstanding, and the Federal National Mortgage Association, which holds some $42 billion in housing debts.

It is estimated that in the 1979 fiscal year about $160 billion will be advanced to borrowers where the federal government is the guarantor, said funds never showing up in the visible federal budget. By the end of 1978 outstanding federally guaranteed loans totaled more than $240 billion.

These guaranteed loans climbed thirty percent during the years 1977 to 1979. And from 1974 to 1979 such funds raised under federal auspices have ranged from twenty-five to forty percent of all borrowing in the U.S. economy.

The tragedy of this type of expenditure is that it siphons off desperately needed capital from the private sector, which then prevents the economy from expanding and the creation of new jobs. Sidney Jones, an economic consultant to the Federal Reserve Board, estimates that in the decade ending 1977 the federal government took a "half trillion dollars out of the capital markets—approximately $260 billion in cumulative deficits and about $225 billion of net borrowing for other programs." (e.g., The borrowing was, more specifically, for off-budget programs and for over one hundred federal credit programs, nurturing housing, agriculture, students, veterans, trade, and the like.) *Fortune* magazine points out, "This year's increase (1979) in federal credit demands by the Treasury and other federal agencies—perhaps as much as $10 billion—could soak up almost all of the increase in new private savings, estimated at about $12 billion."

A primary means by which the off-budget federally guaranteed loans are effected is the Federal Financing Bank (FFB), founded in 1974. This bank is really a fiction, allowing the government to do what amounts to off-the-balance-sheet borrowing. It does business out of a tiny office, has no full-time employees, and its boss, Roland H. Cook, does other jobs as well for the Treasury. How it operates is really very simple:

Supposing Congress authorizes some branch of the government to sell equipment to a foreign country. The Federal Financing Bank borrows the money and lends it to the foreign country. Or, say a government agency wants to borrow money to expand its regulatory operations. Ordinarily, the agency would borrow directly from the Treasury and thus create a larger federal deficit. The new way, the agency borrows from the FFB and the loan doesn't appear on the federal budget. It so happens that there is a saving to the taxpayer in that a borrowing agency will pay a slightly lower rate if borrowing from the FFB instead of directly from the Treasury (the FFB pays the going rate for Treasury securities). But the fact remains that the FFB is competing with the private sector for credit, to the detriment of the U.S. economy as a whole.

In 1978 the FFB bought nearly one-quarter of about $65 billion in loans the government guaranteed that year. Since the FFB is outside the federal budget, the government has no control over the volume of loans that will be converted.

Federal Debt

Since, in the final analysis, the consumer pays for everything including the federal debt, it should be a cause for concern that the federal debt has increased more in the 1970s than in the entire previous history of the United States. By the end of 1978 the public debt of the U.S. government was $800 billion—more than one-third of the Gross National Product! Interest costs are running about $50 billion. Years ago the federal debt was owed mainly to Americans themselves, but this is no longer true. Foreign holdings of American debt in 1978 were approximately $123 billion, with interest payments running at about $5 billion a year. In 1968 such foreign holdings came to no more than $11 billion. Needless to say, current interest payments to foreigners on our debt gravely affects American balance-of-payment deficits.

It is also worth noting that should the American dollar

decline precipitously, or faith vanish in our ability to curb inflation, the foreigners who hold our indebtedness will seek to unload those dollars, with catastrophic results.

The Annual Price Tag on Income Transfers: $250 BILLION

4

For many, "welfare" still conjures up a picture of destitute, undernourished people, anxious to be of service to society but prevented by involuntary unemployment, illness, or old age. Of course, there will always be those, but for the most part the picture is obsolete. In 1979 the federal government, in its role of the Good Fairy to nonproductive Americans, distributed more than $250 billion via income transfer programs—almost one-third of the national budget. Included in this vast sum was welfare, a mere drop in the bucket when one considers that President Carter sent a $5.7 billion proposal to Congress for welfare.

As of last year the largest single spender on income transfer and related programs was the Department of Health, Education and Welfare (HEW) with its annual budget of $182 billion. For those who appreciate statistics, HEW spent $500 million every day, disbursed by an army of 1,250,000 bureaucrats. In a moment of candor, the agency acknowledged that between $5 and $7 billion a year was wasted.

Only the most calloused would suggest that the impoverished should not receive help. The problem is that the federal income transfer programs have exploded in recent years to the point where the working sector of the population is being grossly penalized to provide for the nonworking. One result has been falling productivity. After all, who wants to work hard when inflation and higher taxes deny a worker the fruits of greater efforts?

What the federal government does with the $250 billion a year allocated for income transfer is revealed in a book aptly called *An Inventory of Federal Income Transfer Programs* based on the year 1977 issued by the Institute for Socioeconomic Studies, in White Plains, New York. A synopsis of the book's findings shows that there are five ways in which the federal government distributes benefits. One, of course, is welfare. The other four are tax relief through a reduction in personal income tax liabilities; essential goods and services, either free or at reduced prices; credit; and insurance at terms more favorable than those available in the private sector.

The recipients of the public income transfer benefits are not required to provide the government with any product, service, or asset in return for the benefits received.

The 182 federal programs listed for 1977 fall into four broad categories. The categories include programs that provide benefits to: (1) replace earnings lost due to the age, disability, death, or other absence of the primary earner; (2) supplement the earned income of the family; (3) supplement the general income of the family; and (4) improve the earning potential of the individual.

There are innumerable individual programs in each category. One is struck with not only how much money the individual programs soak up in tax dollars, but who are the beneficiaries.

Let us examine some random annualized examples:

Railroad retirement insurance, providing certain workers with monthly cash payments to replace income lost through retirement: $2.250 billion; civil service retirement pensions, providing certain civil service employees with monthly cash payments to replace income lost through retirement: $6.370 billion; railroad disability insurance, replacing income lost through loss of work: $551 million; Medicare—hospital insurance: $15.314 billion; unemployment assistance: $691 million; agricultural stabilization programs of various types: $600 million; earned income credit to low income workers with dependent children: $1.070 billion; school lunch programs: $2.2 billion.

One program that has inflated enormously since its inception is food stamps, a $5.5 billion operation in 1977. The concept was created in 1964 as a specialized nutrition program for some 360,000 needy people. Before 1977 food stamps were sold at discount prices to qualifying families, but in that year they were made free. By 1979 the number of Americans getting food stamps had risen to 19 million, and federal agricultural committees have proposed a nineteen percent expansion of the food stamp program for fiscal 1980. Out of fear that food stamps might become a runaway program, Congress placed a cap of $6.18 billion on the program for fiscal 1980.

In 1979, food stamps fed one out of every twelve Americans.

There are other food assistance programs besides food stamps. All told, these programs cost some $10 billion annually. As might be expected when one considers federal spending habits, there are overlapping programs. It has been admitted by the General Accounting Office that "some low income families participate simultaneously in as many as six different programs providing federal food assistance." There seems to be no illegality in such participation.

Psychologically, how are the beneficiaries of welfare programs affected by their status?

One would imagine the answer to be self-evident: Anyone taking government handouts provided by the taxes of working fellow Americans would be most anxious, conditions permitting, to become self-sufficient. Of course, there are those who, because of age, illness, or other good reasons, must look to government for sustenance, but what about those who do earn something, although little, and therefore qualify for income maintenance?

To get some answers, the federal government sponsored a

number of studies in welfare research over the ten year period 1968 to 1978. Welfare rolls were growing and no one seemed to know why. The sum of $150 million was allocated.

In November 1978 the Subcommittee on Public Assistance held hearings on the findings of the federally sponsored studies and on other important research related to welfare programs. Some of the findings were quite surprising.

The income maintenance experiments had been designed primarily to find out how such programs affect the work behavior of low income people.

What was learned?

Dr. Irwin Garfinkel, director of the Institute for Research on Poverty at the University of Wisconsin gave this answer: "We learned that simultaneously increasing the unearned incomes and reducing the rewards for work of low income people will induce them to work less. We also learned that how much less low income people work depends upon how much we increase their income and how much we decrease their net wage."

Senator Daniel Patrick Moynihan (Democrat, New York) echoed that finding: "Instead of encouraging work and self-sufficiency, the kind of plans tested appeared to produce substantial reductions in work effort and corresponding increases in dependency on public subsidy. Ten years ago, we expected quite different outcomes from these tests. We must now be prepared to entertain the possibility that we were wrong." (Moynihan office release, November 15, 1978)

And Dr. Jodie Allen, special assistant to the Secretary of Labor for Welfare Reform, summed up the issue as follows: "Transfer programs can affect the overall economy by worsening the relationship between unemployment and inflation. One mechanism is that by raising the return for *not working* relative to *working*, the programs may influence people to delay taking jobs in order to try to find a higher paying job or for other reasons. The delays may lengthen the duration of vacancies, raise the rate of wage increase, or force employers to use less efficient workers. In any case, the result can be less productivity, more inflation, and, ultimately, additional reductions in employment if policymakers attempt to restrain the inflation by inducing an economic slowdown." (December 12, 1978)

Translated in terms of the results of an actual experiment, it was found that recipients of cash assistance from negative income tax (NIT) programs in the New Jersey–Pennsylvania area, worked five to seven hours per week less than workers who went without such assistance.

What the Subcommittee on Public Assistance determined regarding the effect of income transfers on individual beneficiaries, Professor Melvyn Krauss has determined for society as a whole. In a penetrating book entitled *The New Protectionism* (New York University Press, 1978), Professor Krauss writes that while economic growth cushions income transfer programs in the short run, redistribution stunts economic growth in the long run. This is because economic growth and social consumption are really competitive, not complementary.

"The welfare state," avers Professor Krauss, "as it depends on the economic growth it negates, is self-destructive . . . the promise of a secure income is an illusion, because the attempt to achieve it reduces the ability of the economy to produce it." This happens as "the welfare economy becomes increasingly unable to adjust to a constantly changing and competitive environment because its social commitments prevent it from doing so. The result is stagnation and the concomitant shrinkage in the job market . . . The emphasis on economic security leads directly and inexorably to demands for the redistribution of income and economic power from capital to labor and to the death of capital accumulation—the goose that lays the golden eggs."

In the mid-1970s, economist Richard Ensor, affiliated with the Hudson Institute, conclusively showed that overall economic growth is lowest in countries where the government sector is largest; that is, the more government spending there is, the less economic growth there is. The same conclusion was reached by two British economists, Robert Bacon and Walter Eltis, and by David Smith, principal research officer at England's National Westminster Bank. His rule of thumb is that "each five percent increase in the share of disposable income absorbed by state consumption implies a one percent drop in the growth rate."

A graph based on data developed by Hudson Research Europe, an independent Paris-based affiliate of the American Hudson Institute, shows how countries with high government spending have the lowest growth rate. The countries include Sweden, Denmark, the U.S., Canada, Britain, and West Germany. At the far end of the scale is Japan, with the highest annual growth rate and the lowest amount of government spending.

Does this mean that public services should be eliminated? Not at all. It does mean that either the growth of government spending must not be allowed to pass beyond a certain percentage of the Gross National Product, or that people of a country should agree to lower economic growth with all that this implies.

Social Security—Possible Bankruptcy

Of the $250 billion disbursed by the federal government in 1977 via income transfer programs, two out of every five dollars went to the major components of the national social security system; retirement, survivors, disability pensions, Medicare, and Medicaid.

As presently constituted, the U.S. social security system may be termed a study in possible bankruptcy.

Back in the late 1930s, an American workingman earning the princely sum of three thousand dollars a year could look forward to a future retirement benefit that would make all the difference between an old age of hardship and one of some security. In 1935 Congress had passed the Social Security Act, a historic milestone in social legislation. By its terms, a worker paying one percent of salary into the fund, with a matching amount paid by his employer, could retire at the age of sixty-five and begin collecting benefits. J. Douglas Brown, who helped develop the program, said that Social Security was "the most adequate protection possible within the limits of available funds" for older people.

In 1937 the first workers began paying into Social Security. In 1940 the first Social Security checks went out: $35 million to 228,000 retirees. By 1947, 2 million Americans were collecting benefits; by 1951, 10 million; and by 1979, 34 million Americans were collecting $102 billion a year.

However, during the four decades, Social Security had been stretched beyond all recognition. It was no longer the simple plan for people over sixty-five. It had become, like everything else created and manipulated by the federal government, a real monstrosity, rising in cost like a sharply graded roller coaster, with an estimated outlay of $250 billion by 1985.

What had happened, or rather, what was happening?

For one thing, Congress brought more and more Americans under Social Security as the years went by. For another, Social Security benefits paid out rise as the Consumer Price Index (CPI) increases and as the beneficiary population grows: an awesome combination.

By 1979, the law had been amended so that retired people sixty-two years old and over were able to collect benefits. The wives and children of those who had died while collecting Social Security were made eligible. So were dependents of workers who died before retirement age, disabled workers and their dependents; domestics and farm workers; the self-employed; and full-time students. Government workers—over 2 million federal employees—with their own pension plans, were also permitted to voluntarily join the Social Security plan. Congressmen and their aides had no need of Social Security, having their own government-funded plan.

In 1972 an amendment to the Social Security Act was passed, adjusting benefits for both current and future retirees periodically so that they could keep up with rises in wages and prices. But consider: The base on which Social Security taxes are levied rises as wages and salaries rise, but, as noted earlier, benefits paid out rise as the Consumer Price Index increases. From 1974 to 1975 the CPI increased 9.1 percent, while covered wages and salaries increased by only 4 percent. This created a high base on which benefits are calculated, with the problem carried forward each year. In effect, Social Security benefits were rising faster than inflation, and it became apparent even to the most liberal Congressman that unless something were done, the whole plan was destined for bankruptcy.

Benefits are adjusted every six months, and in July 1979 34 million Social Security beneficiaries and 4 million disabled persons began getting a 9.9 percent increase in benefits because of increased prices. This meant an outlay of an additional $10 billion a year. Of added concern was what was happening to the Old Age and Survivors Trust Fund and the Disability Fund, both of which are integrated into Social Security. In 1977 these funds collected $75.7 billion but paid out $80 billion. As of mid-1979, the Old Age and Survivors Trust Fund had only 30 percent of a year's benefits on hand and, at the present rate, is expected to run out of funds by 1984. The Disability Fund may be out of cash by the end of 1979.

As a saving measure, Congress passed a law in 1977 increasing Social Security taxes by a whopping $227 billion over the next decade. It was the largest peacetime tax increase in U.S. history. Even so, it may not be enough. The year 2000 is a scant twenty years away, but Social Security payments between 1979 and 2000 show staggeringly high increases. From a total outlay of $135 billion in 1979, all payments are expected to reach $400 billion by 2000. From 1979 to 1987, payroll taxes will rise 7.15 percent each for workers and employers from the 1977 level of 5.85 percent. In 1977 payments into Social Security by employee and employer was $965.25 each, based on a maximum wage of $16,500; by 1987 this amount will be $3,045.90 each.

In 1979, to administer this vast program, twenty thousand were employed in the Baltimore headquarters of Social Security, with another sixty thousand workers around the country.

It has been estimated that over a period of forty-five years, a private plan could produce retirement benefits double what Social Security would supply during the same period. Here is an instance where special incentives to private plans could attract newcomers to the labor market to such plans, giving individuals a choice. At least it would begin to reduce the role of government in retirement planning. Otherwise, quoted statistics show what lies ahead. Future victims will be today's wage earner (the employer can always pass along his share of Social Security taxes to the consumer via higher prices), his retirement benefits eaten up by inflation, and the next generation, which will be saddled with unendurable taxes.

Britain's Welfare State— Is That Our Future?

The unease which one must feel when contemplating an American economy in disarray surely must lead to the thought: Left unchallenged, where will our federal economic policies take us? A probable destination is the same one reached by Britain in the late 1970s.

Britain, the homeland of John Maynard Keynes, went all the way. The country began with the acceptance of basic Keynesian thinking, and ended up a welfare state.

The British government's policy was one of spending, leveling incomes, imposing high taxes, and even instituting a wage-control plan, which was begun in 1975 and came apart violently in 1979 when pent-up grievances drove millions of workers to strike for higher wages. The British government had decreed wage increases be limited to five percent, but the grim fact, ignored by labor and government alike, is that higher wages without increased productivity is simply inflationary. And for years British productivity had been falling.

As Robert Ball pointed out in *Fortune* magazine (March 22, 1977), "Britain's underlying problem is summed up in one melancholy set of figures. Since the end of 1973, industrial wages have risen by 111 percent and prices by 107 percent— but real gross domestic product by only 4 percent. To point out, as some apologists for Britain do, that in absolute terms the average Briton is better off than he has ever been is to describe a fool's paradise. In a world of international competition in trade, relative decline is defeat."

The welfare state is simply not conducive to enterprise and productivity. Why should a worker exert himself if he knows that the state is committed to supplying him and his family with all basic amenities no matter what his rate of productivity?

The British have wage and price controls, from which they permit only minor deviations. The U.S. imposed wage and price controls itself, under Nixon, and the result was higher prices when the controls were finally removed than what they would have been had there never been controls. The British have also been tinkering with tax rebates, and have relentlessly extended social services from the late 1940s onward. There has been a forty-one percent shift in British employment from industry to services from 1961 to 1975. In their book, *Britain's Economic Problem: Too Few Producers* (London: Macmillan, 1976), Robert Bacon and Walter Eltis wrote that the "serious structural problems" from which the British economy suffers are the direct result of the real costs of maintaining a welfare state. The problem could have been less, they aver, if the private sector had increased capital spending. But British government policies never permitted companies to make enough profits to pay for new investment which would have boosted productivity. Corporate tax rates were, and still are, simply too high.

From 1955 to 1974, the share of market production, excluding defense, taken by the nonmarket sector in Britain, went from 26.2 percent to 31.4 percent. During that same period of time, the percentage change in the United States went from 14.4 percent to 26.2 percent. This road leads to greater demands on the productive sector by the nonproductive, with diminishing chances of meeting those demands because of higher taxes, higher costs of regulatory demands, and lower productivity.

In September 1976 Prime Minister James Callaghan, of England, addressed a Labour Party convention. He said: "We used to think that you could just spend your way out of a recession and increase employment by cutting taxes and boosting government spending. I tell you in all candor that the option no longer exists, and that insofar as it ever did exist, it worked by injecting inflation into the economy. And each time that happened, the average level of unemployment has risen. Higher inflation, followed by higher unemployment. That is the history of the last twenty years."

THE ENERGY "CRISIS"

5

There is no energy crisis in the U.S. today, but there is an energy problem. It was created by political manipulation and price controls in energy markets.
—"Demagoguery at the White House", Advertisement
Signed by Forty-five Economists,
—Wall Street Journal, November 3, 1977

Energy was never a problem for Americans until the government stuck its nose into it. The further in the nose went, the worse the problem became.
—Paul Craig Roberts, Wall Street Journal, April 19, 1979

Residents of countries with planned economies know the reason for a shortage, which is that a government official made another error. Americans have not yet learned this simple explanation, and so they still seek more information.
—Herbert Stein, AEI Economist, July 1979

As the fuel crunch tightens across the nation, a consensus is growing that government efforts to deal with the problem are only making a bad situation worse.
—U.S. News & World Report, July 2, 1979

Federal Culpability

Unfortunately, there is no way to force President Carter, our Congress and Senate, and the Department of Energy to listen to the story of how petroleum replaced whale oil as a primary source of lighting and lubrication, nor to draw the proper conclusions from it. Were it possible, there is a reasonable hope that the federal government would gradually withdraw from the energy field, leaving it to those who had little trouble supplying America with inexpensive energy until the U.S. government instituted controls, OPEC ran wild, and the government compounded the mess with additional regulations.

We'll come back to petroleum versus whale oil later. First, it's important to expose a few myths.

For years now, the rising cost of gasoline and heating fuel has been a strong factor of inflation in the United States. From the public viewpoint, based on media and government representation, there have been two major culprits in what has come to be known as the energy "crisis." Standing condemned is the Organization of Petroleum Exporting Countries (OPEC), whose appetite for profits seems insatiable, and the major oil companies, long accused (unjustly, as analysis shows) of "ripping off" the public.

Nowhere in the picture, or prisoner's dock, as is the case, is the federal government. Yet facts show that policies of federal administrations over the past twenty-five years are most responsible for the country's energy mess.

Years before the OPEC cartel came into existence to bedevil the world with its arbitrary price increases of oil based on little more than greed, the U.S. government embarked on a policy of controls and regulations that inevitably led to energy shortages, disruptions, and distortions. Of course, the intentions were good: Who can fault a policy that ostensibly seeks to protect people from price hikes? In 1954 it seemed like a good idea when the Supreme Court ruled that the Federal Power Commission (FPC), under the Natural Gas Act of 1938, could regulate the price of interstate gas. It was, after all, helpful to the poor. A few years later, in 1961, the same philosophy prevailed and the FPC imposed a price ceiling at the wellhead on interstate sales of natural gas. Intrastate gas—gas produced and sold within state borders—was left uncontrolled.

There really was no excuse for these moves. For the first six decades of the century no other people in the world enjoyed so many energy benefits at such comparably low costs as Americans. Until the Arab oil boycott of 1973, real energy prices in the United States, in terms of constant purchasing power dollars, had been falling consistently from 1950. Edward Mitchell, in a monograph published by the American Enterprise Institute, pointed out that real energy prices fell by 3.1 percent between 1950 and 1955; by 3.7 percent between 1955 and 1960; by 6.5 percent between 1960 and 1965; and by 8.1 percent between 1965 and 1970. On a five-year basis through October 1973 real energy prices in the U.S. fell by 9.4 percent.

In an uncontrolled market subject to the law of supply and demand, exploration and drilling for oil boomed, giving the lie regarding the size of American oil reserves to one federal estimate after another. In 1914 the U.S. Bureau of Mines estimated that future production of oil would amount to only 5.7 billion barrels. In 1939 the Department of the Interior said that the U.S. oil supply would last only thirteen years (we have since discovered more than the total known supply at the time). In 1949 the same department said the end of the U.S. oil supply was in sight, whereas what happened was that domestic oil production was increased by more than a million barrels a day in the next five years. Somehow, known oil reserves kept increasing in the face of the most dire predictions.

Always forgotten by the doomsday criers was that a lot of oil may be uneconomical to recover at prevailing prices, but becomes available when the difference between recovery and profit becomes acceptable. This was stressed by Professors W. Philip Gramm and Richard Davison in a *Wall Street Journal* article in 1977. They pointed out that, as of 1969, the U.S. had 31 billion barrels of recoverable oil reserves at then-current prices; but there was another 285 billion barrels in the ground that were recoverable only at higher prices, and could come on-stream only as prices were permitted to rise.

Obviously, shortages of oil were not going to develop because of low proven reserves. If we were to have shortages, price controls and excessive regulation would have to do the job. From 1960 to 1970 exploratory drilling for oil and gas in the United States declined from twelve thousand wells to about seventy-five hundred wells. The number of natural gas producers dropped from eighteen thousand in 1956 to four thousand in 1971.

Lower domestic oil production was made up by increased imports. In 1970 oil was $2.45 per barrel; in 1973 the average price was $3.14; in 1974 it was $11.11; in 1979 it was about $21.00. The OPEC cartel had taken due notice of the U.S. energy no-program and had gone all the way in charging whatever they felt the traffic would bear. What was it about U.S. energy policy that so buoyed OPEC? It can be summed up as follows: maximum interference with domestic production by holding down the price of domestic crude oil and natural gas; blocking off access to offshore petroleum; imposing environmental and other constraints on the mining and use of coal; and bringing development of nuclear power to a virtual standstill, especially after the unfortunate incident at Three Mile Island in Pennsylvania, when a nuclear reactor was in danger of going critical.

President Carter, in his anxiety to prove his mettle, almost added to the energy mess by submitting a totally unworkable plan a scant ninety days after his election. (The plan was mercifully chewed to bits and discarded by Congress.) But U.S. energy problems didn't start with Carter any more than Watergate type machinations started with Nixon.

The 1954 Supreme Court decision authorizing regulation of interstate gas has already been noted, as has the 1961 price ceiling imposed at the wellhead on the sale of interstate gas. This latter move was especially restricting to the growth of our economy. Years later, with the controls still in effect, W. Philip Gramm, Professor of Economics at Texas A. & M. University, wrote in *Human Events,* July 9, 1977:

> By regulating the price of natural gas at the wellhead, the Federal Power Commmission has produced several undesirable effects. It has stifled the development of a cheap and clean-burning domestic fuel. It has produced a higher price to the consumer because he has been forced to rely on more expensive substitutes. And it has produced foreign dependence because the consumer has been forced to make up for the failure of natural gas supplies to grow by importing petroleum products as substitutes.

In the late 1960s, bowing to populist pressure, the depletion allowance was reduced. In 1971 oil prices came under regulatory control. In 1973, following the Arab oil boycott, the Emergency Petroleum Allocation Act (EPAA) was passed. This brought into being the Federal Energy Office (FEO), which became the Federal Energy Administration (FEA), which in turn became a part of the Department of Energy.

The Clean Air Act of 1970 made it mandatory for utilities to switch from soft coal to oil or gas in order to reduce air pollution. There is no way of measuring how much cleaner our air became as a result of this law, but it is certain that the demand for oil and gas increased sharply while price controls kept domestic production from rising to meet the demand. The result: increased imports.

The emotional reaction to OPEC's quadrupling of the price of its oil in 1974 gained momentum as new and more complex regulations were imposed on domestic producers. An "allocation" program was decreed. Under it, direct customer-supplier relationships were replaced with customer-supplier-government relationships. The federal rationale was that government had to make sure that oil refiners maintained normal service to established customers.

After "allocations" came something called "entitlements," in 1974. Here is this complexity as seen by economists Charles E. Phelps and Rodney T. Smith (*Wall Street Journal,* September 28, 1977):

"Under (the entitlements program) refiners using more than the national average of 'old' oil—oil from existing domestic fields at their 1972 rate of output—were required to purchase monthly 'entitlements' from refiners that use less than the average. The purchase price of the entitlements reflected the difference in cost between the price-controlled old oil and the world price.

"The idea, of course, was to provide a financial cushion for the companies that didn't have much 'cheap' domestic oil. But a corresponding impact was that refiners promptly began to import more foreign oil to run through domestic refiners, thus increasing their volume of crude oil and their share of entitlements . . . The expansion in domestic refining replaced imports of refined products but domestic consumption and domestic product prices were virtually unchanged."

What the entitlements program did, in effect, was indirectly tax domestic production in order to subsidize imports.

Meanwhile, when the 1973 Emergency Petroleum Allocation Act expired, an extension was enacted by Congress called the Energy Policy and Conservation Act of 1975 (EPCA). Against expert advise, President Ford renewed the act when it, too, was about to expire. The new EPCA called for the phasing out of price regulations on crude oil over a forty-month period; however, the attending instructions regarding pricing were such that controls could not be phased out if world-wide market prices went up ten percent or more a year.

From an inflationary point of view, a 1977 Presidential Task Force study on FEA regulations found that since the inception of the regulatory program in 1973, almost $55 million had been spent just for direct regulatory costs. The costs to refiners of meeting FEA administrative requirements were estimated at

$570 million a year. The task force's conclusion: The FEA's costs outweigh any benefits it might yield to the consumer.

Like a Bach fugue, government intervention in the energy industry developed intricate variations. It was decided that domestic production of crude oil should be encouraged, so a two-tier system of prices for domestic crude oil was established. Price controls were maintained on "old" oil, that is, oil discovered prior to the Emergency Petroleum and Conservation Act. A higher price was allowed for "new" oil, as well as for expensive oil derived from stripping old wells of their remaining imports. Imported oil made up the third tier of the price system.

In all the years of bureaucratic bungling in energy, wasn't there a voice somewhere in the bureaucracy calling attention to the possibility of a coming energy crunch? Yes, there was.

Of all the unread reports languishing in federal files, surely the one most likely to haunt every administration since the days of President Eisenhower is a report issued by the Senate Minerals, Materials and Fuels Economic Subcommittee in 1954. Called the Malone Report after Senator George W. Malone of Nevada (*Human Events,* May 14, 1977) the subcommittee chairman, the report was entitled "Accessibility of Strategic and Critical Materials to the United States in Time of War and for Our Expanding Economy." The telling phrase in the report was, "We must recognize that our greatest weakness is our dependency on very distant countries across the major oceans for our resources and pursue intensively our search for resources here at home."

The Eisenhower years were ones of very little inflation, low gasoline prices at the gas pumps, and moderate natural gas prices despite controls. Under those circumstances it was no wonder that the Malone Report went unheeded. There was no incentive for urgent action, and it has been said with a great deal of truth that a democracy acts only when a situation becomes hopelessly untenable. For some twenty years, the time during which fuel prices in the United States were artificially kept below market levels, the country lived with controls because the situation wasn't dire enough to prompt action.

Following the 1976 elections, President Carter had the opportunity of admitting government errors in its regulatory practices, but chose instead to mislead the American people in a manner that backfired badly. In 1977 Carter informed the public that the country was running out of natural gas. This was an indirect justification for the maintenance of controls on natural gas. But what the president didn't say was that a branch of the federal government, the Energy Research and Development Administration (ERDA), had told the White House in a special report that if the price of natural gas were deregulated, the nation would literally be "awash in natural gas."

This was a time when Carter was setting a price ceiling on new natural gas at $1.75 per thousand cubic feet (mcf). His own experts were telling him that if the price was $2.25 mcf, we could have all the natural gas we wanted.

The postscript to this tale in bureaucratic absurdity is that Dr. Christian Knudsen, chairman of the energy supply study committee of ERDA, was peremptorily relieved of his position and a new study of the natural gas situation was ordered. The second study also turned out to be too optimistic for Carter, and a third study was ordered. Even that one showed no shortage of natural gas, provided price controls came off!

More Bureaucracy—and Still More!

The bureaucratic answer to bureaucratic-engendered messes is more bureaucracy. In 1977, by a vote of seventy-four to ten, the Senate passed Bill S826, which established a Department of Energy. The intention was to consolidate three existing energy agencies: the Federal Energy Administration, the Federal Power Commission, and the Energy Research and Development Administration.

The FEA, from a standing start in 1973, had gone from zero employees to a staff of four thousand in less than four years. The Department of Energy started life with a budget of $10 billion and twenty thousand employees. The budget was a sum equal to the profits of all major oil companies. The department has not produced, nor will it ever produce, a single barrel of oil, but its presence is felt by the energy industry via its regulations and a veritable mountain of forms that have to be filled out annually. Its predecessor, the FEA, was already responsible, by 1977, for the filing of some six hundred thousand forms a year.

Economist and Nobelist Milton Friedman saw the dangers in a Department of Energy. Writing in *Newsweek* after the Department came into existence, Friedman said,

> It enthrones a bureaucracy that would have a self-interest in expanding in size and power and would have the means to do so—both directly, through exercising price control and other powers, and indirectly, through propagandizing the public and Congress for still broader powers. The new Energy Department will produce distortions and disruptions, which its secretary and its bureaucrats will take not as evidence of their own malfeasance but as demonstrating the need for still broader powers.

In 1978 Congress compounded the natural gas crisis by passing the Natural Gas Policy Act of 1978.

Even sophisticated people in the energy industry had trouble understanding what the act said. What was certain was that Congress had taken the energy industry deeper into the regulatory jungle. Our legislators showed their determination to prevent prices from finding their own levels. Speaking of the act, Alexander Stuart wrote in *Fortune* magazine (February 12, 1979):

> The bill-drafting process was a series of compromises between those who wanted to promote increased production by letting gas prices go up and those who wanted to hold

gas prices down. The outcome was a measure that provides for slow, grudging, partial deregulation of natural gas in the interstate market, and at the same time imposes price ceilings on the previously unregulated intrastate market, which accounts for roughly 45 percent of the nation's production.

There is a built-in policy of deregulation of natural gas in the 1978 act, but it is unbelievably complicated. The act takes 66 pages to outline, followed by 364 pages of regulations to detail its implementation. There are different prices and deregulation dates for new natural gas; new onshore production wells; high-cost gas; stripper-well gas; gas committed to interstate commerce before the act was passed (classified by the well-drilling date); gas committed to interstate commerce before the act was passed (classified by type of gas); gas sold under existing intrastate contracts; sales of gas made under "rollover" contracts (expired contracts that have been renegotiated); and "other categories."

The federal paper work involved for energy companies is staggering. And it is more costly than usual because only high-priced technical people can decipher the intricacies of the act.

U.S. Helped Create OPEC Cartel

The Organization of Oil Petroleum Exporting Countries, OPEC, was created in 1960. At the time there were twelve countries, and in 1979 there were thirteen: Saudi Arabia, Iran, Iraq, Kuwait, Venezuela, Libya, Nigeria, United Arab Emirates, Indonesia, Algeria, Qatar, Ecuador, and Gabon. Together, their known oil reserves constitute fifty-three percent of the world's supply. Their intention in forming a cartel was to take control of their own oil production. In effect, they sought to take that control away from the world's major oil companies, and so be in the position of setting their own prices for sale of oil to the rest of the world.

There was a good deal of trepidation on the part of OPEC in embarking on this new course. Lacking expertise, they needed the help of the major oil companies to market their oil. Negotiations would therefore have to be held. Also, the response of the U.S. government was an unknown factor. Would OPEC's actions trigger economic sanctions against them or, worse, military reprisals?

The oil companies decided to present a united front to OPEC, and received an antitrust waiver from the U.S. Justice Department. What then happened was recounted by G. H. M. Schuler, director of the European operations for the Bunker-Hill Oil Company, when he testified before a Senate subcommittee in 1974. The gist of it was that the U.S. State Department gave OPEC the courage to insist on their demands by telling those member countries that the U.S. government would not support the major oil companies.

In effect, the U.S. government helped OPEC create its cartel.

The oil boycott instituted by the Arabs against the United States increased prices to this country by some $18 billion. Since oil is a key raw material, the effect was like that of a comet pulling everything along in its train. A drastic price increase spiral was set in motion affecting most products sold and services rendered. It's estimated that higher oil prices were responsible for almost one-third of the increase in U.S. prices between the last quarter of 1973 and the last quarter of 1975.

In the aftershock of the boycott, gas rationing was contemplated by the government, but mercifully not imposed. Wise heads pointed out that human nature is such that a black market would quickly spring up under gas rationing and play havoc with the economy. People in low income brackets, the very ones government professes to want to help most, would be most hurt by rationing since they could least afford the black market prices for fuel.

The OPEC countries sell their oil to the highest bidder. If

the United States didn't meet OPEC's price, we would have to do without OPEC oil. In 1978, this would have meant some 7.9 million barrels of crude oil and refined products every day to meet our total demand of 18.8 million barrels per day. This oil would simply be sold to anyone willing to pay OPEC's price.

Do We Waste Oil? Have We Reserves?

It was inevitable that with oil prices rising, the cry would be heard that the United States was wasting energy in countless ways, and had only to cut back on the use of oil and gas to eliminate the energy crisis. Back in 1973, the year of the Arab boycott, Stewart Udall, former Secretary of the Interior, openly accused the country of wasting global energy resources. His criticism focused on the fact that we consume one-third of the world's energy resources. What he neglected to add was that the U.S. economy produces over one-third of the world's goods and services. The attempt to make Americans feel guilty for having the highest standard of living in the world—thanks in no small part to the harnessing of energy to technology—has never stopped.

Those who preach oil conservation through fear of diminishing oil reserves should know that the proven oil deposits under the surface of the United States are sufficient to satisfy present demand for the next fifty years. And this doesn't include untold amounts in the continental shelves, or the vast deposits of oil shale in the mountain states, which contain more oil than the deposits of the entire Middle East. In February 1979 the U.S. Geological Survey estimated there were 60 billion barrels of undiscovered oil reserves. If oil conservationists want to reduce consumption, they should note that environmental standards are estimated to have increased demand for oil by some five hundred thousand barrels a day. Coal users have switched to oil in deference to clean air laws, and exhaust emission controls have been added to cars, reducing the miles per gallon. The federal government has encouraged the switch-over from oil to coal, but there is a bizarre element involved in this aspect of federal energy policy: Even while utilities and others are trying to comply with federal encouragement to switch from oil to coal, federal environmental authorities refuse to ease pollution regulations to permit more coal use.

Ask any energy conservationist if he wants to reduce employment and production and he will vehemently deny it. But the truth is that it would be impossible to reduce energy consumption by, say, ten percent and still maintain existing levels of employment and production. The dollar cost of converting some $6 trillion worth of plants and equipment to reduce energy use, though never figured out, would surely be staggering. As Professor W. Philip Gramm has pointed out (*Human Events,* July 9, 1977), "There may be those who are willing to pay such a price, but it is important to realize that with 7.2 million Americans unemployed and with 2 million people a year entering the labor force, we are talking about a significant price if this retooling eats up the new investment and employment capacity of our economy."

In 1977 President Carter formulated seven energy goals for achievement by 1985. In his entire speech, there wasn't a single word about encouraging domestic exploration and drilling for oil via less government interference in the energy industry. The speech called for the reduction of the annual growth rate of energy consumption by more than two percent, the reduction of gasoline consumption by ten percent, cutting foreign imports of oil, establishing petroleum reserves, increasing coal produc-tion, insulating homes, and using solar energy. When the president talked about "reduction," he was really asking for higher taxes to achieve his objectives. This was recognized by the *Wall Street Journal* (May 11, 1977), which called Carter's energy program "nothing but a massive tax increase." And the National Taxpayer's Union, in a full-page ad that ran in the *Journal* of November 3, 1977, entitled "Demagoguery at the

White House" and was signed by forty-five prominent economists, declared that Carter's so-called "energy program" was the "largest peacetime tax increase in history."

In July 1979 and following a particularly frustrating period of gasoline shortages at the retail level, President Carter unveiled what was touted as being the administration's master plan on energy. It was a complex plan for reducing American dependence on imported oil. "This nation will never use more foreign oil than we did in 1977," Carter declared to his television audience. It sounded as though the United States was exceeding import levels of oil it had set for itself, but this was not the case. Quotas on oil imports in 1979 were set at an average of 8.2 million barrels a day, a figure below the import levels the U.S. was pledged to meet. The long-range objective in the Carter plan was to cut our dependence on foreign oil by half by the end of the 1980s.

Another part of the president's plan called for the development of alternative sources of fuel from coal, oil shale, plant products for gasohol, unconventional gas, and from the sun. These programs, if ever enacted, are highly expensive and a long way off from fulfillment. Nor, of course, is there any guarantee of success. One criticism immediately voiced was that the energy industry, to whom responsibility for developing synthetic fuel programs would fall, would be highly concerned with the possibilities of future price regulations or taxation, and uncertainties about environmental restrictions. Such fears, unless allayed by the federal government, would surely inhibit the energy industry from making hoped-for investments in synthetic fuel development.

Perhaps the most dismaying aspect of the president's speech was the recommendations to involve the federal government more deeply in the energy picture. For one thing, Carter proposed the creation of an Energy Security Corporation, a federally chartered entity that would oversee development of a new industry with the objective of producing the equivalent of 2.5 million barrels of oil a day in synthetic and substitute fuels by 1990. This corporation, with no need to concern itself with such matters as rates of return, costs, and market prices—factors which play important roles in the free marketplace—could well create serious warps and imbalances, just as did Nixon's wage and price controls for years after they were enacted. Carter contemplated the use of some $88 billion over the next decade to fund the Energy Security Corporation, money obtained from an anticipated $140 billion in "windfall" taxes imposed on the oil companies over the same ten-year period.

The president also asked for the creation of an Energy Mobilization Board to expedite construction of important non-nuclear energy projects. To opponents of excessive bureaucracy, both the Energy Security Corporation and the Energy Mobilization Board sounded like the creation of a lot more bureaucracy. Still not forgotten was the government role in creating the massive gas shortages in the spring of 1979, when the government tried to distribute fuel so that it was equally shared. The bureaucratic nightmare of allocating 17 million barrels of crude oil daily as it passed through two hundred refineries, twelve thousand wholesale distributors, and two hundred thousand retail service stations had resulted in a snafu of gigantic proportions. Would federal allocation of the tremendous sums for energy requested by Carter create any less waste and confusion?

The *Wall Street Journal* of July 17, 1979, pointed out one glaring flaw in the president's program—that it "relies heavily on a network of huge plants to make liquid and gaseous fuels from coal and shale. But there isn't a single operating plant anywhere in the world of the size called for by Mr. Carter."

Other recommendations made by Carter included standby gasoline rationing authority; an extra $10 billion or more over the next decade to strengthen the public transportation system; a mandate to have utility companies cut their use of oil by fifty percent during the next decade and switch to other fuels, especially coal; and authority to set mandatory state targets for saving energy.

Considering that it was less than a decade ago that the federal government encouraged utilities to switch from coal to oil, and the lead time involved in making costly changes of this nature, it's no wonder that Carter's newest recommendations produced shaking of heads and skepticism.

Oil Prices, Profits, and Monopoly

There is a myth that price controls on crude oil protect the consumer. They don't. Prices of gasoline and fuel oil are set by world market prices, not by American prices. The basic price of oil is set "on the margin." This means that the world price will be the cost of producing the last unit necessary to bring supply and demand into balance. The determining factor is not the average price of production, but the cost of the most expensive unit.

The imposition of price controls on domestically produced crude oil doesn't mean that American consumers pay less than the prevailing world price—they don't. They always pay the world price for refined products. What happens is that the oil companies, because of price controls, simply shift their profits to their refining companies and away from their producing companies to get the world price for their domestically produced oil. Such possibilities are denied the small entrepreneur who is trying to make his money from exploration and drilling, and lacks the vertical operation of the major oil companies which can juggle profits from production to refining.

Profit transfer from domestic crude oil producers to oil refiners, because of price controls, has inexorably led to the development of production abroad, with all that this entails in the way of lost jobs, lost income, and reduction of "gain" to the nation.

It is firmly lodged in the public mind, thanks in great

measure to years of unrelenting hostility on the part of the media, that oil companies make too much money. The truth is that between 1968 and 1976, the net income of the major oil companies declined by one-half, as a percentage of total revenue; dividends declined as a percentage of after-tax profits; and taxes increased four times faster than net income. During those same years, U.S. domestic exploration and development expenditures by the major oil companies increased by 272 percent and that of the independents increased by 454 percent. Between 1971 and 1977 forty-two integrated oil companies spent an average of 86.4 percent of their cash flow—a total of $121 billion—on capital investments. The rest went mostly into working capital and dividends. Using thirty leading oil companies as a yardstick, a Chase Manhattan Bank study shows that between 1974 and 1979, capital and exploration outlays of $126 billion exceeded net income by some $59 billion, that is, by 88 percent.

In 1978 the oil industry averaged 14.3 percent return on equity, while the average for all manufacturing industries was 15.9 percent.

In the first quarter of 1979, twenty-three leading oil companies showed a fifty-eight percent gain in nominal dollar profits over the same period last year; however, two-thirds of that gain was from overseas operations. Thus, contrary to what the U.S. government and media would have the American people believe, the much higher oil profits have not been the result of price gouging at home.

From time to time fears are expressed about the tendency of large oil companies to spend cash flow on acquisitions rather than on reinvestment in energy. Treasury Department figures show that the integrated oil companies spent an average of only 5.7 percent of their cash flow on acquisitions of all kinds from 1971 through 1977, and the great majority of these acquisitions have been in energy. So much for the concern about where the oil industry spends it money.

President Carter has often voiced his anxiety over the

additional profits expected to accrue to the oil companies from higher prices over the next three years, a "windfall" estimated at about $6 billion. He has proposed a "windfall" profits tax of up to forty-five percent, effective January 1, 1980, on all oil company revenues resulting from decontrol of U.S. crude production and from future price increases by OPEC. Carter wants these windfall tax revenues to be channeled to low-income housing ($800 million), mass transit ($350 million), and an undetermined amount to energy–research projects. In effect, of the $15.4 billion in extra revenues that decontrol is expected to produce through 1981, the producers would get $6 billion, the state and local governments would get $1 billion, and the federal government would get $8.4 billion. However, Thomas P. O'Neill, Jr., Speaker of the House, and chairman of the Ways and Means Committee, Al Ullman, are seeking to boost the federal share.

An analysis of what happens to a dollar of increased oil prices under Carter's program of decontrol shows the following: Fifty cents will go to the Treasury as a new tax; about thirty cents will go to federal and state governments in the form of increased income taxes, state severance taxes, and royalty payments. This will leave the oil companies with twenty cents on the dollar to invest. But a Banker's Trust study shows that the oil industry will need at least $25 billion annually just to meet projected drilling requirements through 1982.

Another accusation frequently hurled at the major oil companies is that they are monopolistic. Economic experts have, in recent years, gone through records and statistics with fine tooth combs searching for evidence of such monopoly. Not only have they come up empty-handed, but the overwhelming conclusion is that the American petroleum industry is very competitive. This conclusion, by the way, also holds true for the natural gas and coal industries.

Several important studies were cited by Walter J. Mead in the American Enterprise Institute booklet, *Energy and the*

Environment: Conflict in Public Policy, published in 1978: A study prepared for the Ford Foundation Energy Policy Project, "Competition in the U.S. Energy Industry" by Thomas D. Duchesneau, concluded that "the structure of the energy industry and the individual fuels, with the exception of uranium, is not monopolistic. The structure is not perfectly competitive, but it appears to be sufficiently competitive to yield competitive performance . . . Evidence of private monopolization of energy resources by oil companies is lacking."

In "Competition in the Oil Industry," Richard B. Mancke stated that "there is no evidence that the large vertically integrated oil companies are now exercising monopoly power in any of the four stages of the oil business . . . indeed, all available evidence supports the opposite conclusion." Both Mancke and A.E. Kahn, the coauthor of a study of vertical integration and its competitive effects in the petroleum industry prior to 1959, are of the opinion that anticompetitive elements in the industry are the fault of the federal government, the direct result of government-imposed restrictions on free market production. Says Mancke pointedly, "Current energy policies have failed to alleviate any of our four energy problems . . . In fact, they have actually worsened each of these problems."

Plans For Oil Decontrol

In April 1979 President Carter announced a plan for gradually lifting price controls from domestic oil. However, what Carter did not spell out for the American people was something well-known to those in the oil industry: There will always be permanent control of oil prices received by producers. Decontrol may take place, but there will remain a special excise tax on the price of oil, the so-called windfall profits tax.

Lets consider Carter's program of oil decontrol:

There is something called "lower tier" oil, that is, oil produced from fields in operation before controls were imposed in 1973. The controlled price of this oil is six dollars a barrel. Carter would phase out controls on this oil by 1983. Taxes on the oil would be half the difference between six dollars and the new selling price. Then there is oil discovered after 1973 but before the end of 1978, or "upper tier" oil. This oil has been selling at the controlled price of thirteen dollars a barrel. Controls would be phased out by 1990. Again, Carter wants as taxes on this oil half the difference between thirteen dollars and the new selling price. Finally, there is oil which is selling without controls (stripper wells, newly discovered fields, etc.). Here, Carter wants half the difference between the world price of oil, adjusted for inflation each quarter, and the actual selling price.

After 1990, all oil other than that produced on the Alaskan North Slope would become subject to one excise tax, the tax specified for oil currently uncontrolled.

As many have already pointed out, Carter's windfall profits tax really would not cause the oil companies much pain. After all, without doing anything, the companies would come into much higher revenues over the years even if the world price of oil remained constant; and their revenues would be much higher if the world price rose. The Congressional Budget Office estimates that if the real price of oil were to remain constant, the industry's revenues would go up by $82.9 billion between 1979 and 1985. If, discounting inflation, the world price of oil were to rise three percent a year, the total increase would come to $108.6 billion.

The objective of oil decontrol should be to leave the energy industry with the funds to drill and explore for new sources of energy, but politicians, unfortunately, don't see it that way. Their primary concern is to provide the federal government with more and more funds to enhance special interest purposes. Thus, out of the anticipated windfall profits tax, there are to be billions for the poor and other income-transfer programs. No notice is taken of the legitimate requirements of the energy industry in the way of capital investments. The Ways and Means Committee in the federal government wants even more of the government's share of windfall profits than does Carter. Whether or not the country's energy needs are met becomes a decidedly secondary factor. Consciences are assuaged via price controls ("helping the poor"), but it is these very controls that increase our oil imports and encourage OPEC to raise prices.

As for the concept of "windfall" profits as undeserved income and therefore subject to highest rates of taxation:

The concept runs counter to established American traditions. We have income averaging, which allows anyone suddenly earning much more than the previous year to average out his tax burden; he isn't penalized with a windfall profits tax. Profits realized as a result of drastically new market conditions have historically been the responsibility of the recipient. In a free market profits are reinvested, generally in areas of acceptable returns. What we now would have with the federal government's outlook on windfall profits, is a situation where the government would feel entitled to take much more than its already high share of revenues. The government could arrogantly appropriate the right to decide how and where the windfall money would be spent. This is not economic democracy, by any means.

The consensus is that even with decontrol, domestic oil exploration and production will increase only marginally. By how much is, of course, unknown. It's important to realize that decontrol doesn't mean that the world price of oil will shoot up; domestic decontrol has nothing to do with that. It does mean that producers of oil in this country will have the incentive to explore and drill for more oil here, and imports will be reduced. It surely makes more sense to purchase domestic fuel than pay exorbitant prices to OPEC. By maintaining controls, the U.S. government has, actually, been subsidizing OPEC oil.

The White House's Office of Domestic Affairs, the Department of Energy, and the staff of the House Energy and Power Subcommittee are all of the opinion that phased decontrol to mid-1982 will mean a one-time increase in the price of oil. Such an increase would be one-tenth of one percent in 1980, and three-tenths of one percent in each of the following two years, to 1982.

The *Wall Street Journal* (February 2, 1979) declared that "decontrolling the price of oil will have zero effect on the inflation rate, since that rate is determined by the government's fiscal and monetary policies." Chase Econometrics Associates maintains that with decontrol, imports will level off and show a slight decline by 1984. However, should controls remain, imports can expect to rise precipitously from 8.5 million barrels of oil per day in 1979 to 11.2 million barrels in 1984.

Will decontrol of oil in the United States finally come, or will further roadblocks be put up to prevent it? Energy experts like Arnold E. Safer maintain that decontrol is an immediate necessity. To protect the American consumer from ever-rising oil prices, Safer recommends the imposition of greater government regulation on the international side of the problem while dismantling the regulations on the domestic side. "OPEC's monopoly pricing remains the linchpin under which all energy supplies are now priced," he says (*New York Times*, May 6, 1979). "The power of the cartel to continually raise world oil prices would be substantially diluted by simultaneously giving free rein to our greatest energy asset, the highly competitive and efficient domestic oil business, and breaking the link between some OPEC states and a few international oil companies." Further, he urges, "Exempt Canadian and Mexican oil from the quota and bidding system, thereby creating a vast North American free-trade zone in oil and gas."

Those favoring retention of controls, and they are many and powerful, have not given up their struggle despite President Carter's acceptance of decontrol. They are people for whom myth dies hard, if ever. "There is the view of the world," write George and Joan Melloan in *The Carter Economy* (John Wiley & Sons, 1978) "that holds that price controls, no matter how

badly they work, are a protection for the poor and the weak—
they will ultimately transfer resources from the rich to the poor.
No amount of pursuasion will convince holders of this idea
that controls usually transfer resources from a productive
middle class to a nonproductive middle class."

We now come back to the matter of petroleum versus whale
oil.

For close to a millennium, right up to the mid-nineteenth
century, whale oil was an important source of lighting and
lubrication. Whales were hunted all over the world with a grim
determination that gradually depleted the oceans of this mam-
mal. The price of whale oil, like the price of oil in our own
time, went higher and higher. However, no government imposed price controls on whale oil, nor established multi-billion-
dollar agencies to harass the whaling industry with regulations
and restrictions. Man simply went in search of a cheaper and
more abundant source of lighting and lubrication, and in 1859
petroleum was discovered.

By the 1860s, the price of sperm and whale oil was so high
that there was a real profit incentive to develop an efficient
refining process for crude petroleum. Later came the production
of kerosene. By 1863 three hundred firms were refining
petroleum products, and kerosene began replacing sperm and
whale oil, whose prices fell sharply. By 1896, whale oil lamps
were no longer in use, and when lubricants were made of
petroleum residuals, there was no longer any use for whale oil.

The basic story and the following epilogue were recounted
by Professor W. Philip Gramm in a 1977 issue of *Human
Events*:

"The whale oil crisis is a case study of how the free-market
system solves a scarcity problem and circumvents resource
depletion. When demand increased, the price of whale oil rose
and higher prices increased the number of feasible substitutes
. . . Had government possessed the power and volition to
attempt to ration sperm and whale oil in order to hold its price

down or to levy a tax on whale oil to reap the gains from the price rise, the shortage could have been catastrophic and the advent of kerosene and other petroleum products might have been delayed for decades . . . The profit incentive produced by higher prices for whale oil gave an impetus to seek out and perfect alternative energy sources. The end product of this discovery and innovation is the Petroleum Age in which we live. We owe the benefits and comforts of this age to free enterprise and the scarcity of whales."

NATIONAL HEALTH PLAN, ANYONE?

6

If we attempt to graft a national health insurance program onto the irrational, inefficient, unsound system we have, there won't be enough money in the world to finance it.
—Dr. Martin Cherkasky, President, Montefiore Hospital and Medical Center, New York City, quoted in *Business Week*, September 4, 1978

There is no record whether or not the above words were ever read by President Carter, Senator Edward Kennedy, or any others advocating a national health plan. But if they were read, they had zero effect. Senator Kennedy has been quoted as saying that "Health care is a right," and if he and President Carter differ it is only on how soon a national health plan can be established. Kennedy wants one immediately and Carter is for a piecemeal approach—one in which implementary legislation will be submitted to Congress in dribs and drabs. This method of legislating is apparently dependent on the state of the economy and what Carter thinks the American people will tolerate in the way of increased costs to them. Under those circumstances, it seems that the Carter national health plan won't be implemented and funded until fiscal 1983, which doesn't sit well at all with Kennedy.

What we are talking about, be it Carter's plan or Kennedy's, is a national health plan whose cost would be greater than the entire 1979 federal budget. We are talking about a program costing in or around $500 billion annually.

In an age when U.S. government spending has gone beyond all rhyme or reason, the inflationary effect of a national health plan as contemplated by the Democratic party's two leading luminaries simply staggers the imagination. One reads of the federal regulatory agencies adding over $100 billion to the cost of doing business; one hears of the enormous multi-billion-dollar waste in HEW's $182 billion budget; one notes the enormous cost of myriad federal programs intended to eliminate poverty and unemployment and which do neither; but a U.S. national health plan would dwarf by far all such expenditures.

However funded, the American consumer will be the ultimate payee. If business pays part, the result will be higher prices. If workers pay part, the result will be a demand for higher wages. A vicious new round of inflation far greater than anything hitherto experienced would very likely end in the total collapse of the American economy and what remains of the free enterprise system. If fortunate, we could limp along like Britain and Sweden, two welfare states where the preponderant part of personal and business income goes for taxes to pay for federal spending projects.

At first blush, a national health plan seems an attractive proposition. The idea that the state should take care of the citizen from cradle to grave sounds very humane and desirable. After all, who, except the wealthy, is not fearful of an uncertain future in which one might see all of one's life savings vanish in payment of medical bills? When Senator Kennedy calls for nationalized medicine, he is playing on the natural fears of the American people, who are well aware of the explosion in medical costs and what it has done to their pocketbooks.

Everyone wants proper medical care, and in the affluent American society, ninety percent of the people already have some health insurance. They are paying roughly $1,150 per family in annual insurance premiums for comprehensive plans. The trouble is that health costs are increasing at the rate of fourteen percent a year.

During the past twenty-five years, the health industry in the United States has grown to the point where it employs six percent of the country's entire working force, and takes close to nine percent of the entire Gross National Product. Cost of health care went from $12 billion in 1950 to $182.2 billion in 1978. Hospital costs rose from $3.7 billion in 1950 to $65.5 billion in 1977.

Alarmingly, medical costs have risen twice as fast as the overall cost of living from 1950 to 1976. Hospitals, as we shall see, account for an enormous increase in costs: They averaged $16 per patient per day in 1950 and $175 per patient per day in 1976—a 1,000 percent increase. Hospital costs in the first month of 1979 jumped 14.4 percent over the first month of 1978. Outlays for physicians' services went from $2.7 billion in 1950 to $35 billion in 1978; however, these service costs contain the high price of malpractice insurance to doctors. The costs jumped 84 percent in 1975 and another 42 percent in 1976.

In the decade ending 1977, the number of lawsuits filed by patients against their doctors rose fourfold. The Insurance Service Office says that the cost of settling an average claim has risen from $7,472 in 1966 to $19,594 in 1975. Malpractice liability premiums paid by doctors went from several hundred dollars in 1966 to almost $5,000 in 1977.

One reason for this increase is that, in the United States, the lawyers for the plaintiffs can participate in damage awards on a contingent-fee basis. This acts as an incentive to file malpractice suits. Another factor is that American doctors practice defensive medicine to guard against litigation. Rather than run the risk of being accused of taking inadequate precautions, doctors prescribe unnecessary testing and longer hospital stays. One result is that from 1950 to 1979 medical costs rose fifteen hundred percent. Yet only forty-three percent more people are being serviced today than were serviced in 1950.

These are disconcerting statistics, but no less disconcerting than the experiences of such countries as Britain, Sweden, and Canada, which have gone the route of nationalized medicine.

Senator Kennedy has repeatedly held up the Canadian national health plan as a shining example to the United States. It was begun in 1968, with the Ottawa government paying $5 billion annually—half the cost—to the provinces, which administer the program and pay the other half. Canadians have basked in the free health care they receive, but disquieting developments have arisen. For one, health budgets have been climbing drastically in every province, to the point where higher taxes will probably have to be imposed to meet costs. For another, Canadian doctors have revolted against the program. They have been leaving the plan in droves, claiming that their fixed fees are too low. To register their protest, some 1,500 Canadian doctors out of a total of 40,000 migrated to the United States between 1977 and 1979. In Ontario, eighteen percent of the province's 11,700 doctors have withdrawn from the plan and are charging fees as much as thirty percent higher than those set by the government. The doctors have been blamed for increased medical costs, but the fact is that their fees consume less than twenty-five percent of Canadian Medicare costs.

The Ottawa government recently declared its intention of ceasing to fund its share of the health program. Should that happen, the provinces will have to charge their people much more, and private profit medicine will probably boom. Right now, provincial costs for Medicare vary greatly, from $44.00 a month per family in Ontario to $14.10 a month per family in Alberta. But these figures are misleading, because even the charge in Ontario is less than one-quarter of the money needed.

When Senator Kennedy speaks glowingly of Canadian national health insurance, mentioning that country's health costs of seven percent of the GNP compared to the United States nine percent, he fails to mention some important differences between the two countries. In Canada there is almost no patent protection on prescription drugs, so Canadians pay less for pharmaceuticals than Americans. Second, as noted earlier, lawyers for plaintiffs in America can participate in damage awards on a contingent-fee basis. In Canada, such practice is disallowed, thus large damage awards against doctors is a rarity. Of the 287 suits brought against Canadian doctors in 1976, only seven were court losses for doctors. Sixty-four were settled out of court and 216 resulted in no payment whatsoever. Total damages and legal fees paid on behalf of 31,000 doctor-members in 1975-76 were just $2.75 million annually, or $89 per doctor. That $2.75 million could be the damage fee awarded in a single malpractice lawsuit in the United States.

In Britain and Sweden, socialized medicine requires a bureaucracy of remarkable size. It even makes bureaucrats out of physicians, inasmuch as they become overburdened with paper work. For the patient, there are long agonizing delays waiting for the availability of doctors, and service itself is slipshod and indifferent. The costs are wholly disproportionate to the services received. Nevertheless, the health expenditures continue to rise, and more and more, individuals and business enterprises find themselves working to fund government programs.

Once people place the responsibility for a national health plan on the shoulders of government, they place themselves in the hands of a bloodless bureaucracy whose rules are autonomous. The rules of this bureaucracy do not engender election issues, and operate for the most part independently of any political party. Bureaucratic inertia is in control, and differences in administration and administrators amount to mere differences in rules and regulations. Under such circumstances, individual responsibility diminishes and with it comes a process of dehumanization.

In Sweden this has been a slow process, and in Britain a speedy one. Sweden, for instance, still has a high standard of living and a democratic government. Its bureaucracy is not yet as ponderous as that of Britain, but there is no question that the country is being run by a bureaucracy. Even with a change in governments, there has been no change in the trend toward nationalization. As in Britain, the concentration of power in the trade unions has virtually made these bodies the real government. It has not gone unnoticed that in these countries, as well as in the United States, organized labor has been wholly behind a comprehensive national health plan with no cost-sharing involved. Again, the consumer ultimately picks up the tab in the form of higher taxes and higher prices.

Currently, the scapegoat for those upset with health costs, which are rising at the rate of 14 percent a year, are the nation's hospitals. Between 1950 and 1977 hospital charges rose from $3.7 billion to $65.6 billion. In the same period, total health expenses went from $12 billion to $162.6 billion, with hospitals and nursing homes taking 47.5 percent of that total. Joseph A. Califano, Jr., former HEW Secretary, estimates that health costs will double by 1983, which means that health care costs would be close to 10 percent of the Gross National Product by that time. Medicaid, which services the indigent, has risen from $3.5 billion in 1966, when it was first introduced, to $19.1 billion in 1978. Medicare, for the elderly, has gone from $3 billion in 1967 to $24 billion in 1979.

Losses through waste and fraud in the health care field are enormous. HEW itself admits that between the $6.3 billion and $7.4 billion lost through fraud, waste, and abuse of rules for the year that ended September 30, 1977, between $4.5 billion and $4.9 billion involved health care.

Nearly twelve cents of every federal tax dollar is now going for health care, and of that amount, nine cents goes to hospitals. It's no wonder that the federal government, from the president down, is concerned with hospital costs. The price of an average hospital stay has gone from $350 in 1965 to $1,300 in 1978 and is expected to reach $2,600 in 1983.

There are many reasons for escalating hospital costs, but one way or another, they all point to the inflationary spending methods and regulatory impositions of the federal government. Charles Schultze, who was head of the Office of Management and Budget under President Johnson and has held other important economic positions since and before, had this to say in 1976:

"The federal Medicare and Medicaid programs have historically reimbursed hospitals in a way that promotes, rather than discourages the escalation of medical costs. Hospitals were reimbursed individually on the basis of the costs each incurred. As a consequence, there was no incentive to take measures to reduce costs, and given the sources of prestige in the medical profession, there was a positive incentive to add high-cost technology and services. More recently, improvements in reimbursement policy have been undertaken to move the system gradually away from the after-the-fact reimbursement of costs toward one that does offer some incentives for cost control. But progress is slow. And one concomitant of an underemphasis on economic incentives is an overemphasis on centralized controls that attempt to hold down costs by an ever-growing body of detailed regulations." (Gadkin Lecture at Harvard, 1976)

Mr. Schultze was speaking of the situation that existed before 1975. Since that time, under the 1972 Social Security amendments to Medicare and Medicaid reimbursements to hospitals, federal payments to hospitals are limited. Depending on circumstances, reimbursements are sometimes held to the direct cost of the services and sometimes determined below cost. However, the damage was done: Between the federal government and private insurance companies, hospitals enjoyed years of unrestrained spending, building new facilities, upping salaries, and buying any new piece of expensive equipment that came along. HEW has estimated thirty thousand excess hospital beds in the nation's seven thousand hospitals. Each hospital sent in its bills and was paid, no questions asked.

When the change in reimbursement occurred, hospitals frantically sought to make use of what they had amassed, even though this sent medical costs soaring. And to use expensive new equipment, doctors must be encouraged to provide services that are not strictly needed. Nor could the hospitals look to such plans as Blue Cross to make up needed operating funds because here, too, reimbursement was limited. The sole recourse was private patients and commercial insurance companies, and the cost to them was brutally increased. By the late 1970s, two more factors had entered the picture that were, to say the least, as unhelpful to hospitals as they were to everyone else: the cost of meeting federal regulatory demands and inflation.

It has been estimated that hospitals must cope with over 1,000 regulations involving 100 overlapping agencies. If New York State is any criterion, the cost of such regulation is staggering. The Hospital Association of New York State, in a survey based on 1976 results, found that New York hospitals are ruled by 164 regulatory agencies, including 40 federal ones. Costs inflicted by these agencies amount to twenty-five percent of total hospital budgets, or a state average of $38.86 per patient per day in New York State. The fact of such dibilitating costs did not deter former HEW Secretary Califano from railing against hospital "waste." But the *Wall Street Journal,* commenting on HEW's tongue-lashing, noted that "a careful look at hospital cost sheets reveals that the primary source of waste is not maladministration or technological 'frills' or 'overutilization' of hospitals by patients and physicians. It is a massive overlay of federal, state and local regulation that makes hospitals one of the nation's most regulation-burdened industries." (April 3, 1979)

Inflation continues to exact its tribute from hospitals. In its

1977 analysis of hospital costs covering 135 representative hospitals, the accounting firm of Touche Ross stated that "with the present rate of inflation, income from operations can hardly be expected to provide sufficient funds either for the replacement of equipment and facilities or for expansion. In fact, even routine maintenance has been deferred in significant amounts."

Acting on the basis that a national health plan was an idea whose time had arrived, and probably feeling the hot breath of Senator Kennedy on him, President Carter, in the spring of 1978, asked HEW to prepare a memorandum listing alternative approaches to a national health plan. When done, the memorandum listed five alternative approaches. They were summarized by Patricia Connell Shakow in the winter, 1978, issue of the *Journal of the Institute for Socioeconomic Studies:*

1. A consumer choice plan essentially relying on the free market and allowing tax credits for the purchase of private health insurance with vouchers for this purchase being given to the poor by the federal government.
2. A target plan which would focus on those constituencies who do not now have either private or publicly funded health insurance, primarily some of the working poor, children, and persons with catastrophic health expenses.
3. A public corporation which would, through complete federal control, provide all health insurance with private insurers, acting only as intermediaries serving an administrative role. Under the plan, employers would pay seventy-five percent of the cost and employees twenty-five percent.
4. A publicly guaranteed plan which would provide federal insurance directly and allow the consumer a choice between this plan or a federally approved private plan. All citizens would be required to make this choice, and insurance for the poor would be subsidized.
5. The so-called consortium plan, wherein two separate and competing systems would be set up, one to be run by Blue Cross-Blue Shield, and the other by the private health insurance companies, with all citizens enrolled in either plan and the federal government paying some premiums.

There are, in the federal government, ten different departments, agencies, and offices that have responsibilities relating to health care. On Carter's directive, the HEW memorandum was circulated among the other groups for comment. As might be expected, opinions varied, and former HEW Secretary Califano proposed that Carter simply choose between a comprehensive and a target plan. Carter's advisers came up with a compromise, the step-by-step approach mentioned earlier; and in the summer of 1978 he sent HEW a new memorandum directing it to prepare a national health plan embodying ten desirable principles:

"1. The plan should assure that all Americans have comprehensive health care coverage, including protection against catastrophic medical expenses.

2. The plan should make quality health care available to all Americans. It should seek to eliminate those aspects of the current system that often cause the poor to receive substandard care.

3. The plan should assure that all Americans have freedom of choice in the selection of physicians, hospitals, and health delivery systems.

4. The plan must support our efforts to control inflation in the economy by reducing unnecessary health care spending. The plan should include aggressive cost containment measures and should also strengthen competitive forces in the health care sector.

5. The plan should be designed so that additional public and private expenditures for improved health benefits and coverage will be substantially offset by savings from greater efficiency in the health care system.

6. The plan will involve no additional federal spending until FY 1983, because of tight fiscal constraints and the need for careful planning and implementation. Thereafter, the plan should be phased in gradually. As the plan moves from phase to phase, consideration should be given to such factors as the economic administration experience under prior phases. The experience of other government programs, in which expenditures far exceeded initial projections, must not be repeated.

7. The plan should be financed through multiple sources, including government funding and contributions from employ-

ers and employees. Careful consideration should be given to the other demands on government budgets, the existing tax burdens on the American people, and the ability of many consumers to share a moderate portion of the cost of their care.

8. The plan should include a significant role for the private insurance industry, with appropriate government regulation.

9. The plan should provide resources and develop payment methods to promote such major reforms in delivering health care services as substantially increasing the availability of ambulatory and preventive services, attracting personnel to underserved rural and urban areas, and encouraging the use of prepaid health plans.

10. The plan should assure consumer representation throughout its operation."

As is true for so many federal projects in their period of incubation or infancy, the wording of administrative intentions is vague enough to prevent public alarm over the eventual cost implications of the program. By June of 1979 enough had been released of the Carter plan to reveal its broad outlines. Its basic benefits called for all "medically necessary" care at public expense for the poor, including all those eligible for Medicaid, and an additional 14.5 million people living below the poverty level. Total health costs to the elderly would be limited to $1,250 in any single year, and they would still continue to receive Medicare benefits. Free care would be given to all pregnant women and infants up to the age of one. Those covered by private insurance and group health plans could continue their coverage, and their benefit from the federal plan would be that no family be required to pay more than $2,500 for health care in any one year. Children of privately insured families would be covered through their twenty-second birthday and through the age of twenty-six if they remained dependents of their parents or were full-time students.

All benefits are scheduled to begin in 1983.

The Carter plan calls for a limit to be set on the fees that doctors could charge for specific services provided for patients covered under the plan. And a ceiling would be placed on what the government and private insurers would pay hospitals for their services.

Carter says his plan would add around $25 billion to the nation's health care costs once the benefits begin in 1983. These funds would be derived primarily from general tax revenue. However, employers and employees would have to pay over $6 billion in higher health insurance premiums.

Like any other federal plan, there is no way of knowing what's in store for the American people in terms of cost once all the separate pieces of legislation—the Carter approach to national health—have been enacted and massive payments are being made.

Senator Kennedy's health plan is known as the Kennedy-Corman bill (Congressman James C. Corman, Democrat, California). It calls for comprehensive and universal coverage, regardless of income or age. There is no cost-sharing, an approach approved by organized labor, which has given Kennedy its backing. The plan grants unlimited hospital stays, and pays for all physicians' fees, X rays, and lab tests, as well as prescription drugs and dental care. It would also pay for one hundred days of care at home or in nursing homes, and psychiatric hospitalization for forty-five days. Benefits would begin in the third year after enactment of the plan.

Kennedy envisages strict cost-control provisions, with the government "negotiating" the fees doctors and hospitals should charge for their services.

Although Kennedy estimates the cost of his plan at about $36 billion a year, an outside conservative estimate is that the overall cost, including the payments into the plan by employers and employees, added to the $206 billion which is the 1979 national health care costs, would exceed the entire 1979 fiscal budget. We are therefore speaking of a figure of some $500 billion a year!

Employers would have to pay the full premiums for the Kennedy plan: by his calculations, 7.5 percent of employees' wages plus industry's own premium payments of over $33 billion a year. Employers would naturally raise prices to balance their increased health costs, and a new wave of inflation would result.

The end of that game is economic suicide.

The plans by the Carter administration and the Kennedy-Corman bill are not the only ones. Three others exist as bills, bearing the names of the legislators responsible for them, and may well be submitted as alternatives to the aforementioned two. In all three instances, the federal government is involved financially in lesser or greater degree. All would have inflationary effects, although not to the same extent as the Kennedy-Corman bill.

A national health plan is more than what it implies; it's a way of thinking that tacitly accepts the concept of a welfare state. As a matter of fact, a national health plan, as England discovered, is the one greatest single step that takes a society down the road toward becoming a welfare state. Once enacted, it is well nigh irreversible, given the inertial tendency of bureaucracy and the laziness and unwillingness on the part of legislators to undo what they have done even when inwardly convinced of their error.

What a national health plan does is really no different from what welfare does: It saps human incentive to act on one's behalf and leaves it up to the federal government to provide and pay. It never quite registers that a lower pay check or a higher price for a staple commodity is the indirect reflection of what it is costing the consumer. The majority of people find it difficult to relate a government benefit to a consumer expenditure, but that is the fact. And the greater the government benefit in terms of budgetary allocation, the greater the cost to the consumer, and the more vicious the inflation.

There are innumerable ways in which health care for the American people can be improved without saddling the nation with a prohibitively expensive national health plan. A first step lies in a seemingly unrelated area: stabilizing prices by reducing federal government expenditures. People must be left with more of their income in order to reduce their reliance on public assistance. Also, reduced government expenditures via, among other things, the elimination of unnecessary programs and regulatory demands, would reduce health costs. It has already been noted to what degree hospitals are penalized cost-wise by government regulatory demands.

Beyond that, there is the continuing incentive on the part of insurance underwriters to find ways of controlling costs. A modest deductible that requires the insured to pay a small part of his or her medical expenses, plus some co-payment that requires the insured to pay a small percentage of the charges above the deductible together impose a measure of cost consciousness when seeking health care. These are two of several practical suggestions that have been made by insurers, in this instance William O. Bailey, president of Aetna Life and Casualty. Writing in the *National Journal* (1977), Mr. Bailey also advocated coordination of benefits which would "eliminate the economic incentive to over-use medical services by limiting combined claim payments to the actual expenses incurred." Estimated 1976 cost savings to Aetna policyholders were $65 million.

Designing a policy to encourage the development and use of less costly ways of delivering health services is also important. One way is for insurers to maintain a computer file of surgical and dental fees in all regions of the country. Says Bailey about such computer use by Aetna, "Benefit payments within the prevailing range of charges for a given service in that locality are made automatically. If the fee substantially exceeds the prevailing level, we conduct an investigation to determine whether unusual circumstances justified the higher amount."

Carrying this concept a step further, why not, as Bailey suggests, permit insurers to pool and publish data on physicians' fees and utilization and use this information in negotiations with providers in a geographical area? Government permission is required so that the insurers are not subject to antitrust laws.

There is no reason why large corporations should not have their own health care programs. They could be in the form of polyclinics that are organized similar to health centers. Employees and their families could, without paying exorbitant hospital costs, have the benefit of basic health care and even preventive medicine. Costs could be shared between employer, employee, and government—in this instance, the state government—and the program could be operated so that contributions would be adjusted to effective costs. Administration could be handled by retired corporate administrators, paid without reduction in their pension payments. Even smaller hospitals could be operated on a similar basis.

This kind of health system would be far less costly, less bureaucratic, and infinitely more personal than a government-run national health plan.

A step has already been taken in this type of corporate health responsibility via the Health Maintenance Organizations (HMOs), which provide total health care from prevention to hospitalization for one fixed fee. Many companies offer HMOs to their employees and their families, who enroll at a community clinic. HMOs have over 3 million subscribers, operate twenty-six hospitals and sixty-six outpatient clinics, and employ three thousand doctors and twenty-five thousand other medical employees.

The ultimate question about health care is, can massive government intervention with a national health plan do more for the American people than the existing health care system?

The facts about the present system, as cited by Alan B. Miller, president of American Medicorp, are these:

Americans are living longer: an average of 72.5 years. In

1931 low income persons visited a doctor 2.2 times annually; it was 6 times annually in 1975. In 1960, twenty-six infants died per one thousand live deliveries; the number was sixteen per one thousand in 1976. In 1960 there were thirty-seven maternal deaths per one hundred thousand population; the comparative number was eleven in 1975. And in 1952 there were twenty thousand reported cases of paralytic poliomyelitis, but in 1976 there were only eight.

What does a national health plan offer? Based on hard experience of government approach to any problem, the American people could look forward to more bureaucracy; more waste; more regulatory demands; unnecessarily higher costs for all medical services; higher withholding taxes; sluggish, inefficient administration; and indifference and hostility on the part of doctors. Together, the above leads inescapably to slipshod treatment and long waiting periods for medical availability.

All of which is a prescription for a massive new round of inflation.

National health plan, anyone?

THE FOLLY OF WAGE AND PRICE CONTROLS

7

By mid-1979, despite vehement presidential assertions that mandatory wage and price controls were "unacceptable," millions of Americans were convinced that wage and price controls would soon be reimposed on the American economy. If so, it would be proof that, in the words of the philosopher George Santayana, those who learn nothing from the past are doomed to repeat it.

For a period that began August 15, 1971 and officially ended April 30, 1974, the Nixon administration gradually imposed wage and price controls and then just as gradually went through phases of decontrol. During this thirty-two month period, the rate of inflation doubled and warps were created in the economy which, even by 1979, had still not been straightened out. It was a time when the U.S. Wholesale Price Index, using 1967 as one hundred, rose twenty percent between 1971 and the end of 1973. By 1973, the National Association of Purchasing Management reported that "almost everything is in short supply." Prices of imported parts, goods, and commodities were rising, but American manufacturers and importers were helpless to adjust their own prices. Why produce and sell for a loss? And why add to plant and equipment when controls will effectively prevent your business from recouping its investment?

When final controls were removed in 1974, the result was as one might expect: All prices shot up precipitously, creating double-digit inflation. It was a natural market attempt to restore price equilibrium. In 1979 an analysis was completed for the National Bureau of Economic Research entitled "The 1971-4 Controls Program and the Price Level: A Economic Post-Mortem." The authors were Allan S. Blinder and William J. Newton of Princeton University. They demonstrated that the 1971–74 program of controls lowered the price level by only 1.7 percent from what it would have been otherwise. When controls ended and prices soared, any gains made against inflation during the time of controls were eroded, and prices settled at about one percent above the level that would have prevailed had there been no controls at all.

Canada's prime minister, Pierre Trudeau, imposed stringent wage and price controls on the Canadian economy to combat double-digit inflation. Controls were lifted in April 1978. In the interval, inflation had dipped only slightly, not enough to be of any significance. Organized labor was champing at the bit, belligerently waiting for controls to end to demand substantially higher wage increases. In the first ten months of 1978 strikes in Canada cost 6.4 million man-days—double the figure for all of 1977. The average annual increase in wages and benefits since the controls were lifted has been around nine percent. Meanwhile, the average net profits of Canadian companies increased twenty-one percent in the first nine months of 1978, on an eleven percent gain in revenues, a factor that added to organized labor's wrath.

President Nixon, who imposed the 1971 controls, was probably no less concerned with inflation than President Carter was when he instituted wage and price guidelines in 1979. Many felt that guidelines were the first step leading to mandatory wage and price controls. Prices went up in anticipation of an eventual price freeze, raising profits and incensing organized labor, which called for immediate controls. From labor's point of view, there was logic in their demand: The administration had asked that wage increases be held to seven percent; however, prices have been rising at the rate of sixteen percent for essentials and eight percent on the average, creating the impression that business was profiting at labor's expense.

President Carter stressed again and again that the wage and price guidelines were purely voluntary, but there was no mistaking the coercion to which government contractors were exposed by the government action. The sword of Damocles was an executive order entitled "Prohibition Against Inflationary Procurement Practices." Under it, as Laurence H. Silberman, former Deputy Attorney General and Undersecretary of Labor in the Nixon-Ford administration, wrote in the *Wall Street Journal* (November 29, 1978), "government contractors will be obliged to agree to a contractual clause certifying compliance with the President's program. Those who refuse to sign will be deemed unresponsive bidders."

What those who know their law found remarkable about Carter's voluntary guidelines is that there is no statutory authority for his approach to the problem. The Wage and Price Stability Act of 1974 in no way authorizes the continuation, imposition, or reimposition of mandatory wage-price controls; nevertheless, those who should know better clamored for just such controls. Statist economist John Kenneth Galbraith, in 1977, called for a "firm policy on administered industrial prices and on incomes." Keynesian Walter W. Heller urged the Carter administration to "assert the government's presence in wage and price matters." By the end of 1978, *Business Week* reported that "more than half of the 11 members of the Conference Board's Economic Forum—a blue-ribbon group of forecasters that meets in early December to pronounce the outlook for the following year—believe that the current voluntary program will yield a mandatory system some time in 1979." Herbert Stein, former chairman of the Council of Economic Advisers under Presidents Nixon and Ford, declared in the fall of 1978, "We are now on the road to controls," and implored Carter to "turn back before it is too late!"

It was as if the 1971–74 wage and price controls had never existed. Forgotten were the stresses, imbalances, warps, and strong inflationary surges that resulted from those controls. The witty comment, in November 1974, of economic observer Louis Rukeyser— "It was Mr. Nixon, let's not forget, who in 1969, 1970, and 1971 kept telling us that controls would not work and who, in 1972, 1973, and 1974 absolutely proved it"—was forgotten by 1979.

In the early fall of 1978, President Carter ordered an informal review of the Credit Control Act of 1969, which gives the president the authority to determine interest rate ceilings and tell banks how much credit to extend to any one company or industry. The move so frightened the business sector that companies went on a borrowing binge, fearing an eventual credit crunch. With interest rates high, it was inevitable that the high cost of money to companies would sooner or later show up as higher prices.

The *Wall Street Journal* thought it saw the scenario that the Carter administration was following. An editorial on October 31, 1978, said: "The strategy is to pour on the fiscal and monetary coals steadily to boost production and reduce unemployment, and to deal with inflation by imposing wage-price controls at the proper pre-election moment; controls probably would work for a few months, enough time to seem to do something and push the collapse onto the other side of the election."

The idea of wage and price controls doesn't derive from any particular economic theory. It is basically an outgrowth of a way of thinking divorced from the realities of the marketplace. It's a totalitarian concept in its assumption that orders handed down from above by non-market-oriented bureaucrats will be meekly obeyed without untoward economic consequences. In a democracy, where a relatively free market economy does exist, the longer wage and price controls are imposed, the more serious and lasting are the warps that develop. So great is the interplay of economic forces in an advanced economy that any artificial application of force at any point must sooner or later have drastic consequences. This is especially so if federal government spending and monetary policies continue on their unabated inflationary course.

In practice, wage and price controls mean a cessation of incentives and rewards. It is an economic reality that without incentives an economy simply doesn't work. Even in the planned economies of Russia, it has long been recognized that the elimination of incentives is counterproductive. It is a rationale of controls that if wages aren't increased, there will be no excuse for prices to rise, and hence there will be no inflation. It is true that if labor is rewarded without any increased productivity the result is inflationary; but it is equally true that if wages are frozen the result is lower productivity because of the elimination of incentive to produce. Increasing rewards for labor, as an incentive, is a main force for improvement and efficiency. Without incentive there is a decline in morale, with workers deciding that higher productivity has no value to them.

The necessity is to create a work climate that rewards higher productivity and condemns poor performance. Such a climate doesn't develop overnight, but over a period of generations. In the United States we have known this phenomenon as the Protestant work ethic, and it's a tremendous asset of any nation whose people possess it.

Conventional economists, like statist Galbraith, who dream of wage and price controls to solve the problems of inflation leave out of their calculations those very factors which are not quantifiable but which play an enormously important role in the economy: morale, ethics, commitment to work, and general working climate. They subscribe to Pythagorean thinking, whereby anything that cannot be expressed in figures simply doesn't exist.

It should be remembered that when wage and price controls were imposed on the American economy, government bureaucracy burgeoned. It was natural, since only government can enforce control. Remarkably, no one bothered to ask where the inflation came from that required controls. Had the question been asked, the hue and cry over excessive government spending and interference in the economy might have arisen years earlier and, by 1979, forced changes in the role of government in the economy. Those who now call for renewed wage and price controls are once again not asking the crucial question about the reason for a demand for controls. Once again, the business sector is harangued about prices, and once again labor is admonished to hold down wage increase demands. Only the federal government seems immune from criticism; yet the congressional spenders have never renounced their profligate ways. They are operating on the same stand in the same old way, mortgaging the country's future with huge budget deficits in times when government should be showing surpluses.

The last word on the subject goes to noted economist Ludwig von Mises, who wrote in his book *Planning for Freedom* (Libertarian Press, 1952): "The superstition that it is possible for the government to eschew the inexorable consequences of inflation by price control is the main peril. For this doctrine diverts the public's attention from the core of the problem. While the authorities are engaged in a useless fight against the attendant phenomena, few people are attacking the source of the evil, the Treasury's methods of providing for enormous expenditures."

PART TWO

The Legacy

How Conventional Economists Think

8

If we are going to understand the impasse in which the American economy currently finds itself, we must know the thinking of the advisers who have determined and shaped the economic policies of the United States government.

These advisers, both Democrats and Republicans, from every administration dating back to and including the presidency of Franklin Delano Roosevelt, have followed the siren song of John Maynard Keynes. What they have advocated and supported—Democrats to a greater degree, Republicans to a lesser degree—is government interference in the economy in a manner that arrogates to government powers and responsibilities that, as government burgeoned, created giant deficits and fueled inflation.

The problem, then, begins with the way in which conventional economists think about the economy. It is, frankly, bankrupt thinking in that it regards the economy simply as the allocation of scarce resources, and economics as the science that studies this process.

The most glaring fault in conventional economists is that they seek to apply the same scientific methods as do natural scientists: They study the economy in the same way that natural scientists study nature. The law of diminishing marginal utility, the law of downward-sloping demand, the law of scarcity, the law expressed in the labor theory of value (postulated by Ricardo and absorbed by Marx) show how economists are trying to make their laws congruent with the laws of physics. These laws are not derived from socioeconomic reality, but are simply accepted a priori and are based on Newtonian mechanistic thinking.

A physicist who observes the forces of atomic energy does just that—he observes, but makes no attempt to change that force: He simply tries to discover how the force works and how it can be used. The scientist doesn't think of value because the issue is not whether atomic energy in itself is good or bad: The primary goal of the scientist is to determine the nature of atomic energy and its utility.

This is the same approach that conventional economists take toward the working of the economic system. They delude themselves that economics is a "hard" science, even though the distinguished economist, Gunnar Myrdal, who shared a Nobel Prize in economics in 1974, has written that economics doesn't deserve a Nobel Prize because it's a "soft" science in which social and political events disturb any attempt at scientific precision.

Myrdal's evaluation has no effect whatsoever on conventional economists. Paul Samuelson, another Nobelist in economics, claims that the task of economics is to "describe, to analyze, to explain and correlate the behavior of production, unemployment, prices, and similar phenomena" and praises the use of mathematical scientific methods in the field. He believes that all societies must confront the same fundamental economic problems. Presumably, this means that a study of a communist state, a tribe of South Sea Islanders, and an advanced capitalist-oriented society would reveal similar fundamental economic problems. Such a belief is plainly as questionable as many conclusions derived from current econometric models.

Conventional economists refuse to acknowledge that, unlike nature, the economy does not exist independently of human beings, that it is a human creation and can be altered, profoundly if necessary. Regarding man as an automaton rather than as an autonomous actor with abilities to effect change, conventional economists strive to computerize American economic policy by applying obsolete concepts to what is essentially a dynamic system.

By "obsolete," is meant such outdated economic concepts as "money supply," "budget requirements," "government spending," and "government responsibility to maintain and control the economy." Then, too, there are economic "laws" that turn out not to be laws at all.

Suppose an economist sees that unemployment and inflation occur together. His or her concern will be to find the relationship between the two: in other words, in what ways and under what circumstances will inflation affect unemployment, and vice versa. The economist will be "scientific" and one outcome will be the Phillips Curve, named after the English economist, W. A. Phillips. This law tells us that there is a trade-off between inflation and unemployment: High unemployment goes hand in hand with lower inflation, and low unemployment is accompanied by high inflation. Alas for Dr. Phillips, in 1974 the Western economies suffered high unemployment *and* high inflation!

Econometrics, a product of the computer age, uses a system of equations as a means of constructing a model of the economy. Theoretically, what can be more scientific than feeding into a computer all available data—statistics on unemployment, money growth, unused industrial capacity, etcetera—and then have it predict the effects any change in variables, i.e., a tax cut, would have on the economy? It is not conceded that the economy is simply too complex, with too many variables and intangibles, to allow for any precise predictions; particularly, that the intellectual reactions of the participants in economic interplay are unpredictable and cannot be computerized.

Grants are still being given for the construction of new

econometric models: Witness a government grant of $244,500 to Chase Econometrics to build a model aimed at quantifying the relationship between taxation and economic growth. Chase claims that a twenty-five percent cut in capital gains taxes will lead to a forty percent rise in stock prices and generate a significant amount of new capital investment.

As might be expected, there are as many economists skeptical of econometrics as there are convinced of its workability. Arthur M. Okun, chairman of the Council of Economic Advisers from 1968 to 1969, terms the plan "without merit." He believes that a tax-based incomes policy ("TIP," in economic shorthand) would fight inflation. This is an attempt to provide a penalty or reward through the tax system: Offer workers a tax credit or rebate if they accept a limit on wage increases, and provide similar incentives to employers to hold the wage lines.

There is nothing anti-inflationary about such an idea because it doesn't touch on such pertinent matters as government spending. As The *Wall Street Journal* February 2, 1979 pointed out, "By reducing the expected rate of return on new profit opportunities, the TIP penalty would inhibit expansion. A policy that restrains output but not money growth raises the price level."

The *U.S. News & World Report* (October 2, 1978) queried six economists regarding their prescriptions for inflation. The consensus was that the burden of regulation should be lightened, that voluntary wage-price guidelines could help, but that wage and price controls of the kind imposed by President Nixon in 1971 should not be used. All maintained that there is no quick solution to inflation.

Walter W. Heller, former chairman of the Council of Economic Advisers under Presidents Kennedy and Johnson, and one of the six economists queried, declared that "what we need is a 'muddle through' policy, one that combines moderate restraints on government spending and on the money supply, plus strong action to increase supplies, improve productivity and reduce costs."

Other suggestions by the six economists ranged from a recommendation to "break the printing press," because the Federal Reserve has been "creating money too fast," to a new administrative program to promote productivity.

Massive tax cuts along the lines of the Kemp-Roth bill, named for Congressman Jack F. Kemp (Republican, New York), and Senator William V. Roth, Jr. (Republican, Delaware), are also a product of obsolete economic thinking despite their appeal to the public. The bill calls for a thirty percent slash in individual income taxes over a three-year period, with a modest reduction in corporate taxes as well. Without an accompanying reduction in government spending, plus an increase in productivity, the proposed Kemp-Roth tax reductions would simply trigger more inflation and generate soaring deficits. These deficits would have to be funded by new government debt, that is, by borrowing from the public. As economist Milton Friedman correctly points out, a major tax cut isn't "real" because conventional economics dictates that future higher taxes must eventually make up the increased deficits. "The total tax burden on the American people," says Friedman, "is what the government spends, not those receipts called 'taxes.' And any deficit is borne by the public in the form of hidden taxes."

Another economic concept currently trying to come to grips with the problem of taxation is called the Laffer Curve, named after American economist Arthur B. Laffer. The Laffer Curve postulates that there are two tax rates that spell disaster for government revenues: one when the tax rate is one hundred percent, at which point all production stops because no one will work one hundred percent for the government, the other when the tax rate is zero, when production is maximized but government revenue is zero. Laffer advocates tax juggling until the point is reached on the curve where the rate of taxation is acceptable to most people.

The Laffer Curve does not come to grips with the real problem, which is the role of government in the economy and not the amount of taxes collected to pay for government activities. One can imagine the appalling inflationary surge if taxes were lowered to an acceptable point on the Laffer curve while government spending continued to increase without any meaningful rise in productivity. Nor does the Laffer Curve take sufficient account of costs added to prices as a result of the regulatory demands of government agencies. These fuel inflation no less than any increase in individual and corporate taxes.

Arthur Burns, former head of the Federal Reserve Board, suggests the following for dealing with inflation: a moderately restrictive policy by the Federal Reserve without congressional or White House interference; a federal budget cut by a "substantial amount," with a balanced budget within the following two years; a scaling down of projected increases in federal salaries by half; a cut in salaries for the president, the cabinet, and the congress; a two-year salary freeze for top corporate executives; the establishment of labor-management "productivity councils" to boost productivity; plans to blunt current cost-raising pressures; tariffs, import quotas, farm price supports, and minimum wages; plus plans to postpone certain pending environmental and safety regulations.

In June of 1978 some fifty economists of different viewpoints met on Martha's Vineyard in Massachusetts to discuss government action on inflation and unemployment. They duly took note that the government policy of wage and price guidelines, the only anti-inflation policy to emerge from the administration, was faring poorly. The usual shibboleths were heard about slowing down the economy by curbing federal spending and reducing the growth rate of the money supply.

But there was some embarrassment about this old-fashioned approach to inflation because the nation had emerged from the 1969–70 and 1973–75 recessions with inflation still at high levels. There was much talk about using econometric models to create economic policy, but many economists rejected the idea. Nothing substantial emerged from the conference.

Some months later, in the final days of 1978, a group of eighty top government and private economists met in St. Louis at a symposium entitled "Alternative Policies to Combat Inflation." All agreed that inflation was a serious problem; and all agreed that restrictive monetary and fiscal policies were needed. Beyond that, all opinions diverged.

Now and then word seeps out about new economic ideas and approaches germinating somewhere. In *Fortune* magazine (December 31, 1978) under the heading "The New Down-to-Earth Economics," Walter Guzzardi, Jr., wrote about a small group of young academic economists strongly criticizing current government economic policy. One of the group, Robert Lucas, pointed out the fallacy of the Federal Reserve increasing the money supply as a way of correcting possible future problems in the economy. There is no addition to goods or services, only an increase in the money supply, said Lucas, yet a sense of euphoria sets in when people find themselves with more cash to spend. Eventually, people find that they have overspent and overborrowed—a condition which occurred during the sixties. As a result, when the Federal Reserve repeated this tactic in the seventies, nobody was fooled. People didn't spend more, and business didn't expand. All that happened was an inflationary surge. The government, which had hoped to stimulate the economy as it successfully had done a decade earlier, found that people wouldn't react the same way twice.

According to Lucas and others, tax reductions and deficit spending work the same way. When taxes are cut for the first time, people spend; and higher taxes follow. When tax cuts come again, people are more cautious—they know what's coming: eventual higher taxes to service expanded debt. As a result, people don't consume or invest as they did the first time. In other words, a tax cut not balanced by a decrease in government spending signals higher taxes to come.

The new economists recognize that one of the salient fallacies of Keynesian economics is the assumption that people will continue to behave and react in the same way to the same situation. They understand that people do learn from experience and are also highly skeptical of the value of econometric models of the economy. Lucas said: "If in the early Sixties we had asked a designer of macro models what the result would be of a doubling of the money stock and a $60 billion deficit, the answer would have been one percent unemployment. Such predictions were wildly inaccurate—the inflation of the Seventies produced the highest unemployment since the Thirties."

Unfortunately, despite the validity of the criticisms directed against conventional economic thinking, Lucas and others of his group fall back on Keynesian economics when asked for solutions to current problems. With Milton Friedman, they call for government to fix an annual rate of growth for the money supply and to stay with it. They also believe in setting tax rates that would, on average, balance the budget.

It's a fact of life that American economic policy for more than four decades has been controlled by Keynesian economists. They range from the orthodox variety who recommend government deficit spending only in times of excessive unemployment, to statists who would maintain and increase government spending in good times and bad. It's a further fact of life that Keynesian policies are practiced under Democratic and Republican administrations alike, and that such policies have resulted in an enormous expansion of government activities. These activities require higher taxes, which result in still more government activities.

When taxes rise, prices also rise, which devalues the currency. This is inflation, which the Keynesians try to fight by increasing the rate of interest and decreasing the money supply. Starved for funds but with taxes still high, industry retrenches, with a higher rate of unemployment as the result. This frightens the conventional economists, who urge the government to lower the interest rate and release more money into the economy. Business booms, until the Keynesians become frightened of inflationary pressures and urge the government to act. The cycle starts all over again.

As long as Keynesian thinking prevails, there are no other solutions for unemployment and low economic productivity but increased spending, expanding budgets, and higher taxes.

Two schools of thought currently dominate American economic thinking. One school is of the opinion that the government's fiscal policy is paramount, while the other avers that money supply is most important. The former school is represented by Walter W. Heller. The latter group, known as monetarists, have as their best-known spokesman Milton Friedman, 1976 Nobel Prize winner.

Walter W. Heller—Fiscal Emphasis

On January 19, 1979, the *Wall Street Journal* ran an article by Walter W. Heller entitled "The Realities of Inflation." But it did not confront those realities head-on and failed to arrive at any conclusions beyond deciding that the monetarists are wrong. Heller, a Keynesian economist, lamented: Yes, over the years we have indeed worried whether full employment, price stability, and economic freedom of choice can coexist. Heller was pessimistic that they could. He wants to "look at the anatomy of inflation and see how much of it is embedded in our institutional structure or external forces largely beyond the reach of monetary policy and grasp of the monetarists, and how much is truly responsive to a squeeze on demand via tight money."

Heller believes that the underlying forces of inflation are political and structural. He is against "drum-tight money", against an end to federal deficits, and against mandatory controls.

Heller berated the monetarists who claim that the reason for high employment and high inflation coexisting in the 1970s is an overabundant money supply. He summed up the monetarist approach as follows: "Curb federal deficits and slow the increase in the money supply and inflation will wither away." He also asked this question of the monetarists: "How can it be that three years of slack in the economy from early 1975 to early 1978—with the unemployment rate averaging 7-½ percent and operating rates in manufacturing 79 percent—failed to dent the underlying rate of inflation; (b) How is it . . . . that the Spartan policies of tight money they advocate could subdue inflation without a deep, deep depression?"

That Keynesian economists will disagree violently among themselves may be attested by the letter responses to Heller's article. One economist admonished Heller that the rate of inflation fell when money was tightened, and rose when money was loosened. Another writer pointed out that

> . . . we think that the fundamental cause of inflation must be the creation of purchasing power without a concomitant increase in productivity. Those who acquire money without producing its equivalent must be accommodated in one of two ways: 1. Reduce the standard of living for those who are now laboring to produce or 2. Inflate the cost of production, thereby shifting the ultimate penalties to those who have saved some of their past productivity.

In summary, Heller believes that government spending is of greater benefit than spending by the private sector. He advises the government to spend more and that taxes be raised to pay for the increased spending. Although he is also concerned with the money supply, his major emphasis is on the role of government fiscal policy to determine the money supply.

Milton Friedman—Monetarist

If one underlines key phrases in select writings by Milton Friedman, one finds an intellect concerned with more than the value-free econometric models and mathematical equations that obsess Keynesian economists. That Friedman is a Keynesian at all is due to the fact that he is for government control of the money supply and interest rates; beyond that he brooks no government interference in the economy. "What is the basic problem of the United States today?" he asks in a brochure, *The Economics of Freedom,* and answers, "The problem is that government interference is threatening to strangle the true source of our achievement."

He reminds us that in 1975 there were at least twenty-seven major federal government regulatory agencies. They issued sixty thousand pages of rules or proposed rules in the Federal Register. Their regulations occupied no less than seventy-two thousand pages in the Code of Federal Regulations. The expenditures of these agencies have tripled from $1.6 billion in 1970 to $4.7 billion in 1975.

Friedman fears that we are nearing the point of no return with such government interference. If we allow government growth to go unchallenged, he says, "We shall degenerate into a society which will lose that spark of creativity, that spark of independence, of freedom, that we have all loved in our country." He is of the opinion that government spending is the real problem. In addition to recommending slashes in such spending, he recommended indexation of taxes—relating taxes to prices in a fixed percentage way; also, indexation for long-term corporate loans. However, he recently expressed doubt about indexing as an anti-inflation tool.

Friedman terms Keynes's policy of government deficit spending a "road to disaster." He sees it as a path that leads to a state of affairs where "government is the patron, the citizen is the ward," and that this paternalistic attitude is at odds with free man's belief in his own responsibility for his own destiny. Friedman puts great emphasis on the connections between political, personal, and economic freedom.

Political and personal freedom need no explanatory notes, but one is entitled to ask, what kind of economic freedom does Professor Friedman have in mind? A careful reading of his writings reveals that his philosophy of economic freedom consists of two basic principles: 1. The belief that the scope of government must be limited, that it should protect its citizens from enemies outside and inside, preserve law and order, enforce contracts, and foster competitive markets; and 2. The belief that the power of government must be dispersed and not centralized.

Within the scope of his first principle, there is surely no argument about the government protecting its citizens, preserving law and order and enforcing contracts. But what about fostering competitive markets? An example of where this type of interference can lead may be judged by considering the components that determine prices. Basically, there are three: the cost of labor; the profit margin; and the cost of government activities, including taxes and the cost of regulatory demands.

Friedman believes that the cost of labor should be limited by the laws of the free market. Anyone familiar with the cost of labor in the United States today knows that such a hope is a pipe dream. There are built-in factors that effectively prevent labor costs from going down, no matter what other considerations are involved.

There is, for example, a minimum wage rate. There is also the strength of the labor unions. One no longer sees declining labor costs in an area where there is a surplus of labor: The unions won't permit it. Where there is too much work and insufficient help, employers are forced to pay overtime rather than hire additional workers. Sometimes, as is the case with the musicians' union, a minimum number of musicians must be hired for, say, a Broadway musical, even when one or more of them are not required to perform at all. The most powerful unions have just about become independent of the labor market in their negotiations; they can even force increases in wages in situations where the labor demand is far below the supply.

Friedman believes that the profit margin must not be interfered with by government, that the quality of entrepreneurship should be the sole deciding factor. In other words, the price paid by consumers should be free in the sense that the consumer should have the right to "pay it or leave it." As consumers know, in most instances such a choice is both painful and unacceptable.

Government activities bother Friedman greatly. He wants government to withdraw from all economic activities save control of the monetary supply and the setting of rates of interest. That is, he is opposed to a fiscal policy whereby government increases the scope of its activities and consequently reduces the freedom of the individual. This kind of fiscal policy has been likened to the operation of a balance wheel: When private expenditures decline, government expenditures rise to keep total expenditures stable; and when private expenditures rise, government expenditures decline.

Says Friedman, "The chief harm of this 'balance of wheel' theory is not that it has failed to offset recession, which it has, and not that it has introduced an inflationary bias into government policy, which it has done too, but it has continuously fostered an expansion in the range of government activities at the federal level and prevented a reduction in the burden of federal taxes." He argues that if the "balance of wheel" theory should be applied at all it could better be done by raising taxes during a boom and lowering taxes during a recession.

There are many economists today who believe that an

increase in expenditures by government is expansionary, and a decrease leads to a contraction of the economy. Friedman regards this belief as a fallacy. He considers fiscal policy based on Keynes's theory of spending as part of an "economic mythology." However, he does accept the philosophy that "the state has to pay its bills and the people should pay taxes." His objection is that the government pays too many bills for expenses that should not be incurred by government at all.

Some Fallacies in Friedman

Friedman sees in the government policy of redistribution of income a form of coercion that conflicts with individual freedom. From his point of view, the "ethical principle that would justify the distribution of income in a free market society is 'to each according to what he and the instruments he owns produces.' " This overlooks the fact that the majority of people do not own "instruments" and that most of the labor force doesn't engage in the actual production of goods. What does a bank teller, a teacher, or a bookkeeper produce, in the classical sense of production? It's impossible to quantify individual contributions and thereby be able to reward someone according to his or her contribution.

Production in a mature economy is the result of both brain work and physical effort on the part of the entire nation. It is an integrated process and cannot be apportioned individually. The "instruments" to which Friedman refers are at the same time both the product of the effort and the tools used.

Most people will agree that the essence of an economy is production for consumption, and that, consequently, the center of economic considerations should be the consumer; however, Friedman's concept of economic freedom isn't connected with consumer rights at all, but with the rights of the business enterprise. This is a simplistic approach. "Business enterprise" is not an aggregate; it comprises many individual corporations that conflict with each other and whose power relationships change in the process of competition. In the American economy it cannot be denied that freedom of business enterprise means primarily the freedom of the giant corporation. No interference with this "imperfect competition" boils down to no interference on behalf of smaller companies. And this kind of "imperfect competition" is growing.

Then what about the consumer? What protection does he have? Friedman says, "The consumer is protected from coercion by the seller because of the presence of other sellers with whom he can deal." Expanding on this theme, he adds, "The seller is protected from coercion by the consumer because of other consumers to whom he can sell. The employee is protected by the employer because of other employers for whom he can work, and so on. And the market does this impersonally and without centralized authority."

Again, we see the simplistic approach. The kind of situation that Friedman envisions actually doesn't exist: It is merely a model of an economy. Friedman calls his particular model "competitive capitalism." It is supposed to work through voluntary cooperation between individuals. The key word is "voluntary" because Friedman compares this system to the totalitarian concept, which is based on coercion. In this latter system the economic activities of millions of people are coordinated through the use of force or implied force. Of course, this is true. In Russia, or any other communist state, the central planning authority has the right to decide what is to be produced and consumed. It represents an absolute monopoly of power in every field—economic, political, cultural, and social. Under "competitive capitalism," avers Friedman, there is voluntary cooperation in economic transactions wherein the cooperating parties all benefit. A model of such a society is represented in a free enterprise exchange economy.

The unreality of Friedman's model economy is apparent when one considers that different forms of coercion also exist in free enterprise economies. There is no such thing as a clear alternative between absolute freedom and absolute coercion. The coercion of competition, for example, channels economic activity, and the power flows toward the giant corporation.

Employees in the free enterprise system are also under certain forms of coercion. Supposedly, an individual is free to choose another employer if he becomes dissatisfied with his work; in actuality, the worker's age, accrued benefits, fear of the unknown, and so on may keep him in place. Also, he is under pressure to produce far more so than his counterpart under communism, where up to ten persons are required to do the job the one employee does under free enterprise. In this respect, oddly enough, there is less coercion under communism. Of course, there is also infinitely less productivity and far more inefficiency, but that's something else again. The assumption that everyone acts voluntarily in the absence of government coercion is just very simplistic.

Friedman states that the central characteristic of the market technique in a mature economy is fully displayed in a simple exchange economy which contains neither enterprise nor money. This ahistorical approach to economy is typical for conventional economists.

Such an approach reduces a mature economy to a point where it has nothing in common with economic reality. In a "simple economy without enterprise and money"—using Friedman's terminology—production is geared toward consumption by the producers themselves. Only some peripheral surpluses are exchanged. Consequently, exchange takes place on the periphery of the economy. The system in such an economy could exist just as well in the absence of exchange. A modern economy is not based on exchange, and to call it a money-exchange economy is to contradict reality.

Friedman's phrase "individual contracting partners" is also not representative of what typically goes on in an advanced economy. The contracting partners are more often institutions and the individuals employees of the institutions. Only exceptionally is the individual owner a contracting partner.

In the same vein, an employee is protected by a labor union or by law, and not by the fact that he may choose a different employer.

Friedman speaks of an exchange economy that doesn't exist anymore; he speaks of free competition, which is a fiction; he envisages an impersonal market, which doesn't exist; and he takes it for granted that the American system is a "competitive capitalism," but what is the true definition of capitalism? Capitalism, for Friedman, is a free private enterprise economy. The emphasis is on private ownership of business enterprises; in other words, the form of ownership is accepted as the decisive criterion for an economy. Consequently, we have capitalist or communist economies according to the forms of ownership of the means of production. Again, a simplistic approach.

Although basically there are no significant variations of totalitarian economies, there are many variations of "capitalist" economies. The American economy is primarily technocratic, based on a high intellectual level of both production and management. European capitalism has distinct features of its own. The Swedish type, for example, emphasizes social welfare. Britain, too, has become a welfare state. France has a high proportion of nationalized industries. Germany is a combination of American and Swedish versions of capitalism. Japan has developed an economy which combines American technology and Japanese tradition. In every capitalist country there are different degrees of government intervention in the economy. In Sweden, termed socialist, there is private ownership and competition, yet the unparalleled interference of government in the economy no longer makes it logical to say that the country has an economy based on the free enterprise system.

Of particular interest to Americans are the findings of Peter Drucker, well-known observer of the American business scene and author of various books on the subject. In his *The Unseen Revolution* (1976) he coined the concept of "Pension Fund Socialism." Drucker proves that American pension funds now own more than fifty percent of the shares of big corporations and in the 1980s may well become the majority owners of all such shares. Are pension funds capitalist—or socialist? Does it matter? Surely of primary importance is *what* is owned, and what "gain" accrues to the nation as a whole.

For a long time now it has been accepted that in a mature economy, particularly where large corporations are involved, there is a growing divorce between ownership and management. Drucker shows that there is even a divorce between ownership of the means of production and ownership of equity. Shares are bought and sold according to the evaluation of respective enterprises. The basic concern of ownership to improve management performance has been replaced by the concern for earnings-per-share, even though shareholders legally have the right to demand greater efficiency. All of this indicates that who owns the means of production is not really the important consideration in an advanced economy. Inflation, high or low productivity, efficiency, and other tangible and intangible aspects of a modern economy are not a function of production ownership.

In view of the fact that it is credit that makes the American economy function, conventional economists have never ceased being bemused with the "money" concept. "Money matters" is the essence of Milton Friedman's quantity theory of money, and money is the centerpiece of the monetarist economic philosophy.

The monetarists define money in a way that makes it usable as a tool for analysis. Simply put, they assert that the quantity of money in the nation determines prices. In arriving at this conclusion, the concept of money is derived from a model, not a reality. Friedman actually sets up a model of money to fit in with his model of the economy. Consequently, he never sees money as a human creation like all other economic components, and the economy itself as our creation. Money, to conventional economists, has taken on a life of its own.

For all practical purposes, Friedman feels that the increase in the money supply (currency plus adjusted demand deposits and commercial bank deposits) should roughly equal the growth in the national economy. He advocates a growth in the money supply of between five and seven percent.

Friedman and his fellow monetarists believe that by so doing, money, at least, will not be the cause of the economic malaise that afflicts the United States. Neither stable prices nor full employment is guaranteed, nor is any method proposed to prevent major economic disturbances.

The monetary authority, according to Friedman, can make a major contribution to the promotion of economic stability:

A steady and moderate growth in the quantity of money could make a major contribution to avoid either inflation or deflation . . . Still, there would be other forces in the economy that would affect the economy, yet we could create a monetary climate favorable to the effective operation of those basic forces of enterprise, ingenuity, invention, hard work and thrift that are the true springs of economic growth. That is all we can ask from monetary policy at our present stage of knowledge.

One is inclined to ask, "Is that all there is to it?" Will a "monetary climate" favorable to all the best human qualities really solve our economic problems? We are beset with problems in energy, employment, pollution, and welfare, among other areas; shall we believe that a sunny "monetary climate" is all we need? We see in Friedman's approach the mechanistic view no different than the basic view of any other conventional economist. For Friedman, money exerts a "distinct and independent influence of its own if it gets out of order." Thus the money machine would "throw a monkey wrench into the operation of all other machines."

Friedman is concerned with a proper definition of money, although he recognizes that his definition itself is not the important factor, but simply serves "mainly to organize our analysis rather than to determine its content in any important respect." Still, Friedman perceives money as something stable, something added to the economy that can exist and be understood as an "independent individuality."

Monetary statistics, as published in Friedman & Schwartz's *Monetary Statistics of the United States,* may be useful for providing information about the quantitative qualities of money, but nothing more than that. It may be of interest that currency held by the public in January of 1867 was $590 million, but the statistics don't tell of the great qualitative differences that must have occurred in the hundred-year interval. One must look to such facts as the building of the first modern blast furnace in 1859; the production of one hundred tons of steel in 1872; the development of the steam engine; the Edison method of using electricity for illumination in 1876. In 1850 there was a seventy-hour work week, and more than seventy percent of the working population were farmers. It was an America without cars, planes, tractors, trucks, automation, radios, television, banking, and with practically no electricity. Yet instead of looking at the history of the American economy and placing money and credit in context—not regarding them as mere statistics—Friedman and conventional economists generally are content just to define money. Friedman's book of some fifteen hundred pages doesn't deal with money but with an arbitrary definition of money.

The same fallacious approach has been applied to credit. In order to "organize the data" on credit in a useful way, credits have simply been turned into "money supply." It is a concept that permits economists to organize data within the framework of the classical theories, which regards the economy as a system of commodities operating in their own space-time continuum. And in order to prove that there is a causal relationship between the "money supply" and prices, an "ether" in the 17th-century conception has been introduced—that of circulation of money and velocity of circulation.

Circulation of money exists in an exchange economy. In a mature economy based on credits and debits, which are nothing more than bookkeeping entries, neither exchange nor circulation exists. Payments are made by making entries into ledgers or, now that the computer age is upon us, onto tape and stored. The sum total of these credits and debits may be likened to a force field that vibrates.

Of what use is it to measure this type of force field that changes daily and hourly as credits become debits and vice versa? Yet this doesn't stop Friedman from creating equations that prove that price will be stable if money supply, velocity, and volume of production doesn't change. Or that if velocity and volume of production is stable, the money supply determines price. Although the equation $P = MV/T$ may be mathematically elegant, it has no relevance to practical economic problems; still, it's used as the basis of the philosophy of the quantity theory of money.

It must be flatly stated that the money supply can never be determined. It was possible to do so in an exchange economy, but in a credit economy based on book entries and literally billions of transactions, the sum total of credits has nothing in common with the sum total of currency and demand deposits.

What Monetary Policy Can and Can't Do

There is no question that Friedman is a staunch advocate of the free enterprise system and recognizes and appreciates human dignity and the value of the individual. He is a great believer in individual responsibility and attributes the worsening of our moral climate to the change in our beliefs—from that of individual responsibility to one of social responsibility. He accepts that the major goals of economic policy should be high employment, stable prices, and rapid growth. It is evident to him that economic policy must be set by a macroeconomic organ, and that this organ can only be the government. Friedman doesn't oppose government interference in the economy; he simply is against the Keynesian variety and, of course, the Marxist.

In opposition to Keynes, Friedman doubts whether government spending can make up for insufficient private investment. He also objects to the Keynesian view that the role of money should be the minor one of keeping interest rates low in order to hold down interest payments in the government budget.

He is frank in assessing what monetary policy can and cannot do. He asserts that "monetary policy cannot peg interest rates for more than a very limited period and it cannot peg the rate of unemployment for more than a limited period." As far as pegging interest rates, Friedman says that to keep interest rates down, the Federal Reserve should buy securities. This would raise the prices of the securities and lower their yields. Further, it would increase the quantity of reserves available to the banks, hence increasing the amount of bank credits and ultimately the total quantity of money. This is why the layman in general and the conventional economist in particular assume that an increase in the quantity of money—the money supply—tends to lower interest rates.

For Friedman, the above is only a beginning. The rapid growth of the money supply would stimulate spending and probably increase relative prices of cash balances. Rising income would increase the demand for loans, might raise prices, and reduce the real quantity of money. These three effects would reverse the initial downward direction of interest rates in less than a year. Within a year or two the rates of interest would return to their original level. A further effect would be that a higher rate of monetary expansion would correspond to a higher rate of interest. Prices would rise in expectation of a further increase in prices, and borrowers would be willing to pay higher rates of interest.

Friedman doesn't believe that monetary growth will stimulate employment, nor that monetary contraction would retard employment. He maintains that at any given moment there is some level of unemployment. A lower level of unemployment indicates there is an excess demand for labor, that will produce pressure on real wages, while a higher level of unemployment indicates an excess supply of labor. Friedman stresses real wages, as against nominal wages, that can be increased or decreased according to the quantity of the money supply outstanding. Real wages reflect what has been produced for those wages, while nominal wages reflect only what has been paid as labor costs.

Friedman concludes that monetary policy cannot peg either rates of interest nor the rate of unemployment.

What *can* monetary policy do?

Friedman accepts the statement by the nineteenth century English economist philosopher John Stuart Mill, to whom ". . . money is a machine doing quickly and commodiously what would be done, though less quickly and commodiously without it: and like any other kind of machinery, it only exerts a distinct and independent influence of its own when it gets out of order."

Monetary policy, says Friedman, can avert major economic disturbances. It can keep the economic machine well oiled. All this is possible if monetary policy guides itself by magnitudes it can control and avoids sharp swings in policy. But Friedman fails to understand that the United States economy is not, nor has it been for many years, a money economy. It is a credit economy, and it is wrong and dangerous to equate the money supply with the credit supply.

Another factor neglected by Friedman and his fellow monetarists is that purchasing power is backed by economic performance. If the economy doesn't perform, the dollar loses its purchasing power. Since productivity in the United States has suffered a marked decrease during the past years, there has been a concomitant drop in what the dollar will buy.

At one time gold was used as an economic barometer, and paper money was directly related to the price of gold. As long as our money was backed by a commodity such as gold, its purchasing power and the relative value of goods and services were determined by that commodity. Money had purchasing power because it represented a commodity of value; and since the value of gold was relatively stable, the gold standard served as a reliable measure of value for all goods and services and helped to stabilize prices. Once we went off the gold standard the commodity backing disappeared, and what we had left was unbacked paper money, money that had lost its inherent value and represented nothing more than a unit of price. In this situation, the purchasing power of money is determined by the prices of goods and services. When prices rise, purchasing power diminishes, because our money entitles us to fewer goods, services, and man-hours. Without the inherent value provided by commodity backing, money in itself has no purchasing power.

Friedman doesn't see that the concept of the money supply, by virtue of its picayune standing as against credit, is more a fiction than a fact of economic reality. The real issue is one of giving credit of a scope that meets the needs of the economy functioning with full employment.

Galbraith—A Stalinist Economist

One of the Keynesian economists who has popularized his ideas to the point where some rebuttal is necessary is Professor John Kenneth Galbraith.

Galbraith may be termed a Stalinist economist, one who

would maximize government spending, government interference in the private sector, and government controls and regulations. He is of the school that insists that socialist-oriented, theoretical economists can do an infinitely better job making decisions and allocating resources than private industry, despite the dismal record of failure in countries where such concepts prevail. Galbraith's way inevitably leads to total bureaucratic control of the economy with all that this implies: elimination of enterprise, competition, initiative, and of individual thrift and responsibility.

Galbraith is an advocate of price and wage controls as a means of combating inflation, pointing to the "success" of such controls when they were imposed by President Nixon in August 1971. There was indeed the appearance of great success following imposition of controls. After all, if you have federal deficit spending plus a rapid rise in the money supply—both inflationary—and if you forbid any rise in prices, the result is positively euphoric. But then came the rude awakening, about which Galbraith is silent. The government can't control the price of goods Americans buy abroad, nor can it control the price of raw farm commodities. When farmers found they couldn't get the price they wanted for their products in the United States because of the controls, they sold abroad. The result was that farm products were suddenly in short supply at home, and what was available rose sharply in price. The government thought of bringing farm prices under control, but wisely decided this was impossible. At the same time, companies importing raw materials and components from abroad found to their horror that those prices were rising relentlessly, but they couldn't adjust their own finished product price because of price control. Nixon had to begin dismantling the controls or risk a catastrophic disruption of the economy.

Galbraith, calling for a wage and price freeze as a means of creating stable prices and wages, also calls for increased government spending and higher taxes, which are the very factors that force prices to rise. Such price increases in turn trigger wage increases that are totally independent of any increase in productivity. If that's not enough, a wage freeze kills initiative and working morale, the most important inputs in production. The result is that we pay more and more for products and services of ever declining quality.

Galbraith's philosophy calls for the government to be arsonist and fire fighter simultaneously: arsonist, in voting massive spending programs for nonproductive purposes and forcing business to seek higher prices to offset the cost of regulatory harassment and higher taxes; and fire fighter by imposing wage and price controls.

The Warning Flags Are Up

Where does conventional—Keynesian—economic thinking lead?

In a 1977 paper entitled "Can the Corporation Survive?" Professors Michael C. Jensen and William H. Meckling of the University of Rochester, made this gloomy forecast:

"The private corporation has been an enormously productive social invention, but it is on the way to being destroyed. Large corporations will become more like Conrail, Amtrak and the Post Office. One likely scenario begins with the creation of a crisis by the politicians and the media. In some cases, the crisis will be blamed on the 'bad' things corporations do or might do. The remedy will be more and more controls on corporations (something like what has been happening in the transportation and oil industries). When the controls endanger the financial structure of the corporations, they will be subsidized by the public sector at the cost of more controls. When the government brings the industry to the brink of collapse, the government will take over. The details of the scenario will no doubt vary. Moreover, some firms will simply be driven out of business because of regulatory costs and the inability to raise capital."

The authors' opinion is that only a radical change of some sort in the basic structure of our political institutions can alter the course of events at this point.

For the American public, Keynesian economics lead to the destruction of the middle class—the historical backbone of the nation—through higher taxes and double-digit inflation. The monies cruelly siphoned from this productive segment of the population are channeled by government into nonproductive programs which contribute little to real economic growth.

Keynesian economics result in government control of the economy rather than vice versa. In the process, according to William E. Simon, former Secretary of the Treasury, "A mood of dependence on government has increased which feeds upon itself, creating still more demands for benefits without recognizing that the bills must be paid—either directly in current taxes or indirectly through accelerating inflation and economic disruption."

We simply cannot afford a government that operates like a Big Brother. It usurps capital and profits; it spends from the pockets of its citizens out of all proportion to what it should spend; its policies increase prices and fuel inflation; it deprives the economy of basic incentives; and it creates unemployment. But we can't live without a government, because there are areas where only government can act, like national defense, foreign policy, attending to the helpless and indigent, and promoting programs the private sector is simply not equipped to handle.

Clearly, the issue is what kind of government we need. What should be the role of government in a democracy? In the economic field, past performance proves that Keynesian economics is not the answer. W. Michael Blumenthal, former Secretary of the Treasury, himself a Ph.D. in economics, is quoted by *Fortune* magazine as follows, "I really think the economics profession is close to bankruptcy in understanding the present situation" (September 11, 1978).

And the last word as to where Keynesian economics is taking this nation may go to *Business Week* magazine, editorializing under the heading "The Warning Flags Are Up": "The President and his advisers . . . are steering the U.S. toward an inflationary explosion, a total loss of confidence, and a collapse" (September 4, 1978).

THE ACTORS
ARE GONE, THE
PROBLEMS REMAIN

9

How did the United States, the wealthiest economy the world has ever known, arrive at this lamentable state of affairs? What is the thinking and ideology that created the economic climate from which our time of troubles developed? To which economic theorists of previous centuries do present-day economists owe their reasoning? And how is it that the ideas of these long dead scholars steered us onto our present dangerous course?

The original cast has long since gone. One by one, over a period of more than a century, they peopled the stage of history, a curious group that came from many walks of life and were drawn together by a passionate interest in a new mental discipline. There were, amongst others, academicians, a physician, minister of the Church, journalist, editor, theologian, businessman, lawyer, and factory owner. Their names were: François Quesnay, Adam Smith, Jean Baptiste Say, Thomas Robert Malthus, David Ricardo, James Mill, Jean Charles de Sismondi, Friedrich List, Karl Knies, Gustav Schmoller, John Stuart Mill, Max Weber, Werner Sombart, Herman Gossen, Carl Menger, Friedrich von Wiser, Eugen Bohm von Bawerk, Bates Clark, Leon Walras, Vilfredo Pareto, Gustav Knut Wicksel, Alfred Marshall, Karl Marx, and Friedrich Engels.

They were the original economic theorists, and their interest was focused on the new economy that emerged with the coming of the Industrial Revolution in the eighteenth century. It was an infant that literally expanded in scope and complexity before their very eyes. To help them in their own thoughts they drew upon a book written by one of their number, *The Wealth of Nations* by Adam Smith, but each also had his own approach to the subject of economic development, his own variations on the economic theme. All of them questioned, probed, and analyzed like laboratory scientists confronted with a new life form. Mostly they conjectured, using concepts like "labor," "value," "surplus value" and "money." All applied Newtonian mechanistic thinking to what they saw, trying to isolate whatever economic phenomena that intrigued them, in the fashion of the natural sciences. They viewed the economy as a bee sees through multifaceted eyes, noting individual components but missing the organic whole of which they were a part.

They were hypnotized by the productive process, and their concern was the whys and wherefores of accumulation and distribution. Originally, the pressing question had been, "What is the source of a nation's wealth?" and Smith answered "division of manual labor." When, sixty years later, Marx answered simply "manual labor," the question was no longer asked. The new question was, "*How* is wealth created and distributed between the capitalist, worker, and the parasitical landowner?"

We shall meet some of the more important members of the original cast later, in their ideas and concepts; for the moment, it is enough to say that their legacy is still, alas, with us, blinding us to new economic realities that require new solutions to old problems.

Economics—A Man-Made Science

The laws and phenomena of natural science exist independently of man. A scientific discipline such as physics or chemistry develops its own nomenclature and stakes out a methodology through the study of the composition, structure, properties, and reactions of atomic and molecular structures.

There have regularly been remarkable advances in the natural sciences over the centuries, advances that have entailed drastic changes in man's conception of the way things work. But when we come to economics, we find, to our astonishment, that we are dealing with a man-made science trying to ape the value-free natural sciences. Moreover, we find that the underlying thinking in economics is based on observations made over a century ago when the modern economy—that of the post-Industrial Revolution—was in its infancy. Man's creative mind has long since transcended those old economic formulations by bringing new realities into existence. But the obsolete thinking still prevails.

Lay people and trained economists alike are accustomed to thinking of economics as a science like physics, physiology, or chemistry—and no wonder. For two centuries, ever since economics attained the status of a scientific discipline, we have believed in the existence of economic "laws" which seemingly operate like the laws of mechanistic physics, independent of man. For two centuries everyone has been conditioned to think along such lines, to see "laws" at work, even as Adam Smith and Karl Marx did and today's conventional economists still do. This is the way of the natural sciences, where man is reduced to the status of an observer and recorder. Whatever is noted has no connection to man's personal existence. In natural science the methodology is to quantify everything, to count, measure, and bring down to irreducible components. All phenomena not quantifiable are eliminated. The scientist strives to be exact and to express himself in value-free terms.

The conventional economic theorist has striven to appropriate this approach lock, stock, and barrel. He assumes that the economy—its past, present, and future—can be determined like any natural historical phenomenon. By deciding that economic factors can be quantified, he tells us that he sees the economy as a science that can be explained using mechanistic terms of reference. He believes that economic events are repetitive, and all we have to do is lay bare the laws by which the economy operates. Such reasoning goes all the way back to the French economist, Jean Baptiste Say (1768–1832), who theorized that economic laws exist and, once discovered, can be used in the same way laws are applied in the natural sciences. Economists even create the conditions that justify such determinism. For example, there is an economic "law," the Phillips Curve, that decrees a trade-off between inflation and unemployment. Do we want less inflation, asks the "law"? Then we must live with higher unemployment. The rationale is that for prices to come down there must be a greater surplus of labor available. On the other hand, we can enjoy higher employment if we condescend to a higher rate of inflation. Instead of analyzing why the two evils of inflation and unemployment coexist—what errors in thinking have led to such an absurd state of affairs—conventional economists justify the problem by framing it into a "law."

This type of thinking disregards the fact that economic phenomena, by their very nature, can never be exact. They are the products of the creative human mind which ever persists in inventing, combining, and recombining natural forces for new productive use, drawing more and more variables into the productive process, and creating complexity out of simplicity. Man, himself an actor in this dynamic system, brings into play new levels of reasoning that make obsolete the so-called laws which the classicists, Marxists, and Keynesians would have us believe determine economic reality.

No one can be blamed for possessing limited vision. What is interesting to note is the historical background that locked human thinking into the orbit of causality as far as economics was concerned.

Many thinkers view the great tragedians of ancient Greece—Aeschylus, Sophocles, Euripides—with their vision of fate, as the predecessors of the scientific outlook. According to Alfred North Whitehead, "Fate in Greek tragedy became the order of nature in modern thought."

In the same way that man's actions were to be understood within the context of his fate, and his fate understood within the context of his actions, "fate" also became a scientific belief. Any occurrence was seen as being determined by and correlated with its antecedents. With this belief in causality and predictability, dominant from the seventeenth century onward, science could formulate general principles of laws.

While the Copernican revolution dislodged man from the center of the universe, Galileo and Newton removed him completely. Newton saw the universe as possessing perfect symmetry and absolute precision. Space, time, and matter were independent of each other, and the motions and relationships in the universe continued in endless repetition. Since everything had a natural and knowable cause, the ability to know the present and future of each cause was possible. And because everything was determined and subjective, no human act or intervention could influence causality. The world was devoid of all purpose. Only primary qualities—numbers, figures, magnitude, position, motion—were real. Secondary qualities perceived by man—tastes, colors, happiness, odors—were unreal. The latter were names and would disappear if man disappeared. Galileo and Newton explained man as part of nature, in terms of body and motion.

René Descartes pursued this line of thinking by postulating that nature was a machine without purpose or spiritual significance. Thomas Hobbes saw reasoning and imagination as nothing more than motion in certain parts of the body; for him, only matter existed and everything could be predicted with exact laws. Spinoza saw the universe as a relentless chain of effects without final cause. He looked upon human actions and desires as though they were lines, planes, and solids. For Laplace, all phenomena were subsumed in a giant universal mechanism, and what didn't fit was only superstition.

The deeply felt assumption of universal harmony and unity was a natural corollary of the religious belief that has always dominated natural science. According to the monotheistic Judeo-Christian philosophy, the world is created by God, and owing to the absolute perfection of God, is itself perfect and harmonious. There is One thought, One will, One wisdom on which the world is based. Einstein's famous statement that "I don't believe that God plays dice," expresses the conviction that all phenomena can in the last instance be explained by a single principle.

If society, being a creation of God, is governed by laws, why not the economy? Adam Smith, foremost economic theorist of the eighteenth century, expressed his religious convictions by assuming the existence of a harmonizing "invisible hand" in the economy. If he didn't use the word God, it was because he didn't want to formulate too close a link between God and an economy that was, in his view, motivated by greed and egotism. Coming after Smith, another great economic theorist, David Ricardo, spoke of laws and not of invisible hands. Thus were the principles of mechanistic physics introduced into economic thinking. The atheistic and materialistic Karl Marx accepted the philosophy that a universal law exists, dialectics, that controls the evolution of human society, the economy very much included.

J. Robert Oppenheimer described the world of thought in his *Science and Common Understanding* (Simon and Schuster, 1954): "There was the belief that in the end all nature would be reduced to physics, to the giant machine. Despite all richness of what men have learned about the world of nature, of matter and space, of change and of life, we carry with us today an image of the giant machine as a sign of what the world is really like."

But this world disappeared. In his book, *Out of My Later Years,* Einstein wrote (Philosophical Library, 1950):

"For several decades most physicists clung to the conviction that a mechanical substructure would be found for Maxwell's theory. But the unsatisfactory results of their efforts led to gradual acceptance of the new field concepts as irreducible fundamentals—in other words, physicists resigned themselves to giving up the idea of a mechanical foundation."

The belief in determinism also declined. Erwin Schrödinger deals with this in his *What Is a Law of Nature?:*

"Simply, the custom inherited through thousands of years of thinking causally, makes the idea of undetermined events . . . complete nonsense, a logical absurdity." He further states that this way of thinking came about after "observing for hundreds of thousands of years precisely those regularities in the natural course of events, which in the light of our present knowledge are most certainly not governed by causality."

Modern physics began to deny the principle of the uniformity of nature, according to which like causes produce like effects, with the emergence of the quantum theory. This great change in thinking came about as a result of work done by Michael Faraday, James Maxwell, and Heinrich R. Hertz. The Newtonian principle of actions at a distance, the basis of the mechanistic world view, could not provide an adequate interpretation for phenomena connected with the electromagnetic field. Actions at a distance were replaced by fields, including that of gravitation, which was no longer regarded as a mechanical force but as a mathematical formula governing the curvature of space and the acceleration of moving bodies. Matter and energy ceased to be the basic data of intuition. Space came to be seen as lacking objective reality. Nor was time regarded as having any objective reality apart from the order of events by which we measure it.

Max Planck's discovery, at the beginning of the twentieth century, that energy is emitted in discontinuous packets or quanta, lead to Niels Bohr's atomic theory, which provided the basis of the hypothesis of indeterminism in nature. Werner Heisenberg's principle of uncertainty, or indeterminacy, has been enhanced by the discovery that the prerequisite of classical physics, or the simultaneous knowledge of position and velocity, was impossible.

While the Newtonian *Weltanschauung* was based on the concept that nature is an independent reality, observable without reference to the observer and the means of observation, the new view is that we cannot observe nature without disturbing it. Bohr formulated this concept in a manner that showed man as being simultaneously an actor and spectator in the drama of existence.

New views, concepts, and methods have been introduced into physics, all of which have established the theoretical basis of our age of electronics, automation, and atomization; but in economics the concepts and frames of reference have not changed at all from what they were two centuries ago. Man is still regarded solely as an observer, studying a system of objective and determined phenomena, and one devoid of all purpose. We only need open any economic textbook to see that the methodology of physics is still applied to economics. We find an endless number of laws, equations, and curves reflecting the view that the economy is a giant machine in which it is possible to isolate the components and bring them into causal relationships. The formulation of a two-variable, linear-causal relationship, such as supply and demand; quantity of money and prices; employment and inflation; saving and investment; et cetera has become the principal mode of economic thinking. It is a method of atomization, mechanization, and reduction. Any changes in the economy are perceived only in the number, scope, structure, qualities, and properties of scarce resources and the methods of allocating them.

In the late 1920s an important concept was formulated in biology which should have inspired economists to think along similar lines in their own field, but didn't. Ludwig von Bertalanfy perceived the organism as an open system. He pointed out that the "chief task of biology must be to discover the laws of the biological system." From this theory it followed that holism— the theory that a living organism has a reality other and greater than the sum of its constituent parts—has to be seen as a methodology. This was a revolutionary approach that became embodied in the General Systems theory. Bertalanfy wrote: "Complex phenomena proved to be more than the simple sum of properties of isolated causal chains, of the properties of their components taken separately." Such phenomena, he pointed out, must be explained not only in terms of their components, "but also in regard to the entire set of relations between the components . . . sets of related events that can be traced collectively, as systems, manifesting functions and properties on the specific level of the whole."

One American economist, Kenneth Boulding, sees the economy as a system. He assumes that the General Systems theory of Bertalanfy applies to any system, including economics. In his essay, "Economics and General Systems Theory," Boulding complains that apart from himself, the only economist who has advocated the General Systems theory argument is Alfred Kuhn. Says Boulding, "Just why the economic profession has viewed the General Systems theory with such massive indifference, I really do not know. Like physicists, economists are so bound up with the elegant framework of their own systems, that they find it hard to break out into a broader interest."

The concept of laws used in the natural sciences expresses a deterministic, repetitive process. Applied to the economy, it emphasizes determinism and underestimates the active role and responsibility of human beings. This elimination of the human dimension contradicts the Judeo-Christian philosophy that envisages man's control of nature. Nature, it says, has been created for man, to serve him. This philosophy, which has shaped our civilization, has emphasized the creative role of man and his responsibilities. Not until the economic approach of Eugen Loebl and Stephen Roman in the 1970s, was there any note taken of the need for the Judeo-Christian philosophy in economics.

The further away we move from a historical event or epoch, the more we tend to regard it in terms of the salient factor which history ascribes to it. Imperial Rome is a time of marching legions and conquest; Ancient Greece is a flowering of philosophy; there is the birth of Christianity, the Renaissance, Reformation, world wars, and the genocidal policies of Hitler and Stalin. All, sooner or later, are reduced to point-events in the human mind. A million individual incidents are forgotten or neglected, and one remembers only a war, a natural calamity, or whatever.

When we come to the economy, we find our history books filled with point-events. There was a time when agriculture came into being, when towns began, when some great invention changed the manner of living, or when the Industrial Revolution came along. In all this rolling splendor of economic history, the perceptive mind notices an astonishing phenomenon: There is no mention anywhere of the role of the creative human mind weaving the economic web throughout the centuries. An average person is apt to exclaim, "But that's obvious! Of course the human mind was responsible for everything!" Obvious, but not to the conventional economic theorist, not even to such brilliant minds as Adam Smith and Karl Marx. They didn't consider the human mind as an economic factor at all. Smith saw an "invisible hand" at work, smoothing out the differences between worker and producer, and Marx saw the formation of social classes battling each other over ownership of the means of production. Today's economists talk in terms of econometric models, curves, trade-offs, and limits of taxation. Always, the thought form of mechanistic physics prevails, and the creative mind process is disregarded.

Primitive Economic Relationships

Before there was economics, there was economy. Only when the economy reached a certain level of development did it become a subject for scientific thinking at all. A primitive economy in which producers were also consumers of their own products, and where only a small proportion of the produced goods were exchanged, posited no problems that required scientific methods. Not until the sixteenth century did the economy achieve a level where it became more than the mere sum total of individual economic components, when it became a distinguishable force.

Millennia ago, man in his nomadic state devoted all his energies to the search for food. There were no hidden laws operating when man left his nomadic life behind and, over an indeterminate period, entered Neolithic times. There was simply an overwhelming desire to be independent of nature. With this motivation, agriculture was begun and man learned to domesticate animals. The wheel was invented and construction was begun using wood and stone. It was discovered that stone implements could be ground to produce smooth edges, thus creating more efficient tools. Pottery, spinning, weaving, and basketry came into being. A beginning was made in irrigation techniques and field agriculture. Routine work was established. A rudimentary calendar system was invented. Writing originated. Long distance commerce on the basis of barter was introduced, and there were the first economic surpluses. Social classes formed as a natural result of those who had and those who didn't have; and when the have-nots tried to take from the haves by force, organized warfare came into being.

We would be remiss not to pay our respects to defunct civilizations that contributed to the development of the scientific spirit, if not to the scientific method itself, which is the essence of the modern economy. Though individual names are lost to us, for the most part, we must gratefully nod in the direction of the Muslim civilization of the seventh and eighth centuries A.D. At a time when Western Europe possessed only a crude agrarian economy, the Muslim economic life was already highly developed. They knew how to manufacture paper (the West learned from them) and how to make use of manures, irrigation, and grafting—the requisites of scientific farming. They were excellent traders, and used partnerships, trade associations, and credit instruments, all marks of an advanced commercial society. "Traffic" and "tariff" are Muslim words.

From the mid-sixteenth century onward, we already know the identities of some of the remarkable individuals who were responsible for the revival of science, which eventually led to the Industrial Revolution. Roger Bacon (1214–1294) set forth the limitations of the dialectical method and suggested the possibilities of the observational or experimental method of obtaining knowledge. The Italian, Peter of Abano (ca. 1250–1316), propounded the inductive method. The Scholastic philosophers and theologians, the humanist translators of the Greek and Roman classics, and the minds of the Renaissance, all contributed in their own way to the establishment of natural science in Western Europe during the sixteenth century.

Francis Bacon (1561–1626), one of the greatest intellects of his age, did most to spur the advancement of the scientific method. Though he didn't discover the inductive method, he did seek the replacement of metaphysical thinking with the scientific method of collecting and classifying facts. In his *Advancement of Learning* (1605) and *The New Atlantis* (1627) Bacon described the scientific method and suggested its vast possibilities.

Before applied science came into being and was integrated into the economy and afterward, when the Industrial Revolution occurred, it was always the creative use of man's mind and not hidden laws that was the primary factor in economic evolution.

In fact, there was no talk of laws until man himself decreed those laws into existence and then strove to adjust reality as though the laws actually existed. This process of quantification began at the time of the Industrial Revolution and has continued until this day.

Centuries of Empirical Thinking

There is no record of when man learned to think in terms of cause and effect, but one can be sure that the process was slow and tedious, requiring extensive periods of observation that probably ran for centuries. During that time the working process was based on experience, not theory; in other words, on empirical observation passed down from one generation to the next: from father to son, or from master craftsman to apprentice.

Empirical knowledge, that is, knowledge derived from sense impressions, provided man with more food and better shelter, but achievements were severely limited. At the outset of human history, man used his own body to harness natural forces for his own use. Acting on nature and being acted upon in turn, thus developing intellect, man came to a point where he was able to harness natural forces outside his body for productive use, thus ushering in a new historical situation.

Progressively freeing himself from dependency on nature, man sought economic relationships with his fellow man, as well as cultural and political ones. Society divided and subdivided. Out of the peasantry and distinct from it arose the artisan class, in the eleventh century. Like the merchant class, already plying their trade, the artisans were townsmen free to choose their crafts and dispose of their products as they saw fit. Craft guilds sprang up, emulating the merchant guilds already in existence. Guilds regulated wages, fixed prices and conditions of sale, determined hours and conditions of labor, and inspected workmanship and quality of materials.

This was a giant step forward from the feudal system, which began to phase out when the Crusades of the eleventh century came along. Before that, in the shattered Western Europe of the sixth and seventh centuries, there were no laws, no administration, and practically no education. It had been a time of brigandage and fearful insecurity, of universal chaos, when people sought protection in numbers. Where possible, they allied themselves with power. Thus, a freeman sought the protection of a powerful lord. The result was a new social structure that brought some order into an otherwise lawless milieu. This was the beginning of feudalism.

The Crusades not only increased the power of the Church, but also contributed to the economic progress of Western Europe. Italian trading centers prospered, and there was a surge of interest in travel and exploration. Merchants joined the Crusades to seek new markets. In effect, a movement motivated by spiritual considerations brought about an intensified interest in worldly affairs and oriented the human mind toward practical existence.

By the late seventeenth century, the Age of Reason had elevated man's mind to primary stature. Trades and crafts developed, towns sprang into being, and a new social stratum— the bourgeoisie—entered the economic world. For the first time, probing minds began to pose the question: What is the source of wealth of the economic system?

Mercantilism—A Mechanical Form

Scientific methods didn't exist as yet, but the mercantile system, which had superseded feudalism, was indicative of how higher levels of society thought about the nature of wealth.

It was known as mercantilism in England, Colbertism in France, and cameralism in Germany. It didn't represent a theoretical body of thought, only practical considerations, but the guiding motive was the same wherever it was practiced: the domination of trade and industry in the interests of the national state. In effect, the prosperity of the state was believed to be dependent on the ability to increase exports and decrease imports, monopolize the trade of colonies, and restrict the commerce of rivals. The system was an expression of the absolute power of the state in the seventeenth century.

The human mind saw gold and silver as the incarnation of wealth at that time. Since a nation was equated with its ruler, it was judged rich or poor by the amount of gold and silver owned by the ruler. The importation of these precious metals in payment for goods exported became the acknowledged system. Gold and silver were exchanged for products, and products were exchanged for human labor.

To effect such a growth of wealth, the system had to be manipulated: a plethora of regulations were introduced to increase exports and decrease imports. National governments created commercial monopolies, regulated companies like the English and Dutch East India companies and the Hudson's Bay Company. As a result of such state intervention in the economy, an important development took place: The nation-state, hitherto only a political unit, now became an economic unit. The economy operated within the framework of a geographical area clearly defined by boundaries, and exports and imports greatly enhanced the importance of frontiers.

History books record that the mercantilist system created a political superstructure. Not so. It was an interaction of a great many facets of social life, the result of creative human thinking exposed to situations which it changed even as it reacted to them. This action-reaction process brought to bear by the human mind is true today, too, just as it will always be true. Only the level of thinking has changed.

The mercantilist system, and all economy preceding the Industrial Revolution, had a mechanical form: It was the sum total of autonomous components engaged in cooperative undertakings, and not the kind of integrated, interrelated organism it is today. The farmer could sell corn to the miller, hides to the tanner, and so forth; but he could also make his own flour or tan skins. Every part of the operation could be understood as such, and cause and effect relationships were clear. Educated people thought in terms of the Newtonian *Weltanschauung,* with its underlying mechanistic philosophy. And so, when the first economic theorists appeared, the economy was perceived in the same vein.

Physiocrats on the Attack

In the eighteenth century mercantilism was ferociously attacked by a group of French writers we know as the Physiocrats. They espoused a system of economic liberalism, a way of thinking associated with the laissez faire philosophy made famous by Adam Smith.

Like economic theorists right up to our own day, including Smith, Marx, and Keynes, the Physiocrats accepted a priori the notion that the economy was a part of the natural order and was therefore governed by economic laws. They adamantly opposed government interference or manipulation of the economy in any way, as practiced in mercantilism. In their thinking they were totally influenced by the mechanistic ideas of Copernicus, Kepler, and Newton, that there was a natural order God created and maintained in the universe, and laws were at work regulating, adjusting, and administering God's will. Any interference by legislative bodies only disrupted the economic process. If there was unhappiness or misery in the world, it was because archaic and restrictive laws hindered the operations of natural law. Unlimited competition would set matters aright because natural laws would then be working freely. As for the state, asserted the Physiocrats, it should confine itself to the protection of life and property, construction of public works, and the promotion of education.

Leading Physiocrats were François Quesnay (1694–1774),

Jean Vincent, Sieur de Gournay (1712–1759), and Pierre Samuel Du Pont de Nemours (1739–1817). Of these, the most notable was Quesnay. He is still regarded as the first economic theoretician and founder of economics as a discipline.

Quesnay was a court physician to Louis XV and Madame de Pompadour. He began writing on economic problems when he was in his sixties. The theoretical approach he took to economics was predictable in view of his calling, so far removed from the marketplace. He created an economic model based on the human internal system. Economics, he said, is a matter of three organs: the productive class, circulating like blood through the system; the proprietary class; and the sterile class. The productive class were the farmers, cultivating the land and producing the real wealth of the nation; the proprietary class were government officials who owned the land and collected tithes; and the sterile class were the tradespeople who fashioned agricultural products into final forms, adding nothing (in Quesnay's view) to the national wealth. Quesnay saw this arrangement as *l'ordre naturel,* and declared that man should do nothing to interfere with this state of affairs. *"Laissez-faire; laissez-passer"* was his admonition: Let things alone; let everything run its natural course.

In effect, what Quesnay did was carry the religious approach to life into economics, the same way Newtonian mechanistic physics did. Since religion and physics accepted a divine presence and universal harmony in life, why shouldn't economics?

Quesnay's claim to fame, therefore, is based on being the first to assume the economy is a part of the natural order. Here, for the first time, was the intrusion of Newtonian mechanistic thinking into the economic sphere. His view that agricultural work was the source of wealth of a nation would be discarded by Smith, Marx, and others, but the mechanistic thinking would remain, right up to the present time.

THE REAL
SIGNIFICANCE
OF THE INDUSTRIAL
REVOLUTION

10

The prevailing level of thinking engrained in a society and its economy is reflected in the manner by which that society fulfills the requirements of human life. The higher the level of thinking, the greater the ability to transform natural forces into human benefits.

This economic *leitmotiv* runs through the entire history of mankind, but sometimes it is more apparent than other times. Normally, economic evolution is a subtle and gradual, although continuous, process, but there are periods that mark radical departures from past procedures. When these occur, society undergoes a profound and comprehensive transformation. Certainly, one such transformation took place in England from the mid-eighteenth century through the mid-nineteenth century. That was the Industrial Revolution.

Even today, two centuries later, the significance of the Industrial Revolution has never been properly understood. It wasn't understood by Adam Smith, whose *Wealth of Nations* is still considered the definitive exposition of the capitalist system of economics. It wasn't understood by Karl Marx, whose theories derived from observation of conditions at the time are today the base of communist economics. Nor was it understood by John Maynard Keynes and the Keynesian theorists whose economic thinking has dominated the West for some four decades.

The tendency is to regard the Industrial Revolution as one where the introduction of machinery was coupled with the division of labor to transform the productive process. Actually, it was far more than that—it was an intellectual revolution of the highest order that found expression in the social and economic spheres. It wasn't a matter of adding additional components, such as machinery and the division of labor, to an existing form; what happened was that a dynamic new factor appeared on the economic scene—the organization of workers, equipment, and materials. All was integrated, and the result was a completely new socioeconomic system, manifested by a much higher level of thinking than had previously existed.

The nature of everything connected with the productive process changed drastically: The economy assumed the form of a dynamic organism. Logically that should have put an end to mechanistic thinking about it once and for all; but it didn't. Adam Smith picked up from where the Physiocrats had left off, Marx and Ricardo had their own mechanistic views, and Keynes and the monetarists altered and adjusted. But economic thinking remained mired, for all of that, in the concepts of classical economics, which became obsolete with the coming of the Industrial Revolution.

A Backward Look: The Agrarian Economy

The impression of economic somnolence that prevailed before the coming of the Industrial Revolution is accurate relative only to our own age. The modern sociotechnological society is a pulsating, dynamic, highly integrated entity. Here the whine of turbines, roar of machinery, and silent, awesome efficiency of computers have effectively severed our sense of association with a primitive world that existed before labor, machinery, and applied science were combined to usher in a fantastic new age of economic development.

Prior to the Industrial Revolution, man's ability to transform natural forces into productive uses was, by our standards, maddeningly slow. Agricultural technology, the mainstay of the productive process, was underdeveloped. Poverty was widespread. The nature of societal institutions reflected the leisurely pace of life. Guilds maintained a fixed way of doing things rooted in the simple medieval principle of cooperation between members. Governments protected monopolies by placing statutory restrictions on industry and trade. The medieval concept that profitmaking was sinful still prevailed, and had the approval of the common people. Human and animal muscle provided whatever power was required in the productive process, augmented by waterwheels and windmills.

The predominantly agrarian economy was stagnant, as evinced by the absence of sustained increases in per capita income. What production there was had a commercial orientation: Almost all the farmers produced beyond the subsistence level, if only to provide for the payment of rent. The low level of agricultural technology placed great strains and limitations on the capacity of the agricultural population to sustain a nonagricultural population. And without the latter, the demand for nonagricultural goods was severely limited. Poor market conditions aggravated by the lack of an efficient transportation system and poor communications confined trade to rigorously circumscribed markets.

In the comfortable orbit of cause and effect, we can follow the thinking of a farmer of pre-industrial England. To him, grain was his most important crop. It served as corn bread for the poor, fodder for animals, and was also useful in brewing and distilling. From grain the farmer's thoughts went to his livestock, raised for the market and providing products that were a major source of farm income. Wool, hides, and skins were cash crops. Other marketable farm products were bones for glue, hair for plasters, and tallow for soap and candle manufacturing. Manure, not offered for sale, was another important by-product.

Farming techniques varied according to regional and environmental diversities—not surprising since the techniques were the result of empirical observation. Environmental factors associated with climate and soil variations resulted in different husbandry systems. The emphasis on the cultivation of oats in certain regions, for example, was determined by their capability to grow under poor soil conditions.

In the nonagricultural sector, the process involved in the manufacture of shoes was indicative of pre-industrial production techniques. It began with the farmer who raised the cattle for leather and grew the grain to feed them. Processing the hides was the tanner's work: He purchased them from the farmer either for money or in exchange for goods, such as finished leather. Once the hides had been tanned, the shoemaker's work began. He was responsible for cutting and stitching the leather and the completion of the final product. Thus, through the cooperation of these three autonomous economic participants— the farmer, tanner, and shoemaker—one or two pairs of shoes per week would be delivered to people who had ordered them.

This type of economy was characterized by the absence of a "market," inasmuch as production was exclusive for a limited number of individuals. The road from raw materials on the farm to refinement by the tanner to the finished product was neither long nor complex. The process was based on the exchange relation of each unit, with the exchange value of each commodity based on the amount of labor required in the process; and since the method of production was based solely on manual labor, value could be determined. Even the tools used were for the most part produced on the farm. There was no machinery to complicate the low intellectual level of the process.

The Industrial Revolution
Quickens the Pace

With the advent of the Industrial Revolution, the labor process was divided into a number of simple operations, which in turn made possible the use of new tools. Machinery became more and more complex, and with the simultaneous development of new forms of energy, began to revolutionize the productive process.

The farmer now had the advantage of an increased knowledge of agricultural techniques, and perhaps a few hired hands to help with the running of the farm. His production of grain and cattle increased; consequently his ability to supply raw materials for the production of shoes (coming back to our pre-industrial example) was considerably enhanced. The tanner also gained knowledge and experience, and benefited by the contributions of inventors and organizers. Perhaps he ran a small factory staffed with a few men. He used new chemicals, new techniques, and machines provided significantly more finished leather of a better quality. The shoemaker himself now employed more men to run the machines, which saved time and provided increased production.

With his output significantly expanded, it became possible for the shoemaker to provide sufficient quantities and types of shoes to supply the "market," itself created by the increase in productivity. He was no longer limited to producing for individuals. The market developed and acquired radically new properties. The road from raw materials to finished products became longer and more complex. No longer was the production of shoes the result of cooperation between three autonomous participants—farmer, tanner, and shoemaker.

With the use of machinery, which required the production of the means of production, the productive process and economic relations were revolutionized. Shoe production now required the use of the instruments of production. The mining, steel, and machine tool industries all had to be integrated into the productive process. A comprehensive educational system had to be established which could support the expanding needs of the new social stratum, the "brain" workers: innovators, organizers, and entrepreneurs who were responsible for the higher level of economic thinking. To provide the increased production of consumer items with a proper outlet into a vastly expanded market, new systems of transportation and communication had to be developed. Forms of credit had to be instituted to allow producers to buy machinery and pay for it later from the sale of their products.

The market bifurcated—one for the consumer and another for the producer. Exchange was no longer applicable. The steel industry couldn't exchange its products with the machine tool industry, nor could the mine owner exchange coal for clothing. Hereafter, products were bought and sold. It didn't matter whether they were sold for gold money, gold-backed money, or fiat money; there was now payment instead of exchange.

The nature of the market also changed: It became the sum total of distribution agencies spread throughout all cities, instead of just a meeting place. In this new market, the distributor and the shopkeepers were the actual participants, not the producer. The producer and consumer no longer confronted each other with products to exchange. In the consumer's market, goods were produced and prices fixed long before the goods were actually distributed. In the producer's market there were the producers of the means of production and the producers who sought to purchase those means. Producers manufactured for an unknown market and became totally dependent on market conditions. The market became more and more specialized with time, and eventually, through necessity, a capital market evolved.

Such concepts as "value," "surplus value," and "division of labor" were transcended and lost all meaning once the Industrial

Revolution came along with its integration of labor, organization, and applied science. Those concepts may have been applicable to a slow-moving, pre-industrial economy, but not to an economy that experienced a sharp leap in integration and complexity. However, to Adam Smith, just appearing on the scene, and to Ricardo, Marx, and the Keynesians still to come, the basic concepts were never transcended. Economics sailed serenely into the nineteenth, then the twentieth century, very much the prisoner of Newtonian mechanistic thinking.

ADAM SMITH AND LAISSEZ-FAIRE

11

What is higher will prove inexplicable if the platform chosen for departure is one which belongs to a lower order of reflection.

—Viscount Haldane,
The Reign of Relativity (1921)

No matter how brilliant the mind, a conceptual leap to a level of thinking involving key components that don't as yet exist is a formidable, if not impossible, task. How could Adam Smith, Karl Marx, or any of the economic theorists of a century and more ago conceive of an economic system where manual labor would be reduced to an insignificant factor, and where computer and nuclear technology, sophisticated production and banking techniques, and the role of government via taxes and regulations would make it impossible to determine the real value of a product or the labor required to make it? They could not derive from the observation of *their* economy the source of wealth typical for *our* economy.

When Adam Smith (1723–90) set himself the task of writing his monumental *Wealth of Nations,* which appeared in 1776, his mind was already set in the Newtonian way of thinking, the way of natural laws. This was not surprising, since the universities, scientific societies, and academies had, since the mid-seventeenth century, been busy creating the intellectual climate for economic progress via the scientific method. By the end of the seventeenth century, each of the major countries of Europe had at least one society for the advancement of scientific learning, and there was a feverish preoccupation with research and experimentation.

As a deeply religious man and professor of moral philosophy, Smith saw the universe as a self-contained, perfect system, a cosmic machine with God as creator-ruler. There are laws for physics, reasoned Smith, and there are laws for the economy. They may not be as readily discernible as physical laws, but they are there, and, said Smith, the best man can do is not interfere with their operation.

This, of course, was laissez-faire, earlier popularized by Quesnay in France, and the logical consequence of Newtonian thinking applied to economics. Laissez-faire was the freedom of all participants in the economic process to act within a system governed by natural laws. It was the answer to mercantilism, which practiced gross government interference in the economic process to enrich the monarchy.

As Jacob Oser noted in his book *The Evolution of Economic Thought:*

"The rising businessmen required a set of ideas to help dislodge the lingering feudal institutions and the restrictive controls of mercantilism that had become unnecessary. For them, Newtonian science furnished a nature fully as effective as the earlier Will of God. If the Divine Will had created a mechanism that worked automatically without further interference, then laissez-faire was the highest wisdom in social affairs. Natural laws would guide the economic system and the actions of men. These ideas were new and revolutionary. No longer would men accept the ancient truths without question, such as the immorality of interest, the virtue of charity, and the requirements that men should be satisfied with their inherited station of life. Society would be served best if men were free to follow the natural law of self-interest."

Smith saw the economy as a matter of a value-free relationship between production and consumption, supply and demand. He envisioned an "invisible hand" working tirelessly to smooth out differences between the two components and creating a sort of rough equilibrium.

The existence of a force dominating the economic performance, and the idea of equilibrium, are concepts borrowed from the natural sciences, where it is possible to observe, measure, and prove.

Man's primary motivation in the supply and demand relationship, averred Smith, was profit. He ascribed to it the highest economic value. Granted, the producer of goods was greedy, but the "invisible hand" would force him to channel his productivity in such a way as to satisfy the consumer. To Smith, laissez-faire meant first and foremost freedom of the consumer: The consumer was sovereign in that he represented demand, and it was up to the producer to meet that demand. In effect, Smith assumed a perfect competition and a perfect accommodation of a business enterprise to the desires of the consumer. He took the freedom of the consumer for granted at all times; it was the producer whose freedom had to be ensured by the government.

In laissez-faire economics, everything was justified—greed, egotism, chicanery. Eventually, free enterprise became nothing more than the undue accumulation and concentration of capital in the hands of producers. Competition became less and less a determining factor as the economically powerful dictated market conditions to ever growing degrees.

If Smith agreed with Quesnay regarding the merits of laissez-faire, he disagreed with him about the source of wealth of a nation. Quesnay said it was agriculture, not an unreasonable supposition in view of the great importance of agriculture in pre-Industrial Revolution times. Smith said it was the division of labor, and this concept became the cornerstone of his new economic system, the driving power of his laissez-faire philosophy. His concern was with such variables as the number of workers, the extent of their working hours, and the effort with which they worked. Since, in pre-industrial times, production was essentially the production of consumer goods, and the value of these goods was dependent on the number of hours of manual labor involved, it was a fairly simple thing to determine value by calculating the working hours put in to produce a product. Physical labor was considered as the primary variable in the work process, and concern with mental labor, "brain" work, was ignored.

Smith, subconsciously applying Newtonian mechanistic thinking, broke down the economy into individual components. He looked out upon an expanding productive process, saw manual labor divided into specialized activities, and concluded that this was the reason for increased production.

Smith Misses the Role
of the Organizer

Smith's famous example of pin production will show what Smith—and Marx after him—didn't see, though it was the essence of the Industrial Revolution.

Smith noted that a worker "with his utmost industry" could make one pin a day, but that the trade was now being divided into a number of "branches of which the greater part are likewise peculiar trades. One man draws out the wire, another straightens it, a third cuts it, a fourth points it, a fifth grinds it at the top for receiving the head; to make the head requires two or three distinct operations; to put it on, is a particular business, to whiten the pins is another; it is even a trade in itself to put them into paper." Thus, the making of a pin is divided into about eighteen operations. According to Smith, a group of ten workers could produce forty-eight thousand pins a day, or, forty-eight hundred pins per worker—a remarkable achievement compared to the previous productivity of one pin a day per worker.

Smith ascribed the increase in productivity to three circumstances: the dexterity of the workmen; the saving of time "which is commonly lost in passing from one species of work to another"; the invention of a great number of machines "that enable one man to do the work of many."

As an afterthought, Smith says "many improvements have been made by the ingenuity of the makers of the machines . . . and some of those who are called philosophers or men of speculation, whose trade is not to do anything, but to observe everything; and who upon that account, are often capable of combining together the power of the most distant and dissimilar objects."

One cannot blame Smith for having failed to see that the new productive process was not based on the experience of the worker at all—the "proletariat" that Marx saw as the producer of wealth. Smith, and Marx, failed to grasp the importance of the emerging role of the organizer as an economic factor. This individual was taking the fruits of applied science coming out of the laboratories and integrating them into the productive process, thus literally revolutionizing society. Neither Smith nor Marx saw the "brain" worker as an economic category—actually, the most important and decisive component in the economic process. Smith—and Marx—saw science as something external to the economy, as something added to it, a part of the Marxian "superstructure." They did not see it as being the essence of the new economy.

The contribution of the organizer was to apply a higher level of thinking to the economy. His intellectual contribution was the cause not only of the division of labor, but of the new level of wealth for the nation. When Smith stated, in his pin production example, that the productivity of the pin maker increased 4,800 times, a more correct statement would have been, the productivity increased 4,800 times thanks to the contribution of the organizer-innovator. In other words, the higher level of thinking introduced into the productive process transcended the level gained in the working experience of the common worker. If we apply Marxist thinking to this new productivity, and as absurd as it may sound, we would concede the pin-making worker wages based on the production of one pin per day, and the organizer-innovator wages based on the production of 4,799 pins per day, his contribution to the new production process.

If one wants to see how the "division of labor" concept became wholly inapplicable in determining value, which also became an obsolete term, one has only to carry the pin-making example into modern times.

Going back into the pin factory, one no longer finds that division of labor that played such a central role in Smith's understanding of the source of wealth. As a matter of fact, we probably won't find a single worker actually producing a pin. We would see a lone employee periodically manipulating some wheels and buttons on a machine, from which would emerge hundreds of thousands of pins neatly stacked and packed and brought by automatic conveyor into a storage room.

No labor, no division of labor. We are not even mathematically able to express the share of manual labor involved in the production process. If we want to trace who actually produced the pins, we would first have to determine how the pin-making machines came to be produced. We would find that the wire was produced by machines; coal, ore, and steel have been mined, refined, and produced with the help of machines; engines have been produced in a machine tool plant. Ergo, machines have produced the pins. But behind the machines, unseen but very much there, is an army of designers, research institutes, and an educational system turning out these designers and researchers—in effect, a schooling system integrated into the productive process. There are managers, bookkeepers, clerks and workers, and with them the operations of an electronics industry; also, banking, transportation, and distribution systems are required. We can actually trace practically all professions in our nation—sometimes even those of other nations—to find that the integration of a fantastic number of components had to take place in order to produce, in a mature economy, even such a simple product as a pin.

To further illustrate the obsolescence of such terms as "division of labor," "value," "surplus value," and "theory of labor," can there be any determination of what share of the production to allocate to what or whom in the pin-making process? How much should we allocate to the designer of the mining equipment, engines, or computers, the educators, bankers, or bookkeepers, or any of the other myriad individuals who, one way or another, had a hand in producing the pins? It's obvious that the concepts of division of labor and value are hopelessly outdated: They simply don't exist any more and reflect no reality whatsoever. They were pertinent only so long as manual labor was the decisive creator of commodities. We may in one way or another determine rewards for labor, but there are no means to determine the exact share of individual labor processes in a technical, integrated society where applied science is densely interwoven in production. Consequently, there are no means of determining value. The concept of value as the basis for price thus becomes meaningless.

Today, simple common sense tells us not to waste time trying to determine how much "value" there is in each part of the productive process. We recognize the organic fluidity, the intermeshing and continually changing conditions of production, and we know of the many variables that enter the picture: advertising and promotion; royalty arrangements; middlemen; taxes; and the cost of government regulations. What businessman would try to break down the productive process to determine "value" for each variable? Yet this is precisely how Smith and Marx thought, and how many conventional economists of today still think.

Smith never recognized the process of productive integration—a natural omission—since it existed only in embryonic state at the time and was of no importance to the economic problems of the day. Unbelievably, nearly a century after Smith, when integration of production with its use of applied science had become obvious, Marx still continued to apply Newtonian mechanistic thinking to the economy. And, two centuries after Smith, in our own time, conventional economists still haven't transcended mechanistic thinking, although their terms have changed and now include such meaningless phrases as "monetary value," "monetary supply," and so on. We still find the definition of money in textbooks as "the measure of value."

What Adam Smith Never Realized

Adam Smith was confronted with a specific situation, an embryonic industrial economy, and drew conclusions from it as best he could. These conclusions were strongly conditioned by the Newtonian *Weltanschauung* that dominated the thinking of the times. And the thinking, in turn, was influenced by the Scholastic philosophy of an orderly, machinelike universe created and run by God.

It's not surprising, given those limitations and considering how close Smith was to the industrial beginnings, that there was much he didn't perceive.

Most obviously, Smith never realized that his basic approach to economy began from the erroneous premise that economics was a matter of causality; he saw laws at work.

He saw the division of labor as the source of a nation's wealth. There was no way he could foretell the tremendous impact that a new source of energy—the steam engine—would have on the economy as it replaced human labor. Nor could he possibly conceive of a situation where manual labor would be the least important component in the kind of dynamic, highly complex, sociotechnological economy of the late twentieth century. Further, had brain work been recognized, Smith would have perceived that, with the coming of the Industrial Revolution, a nation's source of wealth was man's creative intellect and not a priori universal laws.

Smith didn't see the market as a rational expression of conflicting interests that created a rough equilibrium. Rather, he saw the market as a relationship between supply and demand, and not as a dynamic interaction of human beings. Nor did he see the producer or consumer as anything more than one dimensional entities. He never posited the question, "What has to be done by government to make certain that the concept of free enterprise will guarantee optimum freedom to all participants in the economic process?" He really advocated an anarchistic economic system by assuming that an "invisible hand" would create the necessary harmony. By so doing, he isolated the economy from the sociopolitical environment.

Neither Smith, Marx, nor latter-day economists have ever been able to understand or explain what is going on out there in the "market" because they refuse to concede that the market is a meeting place for thinking human beings with conflicting interests. In time, economists, unable to abide Smith's quasi-religious concept of an "invisible hand" guiding the economy, but no more able than Smith to understand the market process, substituted "laws" for "invisible hand."

Thinking mechanistically as they do, conventional economists cannot tolerate random patterns and creative processes which don't permit quantification or formulation into eternal laws. They fail to see the simple truth: that if the market brings about prices and conditions favorable to most of the participants in the productive process, it is because the rational expression of conflicting interests has created an acceptable equilibrium.

Laissez-faire—business operating without government interference—is today an outdated concept. However, at the time when the Industrial Revolution was just getting underway, freedom for the producer did result in a notable phenomenon: It opened up the avenue of development for the economy in a spectacular way. Strange things were happening that the theorists couldn't—and still can't—explain, such as how the economy grew as it did, and why it stopped growing periodically (those periods we see as the troughs of the business cycles, the "no-growth" times). But theorists firmly believed that there were laws at work, and that sooner or later we would know them and apply them like the physicists or the chemists do in their fields.

Karl Marx Takes Note of Capitalism

12

In the history of ideas, there is nothing to compare with Marxism as a concept that became a powerful political force in so short a time.

In the century following the advent of the Industrial Revolution it seemed apparent enough to compassionate observers of the economic scene that workers—men, women, and children—were being cruelly exploited. The "dark, satanic mills," as the English poet William Blake described them, were everywhere, churning out products amid clacking machines and chimneys belching smoke. The human beings laboring under these conditions were accorded no consideration apart from their contribution to the productive process.

All this was duly noted by Karl Marx, and indeed by thousands of others, but misinterpreted in a manner that has plagued the world to this day.

As noted, the Industrial Revolution brought with it an entirely new type of economy. There was an increasing use of machinery; there was a gradual but continuing integration of applied science into the productive process; most important, there was the emergence of the organizer as an economic factor. The organizer combined labor, applied science, and productive techniques to set in motion an organic economy which drew all aspects of life into its operation. It was like the beginning of a nuclear chain reaction of production and integration that is still going on in the advanced societies of today.

With the above factors acting as a driving force, the creation of wealth became the obsession of the times. Given the relatively low level of conscience, it is not surprising that the Judeo-Christian emphasis on the value of the individual went by the board. The economy became wholly enterprise-oriented. The emphasis was on production and still more production.

What happened was that all factors involved in the economy, including human beings, came to be regarded only in terms of their ability to contribute to the creation of wealth. That is to say, everything came to be viewed either as capital or as a means of acquiring capital. There was no humaneness in such a system because humans were equated with money, machinery, land, and natural resources. The sanctity and dignity of the individual, the Judeo-Christian concept of man as a spiritual human being created to be the master and not the servant of nature, was forgotten. Humans were assessed solely on their ability to produce, as were machines. And like machines, humans were discarded when they could no longer produce.

The conditions which this type of thinking brought about— the unrelenting misery and impoverishment of workers— were not intentional on anyone's part. The philosophy of laissez-faire, promulgated by Adam Smith, did not decree that grinding poverty had to accompany the Industrial Revolution. Laissez-faire was simply a way of excluding government from interfering in the productive process. It was pleasant to think that there was an economic law, an "invisible hand," operating in the marketplace that produced an equilibrium between production and consumption, supply and demand. Anything else—including the condition and welfare of the human component in the economy—was simply not considered.

Marx painted unforgettable word pictures of the dehumanizing process of the industrial system. On one side was the disembodied force called "capital," with its "vampire thirst for the living blood of labour," and on the other side was the brutalized worker, ground down in abject poverty and misery.

Marx's description of the factory system of the time is like a portrait of hell. The machine turns the worker into an automaton—a robot gradually sucked dry by the instruments of labor. The worker is ever under the control of an "alien will," i.e., the "capitalist." He is degraded by being forced to repeat endlessly a minute operation in a productive process he doesn't understand. This division of labor, wrote Marx, "mutilate[s] the worker into a fragment of a human being, degrade[s] him to become a mere appurtenance of the machine, make[s] his work such a torment that its essential meaning is destroyed; estrange[s] him from the intellectual potentialities of the labour process in very proportion to the extent to which science is incorporated into it as an independent power."

A Philosophy Devoid of
Human Considerations

Marx accepted the axiom that in the process of increasing wealth the worker becomes impoverished. He asked what the source was of this impoverishment. Why is it that the class that, in his opinion, creates wealth has no share in it? He answered that question with a philosophy deprived of human dimensions: that there is a natural historical process going on in which man is just a cog, and manual labor simply an abstract category creating wealth. Within this process, certain laws come into operation which vanish when one economic system replaces a previous one. In the capitalist system it is an iron rule that wages paid to workers must always remain at subsistence level.

This was a leaf out of the writings of David Ricardo, who preceded Marx and reasoned as follows: If the supply of labor is higher than the demand for it, wages, adhering to the law of supply and demand, would fall under the subsistence level. This would lead to a decline in the number of available workers. When the supply of labor falls below the demand, according to the law of supply and demand, wages will again increase. This will, in turn, lead to an increase in the labor force. The cycle keeps repeating itself, and wages eternally fluctuate in or around the subsistence level.

Ricardo felt that no one was to blame for all this—it was economic law. Marx agreed, but said the theory was valid only in the capitalist system. Eliminate private ownership, he theorized, and the law would disappear.

For Marx, the properties of classes and not of human beings play the essential role in the economy and in history. The form of ownership of the means of production, he maintained, determines human behavior. Presumably, then, a more humane society will emerge if we change the form of ownership of the means of production.

The implication that it is not consciousness that determines human beings but social being that determines consciousness is an arbitrary juxtaposition. Every human being is both a social and a conscious entity at the same time, and it is impossible and senseless to think in terms of separating people into two types. Such simple relationships exist only in the realm of Newtonian physics. Nevertheless, Marx averred that men begin to distinguish themselves from animals only when they begin to produce their means of subsistence. The truth, of course, is that men distinguish themselves from animals not by the fact that they are able to produce, but by their ability to think and develop that ability. The importance of the thinking process as an economic category is completely overlooked by Marx.

According to Marx, the main task is not to fight for humanism and develop a more humane society, nor make the means of production and nature serve us, but the reverse: to change the form of ownership of the means of production, and then as a by-product we'll become more humane.

Marx made the form of that ownership a metaphysical category endowed with the power to determine the character of a society. Both capitalism and communism attach a decisive function to the form of ownership. The battle for a just, humane society has been reduced to a battle against a certain form of ownership.

But what does the form of ownership of the means of production really have to do with the nature of an advanced economy? Ownership has become so diffused in the United States, for example, that it isn't clear any more precisely to whom the means of production belong. The larger the corporation, the more difficult it is to determine who owns what. Corporate shares and profits are spread throughout the entire nation, accruing to private individuals, other corporations, labor organizations, trusts, foundations, and foreign entities. Of primary importance is, who is the beneficiary of the gain resulting from production? If the majority of the people are the beneficiaries, then the relatively small part of profits that accrue to the owners of the means of production, whoever they may be, is not of primary importance. If, however, gain accrues to a very few, or to a privileged class, as is the case in communist societies, then the people are justified in changing their form of government.

It should be noted that fascism is not a deviation from capitalism just as Stalinism is not a deviation from Marxism. Both follow from the importance attached to the role assigned to ownership, identifying such ownership as the most decisive factor in a social system.

Marx asserted that a social order perishes only after all productive possibilities in it have been developed.

There is no God in this process, declared Marx, only a natural historical process. He saw feudalism emerging from slavery, capitalism from feudalism, and socialism from capitalism. He stated that history is nothing more than a history of production, and man is the producer. The entire process is inevitable, but can be helped along by forces which have come into existence and are destined to replace existing power centers and institutions.

These forces started out as ideas, averred Marx, and became political forces only after they took command of the human mind. Thus, if we accept that reasoning, we would first have the consciousness of wanting to change society, of formulating new political, legal, and ideological superstructures. These superstructures would then determine the nature of the substructure—economic relations.

But "superstructure" and "substructure" are the results of man's ability to think: They are the organic parts of a single entity, never existing in a way that makes it possible to draw a dividing line between them. Economy is a part of the cultural continuum of a nation and must be viewed and understood from a holistic point of view. Economy does not exist independently of other components of a society.

History is always more than just the story of production. Cultural trends, religious beliefs and a variety of other factors play their part in shaping the tenor of an age. Also, if Marx was correct about capitalism emerging from feudalism and socialism from capitalism, then one should be able to justify the efficacy of his theory by observing countries where different economic systems prevailed. One should be able to observe, in a feudal system, a different economic substructure and a different legal and political superstructure than those one would see in a capitalist system. The truth is that differing economic systems are more a consequence of the effect of legal and political superstructures than a cause.

Is there a natural historical process involved in the transition of one stage of history into another, one in which humans are mere pawns? Or is it a process brought about by thinking human beings?

With Marx, a system develops in a determined way, like a tree growing out of a seed. But human thinking has its own rationale which has nothing to do with systems. It is a free creativeness, and how it molds and shapes the outside world is dependent on the level of creative thinking applied. Turn enough creative minds loose in a society and the results may well be astounding. Hobble creative thinking by stringent regulation of the productive process, and the results will be precisely what they are in any communist society: resorting to parasitical importation of technology and expertise.

Marx's view reflects the antihumanistic outlook that we are dealing with a relationship between a social order and the productive forces in it. It eliminates the human mind as a factor. But there is no historical evidence that mankind ever set itself the task of developing all productive possibilities in a given system.

Marx's aim was to create a humane society based on a philosophy devoid of human considerations.

Hegel Influences Marx

Karl Marx had the kind of intellectual mind that was fascinated with grand designs, be they philosophical, historical, or scientific. The arrangement of facts into some new grandiose concept intrigued his imagination. Added to that was an apocalyptic vision of history, in which ferocious violence was required to move the world from one state of being to another. All this was, in Marx's opinion, part of a process operating according to strict laws. In this approach we see the workings of a mind trained in the methodology of the natural sciences—Newton's way. Man's mind—his creativeness and ability to bring into being entirely new factors via the application of a higher level of thinking—plays no part whatsoever in Marx's system.

Like Adam Smith before him, Marx, once he had his own unique *Weltanschauung,* sought to break down economic phenomena into individual components. But whereas the theories of natural science can be tested with practice, those of economics, a man-made system, cannot. A fallacious economic theory is very often applied to the real world, which then acts as if the laws inherent in the theory actually exist.

The great credence the world has given to Marxist theories literally willed them into existence.

It wasn't until he discovered Hegel that Marx found a theoretical basis for his developing beliefs.

Up to that point, Marx was well aware that he lacked a system, a full-length work that would incorporate the socio-political grand design that had been germinating in his mind for years. He had read Smith's *Wealth of Nations* and Say's *Treatise on Political Economy* and had accepted the classical approach that labor was the source of wealth. He was strongly influenced by Proudhon's *What is Property?*, published in 1840. Proudhon's answer to the question was: Property is theft. His argument was that property was specifically the right of the owner of capital goods to employ the labor of others to augment his own wealth. And it was "theft" in the sense that labor contributed to the enrichment of the property owners. Proudhon anticipated Marx by calling this capital-labor relation an exploitation of man by man. In his own words, "From the right of the strongest springs the exploitation of man by man, or bondage."

Hegel fascinated Marx. Here was a *Weltanschauung* truly worthy of admiration. Hegel wrote of the progressive self-externalization of spirit, both in space as the world of nature and in time as successive cultures and civilizations. He saw history as a record of human suffering caused by man's ceaseless striving to actualize the Absolute in himself, and justified the suffering on the grounds that by striving man would eventually reach his goal.

The materialistic, atheistic Marx was not satisfied with what he considered to be Hegel's religious coloring. In the writings of Ludwig Feuerbach, a political economist of the times, he found the method of utilizing Hegel to set down his own system of thought.

Feuerbach believed that Hegel's system had real truth value, but that it was necessary to turn it upside down in order to arrive at the truth about existence. He averred, and Marx echoed, that it was man himself, not spirit, who underwent a process of self-externalization. This was the "handle" Marx needed for his Hegelian-based system. For Marx, self-externalization was reflected in successive economic systems: slavery, feudalism, capitalism, and, finally, communism. At each stage the superstructures of law, science, philosophy, etcetera developed out of the system.

Feuerbach saw no justification for man's suffering. Man suffers because he oppresses himself, he said. Marx tailored this concept to his own needs by stating that the execrable working conditions which existed were the result of a particular system—the capitalist—and would change only if the system changed, i.e., was superseded.

But how could the system be changed? His answer was by taking the ownership of the means of production out of the hands of the capitalists and giving it to the real creators of wealth—the workers or "proletariat," as Marx named this social class.

Of course the capitalists would not give up their ownership of the means of production without a struggle. Hence, reasoned Marx, there would be frightful clashes between the capitalists and the proletariat before the change in ownership was effected.

No Ethical Content to Marx

There are still those who believe that Marx was motivated by the kind of compassion for workers that motivated the early Russian socialists of the nineteenth century—those populists who were willing to spend their lives, and give them, to improve the lot of the masses. The truth is different: Marx had cast himself in the role of a detached scientist, an observer of conditions who formulated a priori a sociopolitical system and used his interpretations of existing conditions to "prove" the correctness of his concepts. He was a social scientist intent on establishing a system of thought, and was no more for the proletariat than he was against the capitalists. As a matter of fact, he never saw a worker huddled over a workbench or operating a machine, and never observed working conditions firsthand until after he formulated his theory of the proletariat. If he called for revolution, it was to hurry into existence the new society, communism, that he foresaw as the natural out-growth of capitalism.

Also wrong are those who think that Marx's concept of communism had anything to do with the creation of material abundance. What was primary in Marx's new society was the spiritual regeneration of man; material abundance would simply happen as a by-product. The objective of revolution was to change human nature, something that simply couldn't occur, in Marx's opinion, without a change in the economic system. He expressed these thoughts in his *Theses on Feuerbach,* written in 1845. There would be, he said, a "self-change" (*Selbstverände-rung*) coincidental with a change of economic circumstances; and the proletariat would be the midwife to such change.

There never was any ethical content to Marx's theories. Even Karl Kautsky, the leading theorist of German Marxism after the death of Engels, realized that. Marxism simply pos-tulated that socialism was inevitable because the class struggle and victory of the proletariat were inevitable. It is a cause-and-effect relationship applied to history, and there is nothing to indicate that the working class would find the end result desirable. That never concerned Marx, hence the ethical void in his teachings.

Marx Postulates a Historical Process

Studying Marx is like examining a series of photographs taken of an embryo. By mentally trying to isolate observed phenomena, one can postulate laws. But one is forced to amend these laws or disregard or add to them as the embryo changes and becomes a completely new entity, even as a child turns into an adult.

Marx analyzed and criticized a developing economy, one that bears no resemblance to the high-technology, integrated society of today. He saw labor, he saw capitalists, and he saw means of production. These were individual components in a system he had decided had replaced a previous system and would in turn be replaced. There was no science in such concepts, no laws that were provable as is the law of gravity or the chemical law that says that the mixture of hydrogen and oxygen will always create water.

Marx studied philosophy and history, observed economic conditions, and decided there was an inexorable historical process taking place. This process, taken from Hegel, was one of thesis, antithesis, and synthesis: a set of circumstances, its opposite that emerged from it, and a synthesis of the two. It was an a priori concept no less than Adam Smith's "invisible hand" guiding and smoothing out differences in the economy, but it was a much grander design and appealed to all those who sought a theoretical weapon to help change the lot of the working class, and to those who are enamored of a *Weltanschauung* that seems to solve all problems of political and economic development.

The Marxist economists apply to a mature economy the thinking that Marx applied to a developing one. The most militant Marxist scholars use Marxist terminology to criticize the contemporary Western economic system. They blame capitalism—the private ownership of means of production—and multinational corporations in terms Marx used. But Marx didn't criticize a system that had the properties of our system, and multinational corporations didn't even exist in Marx's time.

Marx didn't criticize capitalists, business enterprises, or profits—he criticized the *system,* the philosophy on which the system was based. He saw the participants in the economic process playing their roles despite any subjective feelings on their parts. The capitalist, he said, could not help acting as he did, because if he didn't the nature of the system would destroy him. He thought the owners of the means of production were caught up in a process of rapid industrialization wherein only the greater and more effective use of machines would ensure economic survival against competitors.

Adam Smith had seen the capitalist motivated by the greed for profits, a purely subjective reaction. Marx saw the pursuit of profit as an absolute necessity to accumulate capital in order to purchase more means of production and hire more workers. Actually, Marx was not even concerned with that portion of profits accruing to the capitalist for his personal use. That was the smallest part of profit. Smith would have been right about greed as the spur if *all* profits were used for personal use, but this was not the case. In effect, the owners of the means of production used machines like weapons of war that have to be improved continuously in order to stay ahead of the enemy, the competition. It was a matter of improving on the productive process or risk being driven from the market by a competitor who was using more up-to-date machines and getting more work out of his labor force, women and children included.

"Labor" and "Value" Enamor Marx

With Smith, Marx believed that labor was the source of a nation's wealth. He saw an ever-growing army of proletariat turning out more and more goods, and it was therefore apparent to him that here were the creators of wealth. It simply didn't occur to Marx that prolonged working hours could not make up for the tremendous increase in production taking place at the time, that there had to be another factor involved. That factor was, as noted, the role of the organizer, integrating applied science, labor, and machinery into the productive process. It was his brain, and the creative thinking powers of those inventing machines and scientific concepts, that were really responsible for the increased production. But since intellect cannot be quantified, it was never an economic factor to Marx, whose "natural scientific approach," still practiced by Keynesian economists, simply didn't recognize or allow for man's creative mind. What confronted Marx, who saw only labor and capital, was higher productivity, which was the result of a higher level of thinking applied to the economy. He didn't see it. He postulated the emergence of capitalism from feudalism as a result of historical laws independent of man; yet capitalism could not have emerged at all had it not been for new inventions, machines, and the brain power of the organizer. These were intellectual achievements that had nothing whatsoever to do with historical laws.

From a determination that labor was the source of a nation's wealth, Marx gave his attention to "value." How is anything valued? In his own words, "the value of each commodity is determined by the quantity of labor expended on, and materialized in it by the working time necessary, under given social conditions, for its production." This observation is an excellent example of thinking applicable to an exchange economy and wholly obsolete when applied to a developed industrial economy. In pre-industrial times it was easy enough to determine value in the way Marx did, by noting how much labor went into the manufacture of a product. After the Industrial Revolution, as we saw earlier by projecting Adam Smith's famous pin-making example into a future where automation played a role, the attempt to determine value based on manual labor became increasingly difficult. The economic scene was being crowded with more and more people like inventors, educators, consultants, and entrepreneurs, whose presence was not apparent in the productive process, but whose contributions were indispensable.

Going further in his analysis of the economic system, Marx noted that workers produced, not only to pay their own way, but to provide profits for the owners of the means of production. In his own words, labor power is a commodity that is "a source not only of value, but of more value than it has itself." It is this property of labor, said Marx, that the capitalist used to obtain profits, which is then used as capital to employ and exploit more workers.

Thus, his process works in this way: A worker, in six hours of labor, can provide himself with sufficient commodities to stay alive and reproduce his working power. But he works twelve hours a day. The product of his additional six hours is appropriated by the capitalist. Marx calls this difference "surplus value," expressed as the difference between surplus working time and necessary working time.

By working twice as long as necessary to supply his needs, and receiving only subsistence wages, the worker can only consume half of his production. Does that mean that twice as many commodities appeared on the market as were necessary for the reproduction of working power? Then what happened to the fifty percent surplus? Who bought those goods? Was it the capitalist, the owner of the means of production?

The process didn't work that way at all because something unique happened with the coming of the Industrial Revolution. In the pre-industrial days producers and consumers were one and the same and simply exchanged labor for commodities. After the Industrial Revolution, the capitalist could purchase machinery, the means of production. Indeed, he had to do so to survive in business. Machinery was not an article of exchange, but something that had to be paid for and belonged to a different kind of market than a commodity such as, say, a pair of shoes. It was a part of a producer's market which the Industrial Revolution had brought into being. How was the capitalist to buy the machine?

Out of the surplus value created by his labor force. In the

bifurcated market of the post-Industrial Revolution society, the need for profit was essential to pay for the new means of production that were being released into the market. These machines were "transformers" of natural resources into productive use, operating on a much more efficient scale than manual labor.

Marx saw that there were two types of surplus value. One was the "absolute" type, determined by the difference between the labor necessary to produce what the worker needed for his subsistence and the amount of labor he actually performed. The other type was the "relative" surplus value, resulting from the fact that by using machinery, the worker was able to produce his needs in a shorter period of time, with the difference appropriated by the capitalist.

It can be seen from the above that surplus value is the essence of capitalism. If the worker only put in necessary working time, that is, only enough to pay for his subsistence, there would be no surplus, no profit, and consequently no incentive for a capitalist to be a capitalist.

By the nineteenth century such concepts as absolute surplus value, and relative surplus value had lost all meaning, as had Marx's theory of labor. But economists were so enamored of this type of quantification that they earnestly kept poring over Marxism, trying to figure out ways of applying obsolescent theories to an organic, complex, and scientific-oriented society.

"Exploitation"—Not What It Seems

Even today, the word "exploitation" as applied to labor still has a place in economic theory, and is used as a weapon by communism to cudgel the free enterprise system.

"Exploitation" was one of the concepts developed by Marx, and referred to the excessive working time of the proletariat as measured against wages received.

Marx saw the worker as being cruelly exploited. But in order to speak of exploitation at all, it's necessary to know how much value labor has added to the productive process. One can then evaluate that contribution against the reward received in the form of wages.

In the pre-industrial economy, as has been noted, it was possible to determine the value of labor through quantification. With no machines or organizers on the scene, an employee could be exploited both in his capacity as a consumer and producer. Looking at the laborers working for the farmer or the apprentice for the journeyman, it was possible to determine precisely what their labor added to the product value. They were exploited by receiving less than what they added. Then, in becoming consumers, they could be charged cost of production plus profit, thus being exploited as consumers.

After the Industrial Revolution it was no longer possible to accurately ascertain value in terms of labor expended: There were simply too many new variables to consider, of which manual labor was only one. Nevertheless, Marx persisted in viewing labor as the sole pertinent component in the wealth producing process, and accepted the axiom that in the process of creating wealth in the capitalist system, the worker became impoverished—exploited.

But what if the capitalist had sold his product for a price equivalent to the cost of production—wages, cost of materials, and the wear and tear of machinery—without adding anything whatsoever for profit? Then the idea of exploitation would not have been pertinent at all. There could only be a discussion of whether or not the rewards for production were properly structured among all the participants in the productive process. And to figure that out in an organic, integrated, science-dominated economy is impossible.

Was there exploitation of the worker? Yes, but only when he appeared in the market as a consumer, that is, when he was asked to pay a higher price than the actual cost of the product to the manufacturer. He would then be exploited as a consumer, not as a worker. This is a very important point, relevant to our own society, and in any comparison between our society and a communist one.

The Idea of Alienation
Becomes a Phobia

Man is alienated, cried Marx, and it is the productive process, the capitalist system, that has brought about this state of affairs.

In all of Marx's writings, nothing is more powerfully expressed. And nothing has resulted in more bloodshed and misery for the human race than this basically psychiatric concept applied to the outside world.

The idea of alienated man began, for Marx, from an observation: Workers who had previously been engaged in work where they could see a commodity produced and feel a sense of involvement in the productive process were now reduced to automatons responsible for a minute part of the operation. This was an undeniable form of alienation, and is still a serious problem today. However, no one today would think of creating a purely economic factor out of alienation, as Marx did. He looked at the economic system extant, i.e., capitalism, and saw a "self-alienation process" (*Selbstentfremdungsprozess*) whereby the worker was gradually brutalized to the point where he lost his will, his personality, his spontaneity, and his joy of life.

In *Philosophy and Myth in Karl Marx* (1961), Robert Tucker points out that Marx's description of an alienated man is "clinically accurate." It coincides in all important respects with descriptions by psychiatrists of the symptoms of alienation as experienced by persons in an advanced stage of the neurotic process. The neurotic sees himself as a godlike being with his imperfect empirical self as a stranger. As time goes by an autonomous dynamic force builds up in the neurotic to actualize the godlike part of him. This leads to a depersonalization, a sense of profound alienation, as though all his activities were performed compulsively at the bidding of another. Dr. Karen Horney, the well-known psychiatrist, in her book, *Neurosis and Human Growth,* writes about the alienated neurotic feeling as though he is "removed from himself," of being "driven instead of being the driver," of the "feeling of not being a moving force in his own life."

Going on from this point, one can show, step by step, how Marx's concept inevitably had to lead to the bloodbaths in Russia, China, North Korea, Vietnam, Cambodia, East Europe, and wherever else the communist ideology has come into power. And all in the name of a historical socioeconomic process.

If an alienated worker feels himself to be doing the bidding of another, then to whom does the alien activity belong? Marx, proceeding in the belief that he was dealing with a genuine matter of political economy and not with a psychiatric phenomenon—one originating and confined to individuals tending toward such neurosis—thunders the news that "The alien being to whom the labour and the product of labour belong, in whose service and for whose enjoyment the labour is performed, can only be man himself," but another man outside himself. In Marx's words,

> If he experiences the product of his labour, his objectified labour, as an alien, hostile, powerful object independent of him, he experiences it in such a way that another alien, hostile, powerful man, independent of him, is the master of this object. If he experiences his own activity as an unfree activity, he experiences it as activity in service, under the domination, compulsion and yoke of another man.

Marx dubbed this alien being, "My Lord Capital," and summed up his collective victims as the proletariat. What we had now were no longer human beings, individuals with their own feelings, desires, hopes, frustrations, fears, and preferences, but two nonhuman antagonists engaged in a battle to the finish for control of the means of production, which were the cause of man's alienation. Generic man vanished from the picture, and all that was left were two warring social classes, the workers and the capitalists, wholly alienated from each other.

The proletariat possessed, for Marx, all the positive traits and virtues that were totally absent from the capitalists. Nor did Marx see any differences between the proletariat in one country or another, or in the nature of the capitalists in any country. The division of labor, he wrote, "created everywhere the same relations between classes of society and thus destroyed the particular individuality of the various nationalities."

So strong was Marx's fixation about the nature and burning enmity between the two social classes he had single-handedly endowed with powerful reality, that to the end of his life he refused to see the betterment of working conditions taking place in the factories. He kept right on insisting that the conditions had to get worse.

Only extreme hostile social relations can result from such visions, and this truth was borne out when communism came to power first in Russia, and then in one European and Asian country after another. Armed with the notion that all social classes save the proletariat were enemies of mankind's struggle for "liberation" from economic fetters, communist rulers have been pitiless in their extermination of intellectual, professional, and business classes. They've carried through this bloodbath to wives, children, and relatives of the "enemies of the state." In Russia, some sixty million people were murdered or tortured to death over a six-decade period. These included not only the aforementioned classes, but millions of recalcitrant peasants and entire nationalities. Such books as Aleksandr Solzhenitsyn's *Gulag* series and *Genocide in the USSR,* issued by the Institute for the Study of the USSR in Munich, West Germany, detail the facts of this slaughter of the innocents. The latter book, for example, specifies the complete destruction of the Crimean

Turks, the Kalmyks, the peoples of the North Caucasus and the Volga Germans, all annihilated because they were "enemies of the state."

In China, during the rule of Mao Tse-tung, the number of people put to death because of their class affiliations will never be known, but it assuredly ran into the many millions. In communist Cambodia anyone with higher education, business-men, professionals—and the families of these people—perished at the hands of one of the most barbaric regimes of the twentieth century. What all communist regimes have in common is the face-value acceptance of Karl Marx's assertion that the world is divided between "capital" and "labor" and that the former must be ruthlessly destroyed. Who belongs in which category becomes the responsibility of the ruling communist clique.

Communists still cling to the fiction of the proletariat as the elite and rightful rulers of society. By "proletariat" they osten-sibly mean manual workers, but the ruling groups themselves are by no means proletarians, but political hacks and professional people. However, it's convenient to have proletarians as a means of establishing an artificial yardstick representing all that's best and noble. At one stroke all other social classes and religious and ethnic groups are reduced to the status of second-class citizens. A stamp of legality is thus given by the state to any policy of terror, repression, and annihilation to eliminate its enemies.

To this day, anyone not in agreement with the dicta of ruling communist parties is automatically placed in the "enemy camp." The followers of Marx still see the world the same way their master did, as sharply divided between only two basic social classes, labor and capital, ferociously locked in mortal combat. The human being is never seen as an individual; indeed, under communism he has no rights whatsoever, being wholly subservient to the state which rules in the name of the proletariat. To prevent the formation of any group posing an actual or potential danger to its rule, the state atomizes the population—destroys all social, cultural, and intellectual bonds that unify certain segments of the population. This is in strict accordance with Marxist thinking that the "enemy" must never be given the opportunity to become a force in opposition to the ruling communist party. The capitalist and bourgeois elements must be crushed beyond all possibility of posing a menace.

It has not been lost on the world that the ruthlessness of this approach has destroyed all effective opposition in those countries where communism has come to power. The sole exception in recent times was Chile, but communist analysis is that the deposed, dead communist leader Allende simply didn't act quickly and forcibly enough to annihilate his opposition.

Marx, a visionary, saw in the expropriation of the means of production by the proletariat a gateway to the creation of a new man. This new species of *Homo sapiens,* freed from the fetters of the "vampire" machine, would undergo a self-change and become a real human being, no longer alienated and brutalized.

Dmitri Panin, prototype of a major character in one of Solzhenitsyn's novels, who spent thirteen years in Russian prisons and labor camps as an "enemy of the people," watched the communist attempt to create a "New Soviet Man." He wrote, "A huge country, basically Christian, had been made over into a nursery for rearing a new breed of men under conditions of widescale terror and atheism. A new society, governed by primitives, began taking shape."

How? By murder, torture, starvation, and overwork. In the communist zealousness to exterminate every vestige of real or fancied opposition, Stalin and his secret police fanned the flames of class hatred to white-hot pitch. One special campaign followed another. Panin cites one, a campaign organized "to wipe out by starvation the inhabitants of certain regions in the Ukraine, in the Kuban and along the Don. The number who died exceeded 16 million . . . whole communities were exterminated; mothers ate their children." Comments Panin on the Marxists who made such horrors possible: "Every nation, unfortunately, has its moral degenerates with their misshapen souls and perverted minds."

The Myth of the Proletariat

The Marxist myth of the elite proletariat is simply that—a myth. For a relatively short while at the time of the Industrial Revolution a working class clearly distinguishable from other classes came into existence. That this class lived in misery is not to be denied, but from within and from without forces were set in motion to ameliorate working conditions and lighten the cruel work load of the workers. They fought for rights and were joined by legislators, ministers, professional people, and even factory owners themselves, like Friedrich Engels. And working conditions did improve, more and more. With time, a huge middle class emerged from the working class, wages rose steadily without any diminution of profits (a possibility Marx termed impossible), and the number of manual workers shrank to a minority of the labor force. They were replaced as the majority by white-collar workers and professional people.

What, then, of Marx's vaunted proletariat as a ruling elite a century or so ago? Would it, could it have created the conditions under which science and technology might have developed? Would the proletariat have produced the tractors, telephones, radio, television, jet planes, computers, and all the other trappings of a modern technological society? The answer is that the proletariat would have negated itself as a viable class had it succeeded, turning into the white-collar workers and brain workers who were responsible for these advances and who did become the majority class.

And what would have been the outcome if the proletariat, coming to power and taking over all means of production, turned upon their class "enemies" as Marx urged them to do? Why, then we would have had precisely the situation that came to pass in Russia, China, and Cambodia under communist rule: a mass killing off of intellectuals, professionals, and anyone else suspected of harboring thoughts hostile to the ruling clique. Leaving what? In the case of Russia, a parasitical society feeding off the technology and expertise of the West and generally unrecognizable from any current underdeveloped country save in its war-making capacity. China, its economy having ground to a halt under rulers who tried to apply strict Marxist concepts, is now seeking surcease via a radical shift toward Western economic techniques. Cambodia, having eliminated itself as a civilized society, has no stratum of society left to call upon to create a viable economy, and may have no future at all under the new despotism of Vietnamese conquerors, themselves the victims of Marxist economic thinking.

Look where you will in any part of the communist world. It is not a liberated proletariat that rules and is busy creating a happy society of material abundance, as envisioned by Marx: It is the dead hand of a cruel, conscienceless bureaucracy that rules, one which, as the astute Yugoslav, Milovan Djilas, himself a communist, has pointed out, is the new privileged class in the communist world, usurping all privileges and living off the labor of the workers.

What If the Proletariat Had Won?

An interesting point that deserves elaboration is, what would have been the practical outcome if the proletariat had made a successful revolution a century ago and expropriated the capitalists? Would workers have worked less? Would they have had more purchasing power? Would they enjoy more benefits? Would productivity have been greater because the worker was, in a sense, working for himself?

It is of primary importance to note that this was a time of rapid industrialization, with all that it implies in the way of cruel hardships imposed on working people. As will be shown, even worse hardships were imposed on the Russian people after the communists came to power in that regime's exertions toward the same kind of rapid industrialization that took place in nineteenth-century England.

Marx declared that profits were the result of low wages, and higher profits were achievable only through lower wages. Contrary to popular belief, however, Marx was not concerned with that part of profit accruing to the owners of the means of production for their own personal use. Although it did allow the capitalists to live on a much higher level than the workers, it was not the important factor in the productive process. What was salient was the expenditures of profits derived from "surplus labor" for the purchase of additional machines and means of production and the hiring of additional labor to man the newly acquired machines.

Following a Marxist revolution, with the means of production taken over by the proletariat, the possibilities would have been as follows: (1) If the process of rapid industrialization was to continue, profits would have to be engendered to pay for new machinery and equipment appearing on the market. The difference would be that the profits would belong to the proletariat and not to the former capitalists. However, there would be a relatively modest savings—that part of profits which formerly accrued to the capitalists for their own personal use. (2) Rapid industrialization would be slowed or come to a complete halt so that profits could be used to better the working conditions.

Marx was in favor of bettering the workers' lot, and made specific suggestions toward that end in his *Critique of the Gotha Program.* He wrote that from the total social product there should be deducted the following:

One—enough to cover the cost of the means of production used up;

Two—enough to cover expansion of production; and

Three—reserve of insurance funds to provide against accidents, dislocation caused by natural calamities, etcetera.

Following the above deductions, there would remain that part of the product serving as means of consumption. Before this was to be divided between the owner-workers, further deductions were necessary, to wit:

First—the general costs of administration not belonging to production;

Second—that which was intended for the common satisfaction of needs, such as schools, health services, etcetera; and

Third—funds for those unable to work, i.e., funds earmarked for relief and welfare.

In passing, it might be pointed out that all the above conditions have been met in advanced free enterprise societies, with the exception that profits for personal use are still taken by owners of the means of production. These are, however, a relatively small part of the Gross National Product.

We can safely conclude that because of the relatively low level of productivity a century ago compared to our own times, workers would have had to work the same long hours and suffer the same hardships as did the workers in the capitalistic society Marx criticized in order to provide themselves with the social benefits enumerated by Marx. The prices for consumer goods would have had to consist not only of the direct costs of production, plus the cost of administration of the factories, but also of additional administrative costs (not a part of the cost of production of commodities or of the machinery used in the productive process); the cost of additional expansion of production; the cost of insurance funds, schools, health services, etcetera. Total it all up and call it profit, overhead, sales tax, or whatever. The result would have been to burden the consumer in exactly the same way it did under the conditions Marx criticized as being exploitative.

MODERN RUSSIA: WHAT MARX HATH WROUGHT

13

In contrast to earlier revolutions, the Communist revolution, conducted in the name of doing away with classes, has resulted in the most complete authority of any single new class. Everything else is a sham and an illusion.
—Milovan Djilas, *The New Class*

The danger of building words into concepts and assigning to them values and a scientific base is that these concepts become reality when they are accepted by enough people who then act as though the concepts are facts.

The writings of Karl Marx abound in such a priori concepts. The very base of Marx's *Weltanschauung,* his assertion that specific social classes—slavery, feudalism, capitalism, communism—grow out and replace, via violence, the preceding class, is an a priori concept. The most damaging concept to the world, in terms of the agony and mass death it has caused during the past century, is surely Marx's theory of the proletariat: the working class pitted against the capitalists, the owners of the means of production.

Marx was virtually paranoid in his idea that during his time there were two social classes vying for dominance in the world. He created an incredibly powerful verbal picture of two

powerful forces armed against each other like two armies poised
for their confrontation in battle. To assign all virtue to one side
and all evil to the other, to assert that there can be no
compromise, that the struggle is to the finish with no mercy
shown, is to invite bloodshed on a vast scale. And that is
precisely what happened.

The revolutionaries who took power in Russia in 1917
knew their Marxism and applied it with a vengeance. Their first
step was to take control of all investments and means of
production. They did so in the name of the proletariat. But
inasmuch as amorphous masses cannot rule, the actual control
of the economy was in the hands of the Communist Party,
which consisted of revolutionaries who made up in zeal,
fanaticism, and hatred for real and imagined enemies what they
lacked in practical knowledge of running a country.

All private ownership was destroyed via such methods as
nationalization, compulsory cooperation, high taxes, and price
inequalities. Heeding Marx's admonition that the proletariat
would be endangered by the deposed classes, the new ruling
class instituted a bloodletting that went on for six decades and
took the lives of sixty million people. Included among the
"enemies of socialism" were entire ethnic groups, intellectuals,
professionals, religious believers, and families and friends of
those arrested.

Although the personal paranoia of the dictator Josef Stalin
played an important role in this mass murder, there is no
gainsaying that the theories of Karl Marx were used as the
theoretical justification of what happened.

The objective of the ruling Communist Party, the new elite,
was to create a classless society through industrialization and
collectivization. In setting in motion a process of rapid industrialization, the communists followed the same path as the
capitalists of a century earlier, but with some notable differences.

Like nineteenth-century capitalism, the communist rulers
of post-1917 Russia were ruthless in their application of

methods to force rapid industrialization. Russia was a backward country, but unlike backward countries of today that receive technological and monetary help from more affluent nations, Russia in 1917 could not expect any help from abroad. That meant the marshalling of all material resources, humans included, to achieve industrialization. The miseries and horrors in store for the nation, the ruling class warned the people, would have to be weathered in order to enjoy enormous material benefits—a shining new communist society—at a later time.

Basically, this is true: Expanded production is made possible only by the sacrifices of the consumer, while at a more developed state of industrialization it becomes the source of an increased standard of living. The horrors of the Industrial Revolution gradually gave way to better working conditions, higher wages, and more material benefits for everyone; however, something quite different happened in communist Russia. The fruits of the laboring masses never accrued to them: All the benefits of the surplus value which a century earlier had, beyond what was needed to purchase machinery and hire more workers, gone to the owners of the means of production, now went to the new ruling class—the Communist Party. In effect, because the party controlled all ownership, it distributed the goods for its own benefit.

The party maintained that ownership was socialist, belonging to everyone. But this was an illusion, difficult to expose because nothing was in the name of a single person or entity easily identifiable, as is the case in free enterprise societies. It was a collective ownership by a ruling class, which used and misused the country's produced wealth as they wished. This is true in every communist society to this day.

Again, as with nineteenth-century capitalism, the Communist Party of Russia was determined to squeeze all possible work out of people at the least cost to the state. This is a classic formula for rapid industrialization: Pay the lowest wages possible for maximum working hours. Here, post-1917 Russia differed markedly from nineteenth-century England in an important respect: Whereas a century ago workers were poorly paid for working long hours, they were at least paid; in Russia, the rulers found a way of not paying millions of people at all: they created a world of slave labor—the infamous "Gulag Archipelago." Through the entire Stalin era and beyond, this slave labor, kept on starvation rations, and consisting of any men, women, and children deemed "enemies of the state," provided the labor used to build roads, operate mines, fell trees, and the like.

In his book *Kolyma—the Arctic Death Camps* (1978), Robert Conquest details the horrors of a Russian slave labor complex where a month's service in one of the lead or gold mines could turn a healthy man into a dying wreck. Three million persons died there: scientists; artists; politicians; educators; and leaders of industry, trade, and government. Conquest quotes from the memoirs of Vladimir Petrov, a prisoner who managed to survive the death camp.

> The boots were always wet, never quite drying out—rheumatism was guaranteed. Then, the air in the pit, where there was no ventilation whatsoever, was filled twice daily with the poisonous fumes of blasted ammonal. Only thirty minutes were allowed for the clearing of the fumes through the entrance of the mine, after which the workers were driven back into the pits to continue their work. Many of them succumbed to the poisoned atmosphere and coughed violently, spitting blood and often particles of lung. After a short time, they were usually sent either to the weak squads for lumbering, or to their graves. Mortality was especially high among the men who carted the wet sand from the barrack after washing. From the steamy, damp atmosphere of the heater the perspiring wheelbarrow-pushers slipped through the opening, which was covered by an old blanket, rolling out their wheelbarrows into the piercing 50 degrees below zero frost. The time limit in this work was, at the most, one month, after which either pneumonia or meningitis dispatched the worker into the next world.

The difference between such horrors and those existing a century ago are slight, as one notes in the following passage from André Maurois's *The History of England:*

> When Engels visited Manchester in 1844 he found 350,000 workers crushed and crowded into damp, dirty, broken-down houses where they breathed an atmosphere resembling a mixture of water and coal. In the mines, he saw half-naked women, who were treated like the lowest of draft animals. Children spent the day in dark tunnels, where they were employed in opening and closing the primitive openings for ventilation, and in other difficult tasks. In the lace industry, exploitation reached such a point that four-year-old children worked for virtually no pay.

It is not the objective of this book to detail the horrors perpetrated on the Russian people by their communist rulers— indeed, an entire library of books would not suffice to do that— but to show that in its quest for rapid industrialization, the communist regime was no less brutal than nineteenth century capitalism had been. Indeed, it was in many respects far more brutal, literally starving, executing, and working people to death with a callousness never before seen in history. The little news of these atrocities that filtered out to the world was either disbelieved entirely or else marked down to the need for just punishment for "enemies of the state," i.e., enemies of the proletariat.

Historically, such has been the excuse of every communist regime to this very day and is in some form still accepted by liberal-left elements in the West. The experiences in North Korea, Vietnam, Cambodia, Angola, Mozambique, and Afghanistan, to name but a few countries that have fallen under communist domination, testify to the readiness on the part of the liberal left to accept the continuing bloodbaths in those countries as manifestations of "justice" being meted out to the enemies of the proletariat.

In their determination to achieve rapid industrialization, the communist rulers of Russia took certain steps which had profound and lasting effects on the Russian economy. There was nothing and no one to stand in their way, once the last remnants of "white" czarist forces had been routed and annihilated. The dictatorship of the proletariat that Marx had propounded as being the next step in the evolution of human society was complete—only the proletariat was a clique of crude revolutionaries. And whereas Marx had based his idea of the dictatorship of the proletariat on the Paris Commune of 1871, which was composed of several political parties, Lenin decreed that only the Communist Party could manage the dictatorship. Later, Stalin amended this to decree that only he could personally make the important decisions for Russia.

One of the steps the new rulers of Russia had to take was to institute a system of economic planning. One says "had to take" because there was no other way Marx's theories could go save in the direction of state planning. Marx had been a prisoner of mechanistic thinking that saw all human development as the outcome of inflexible historical laws. He never gave any credence to the ability of the creative human mind to bring about radical changes that would make theories and "laws" based on outmoded methods of production obsolete. He regarded the economy much as a watchmaker regards a watch: as a mechanism composed of various components which have an intrinsic, unchangeable quality about them.

This kind of viewpoint precludes the existence of a free market economy, incorporating the give-and-take of human beings with conflicting interests. Marx believed that all conflicting interests would automatically cease to be once all means of production were in the hands of the proletariat. People would simply produce for their own benefits and consumption, and there would be no parasitic capitalist class to siphon off surplus value created by the working class. Under such conditions, Marx never dealt particularly with the problem of economic planning. In his *Private Property and Communism,* he made what is probably his only serious effort to explain systematically and in some detail what communism meant to him. One finds that this tract has absolutely nothing to say about planning, distribution, or any other practical question involved in running an economy. Marx disregarded such mundane subjects on the grounds that, since under communism everyone will have an abundance of everything, why bother with problems that will be nonexistent?

The Russian Communist Party, however, found itself saddled with all the problems Marx chose to disregard. Since they were hardened Marxists, the thought of a market economy, one that would be allowed to undergo organic transformation as a result of the application of free human thinking, was simply unthinkable. In that direction lay the negation of Marxism, and of the dictatorship of the proletariat as represented by the all-powerful Communist Party. Only one way was open to the Russian rulers: state planning on a total scale, the handing down of directives on every aspect of the productive process. This included pricing, amount of production, type of production, wage scales, and long-range investments. Lacking the business expertise, it is no wonder that the Russian economy was quickly reduced to a shambles. And inevitably, seeking scapegoats for their own shortcomings, the Communist Party managed to find millions of "enemies of socialism" on whom to fasten the blame for the economic catastrophe.

Any underdeveloped country seeking rapid industrialization, as was England at the time of the Industrial Revolution and Russia after 1917, is dependent on savings in consumption to provide the wherewithal for the manufacture of means of production. Profits must be engendered to pay for industrialization. In post-1917 Russia, the consumer was forced to "save" by consuming less, and this "saving" was equal to gross profit.

The differences between nineteenth-century England and twentieth-century Russia is that the latter is a totalitarian society wherein criticism of the system is punishable by imprisonment or death. Also, with all property and means of production in state control, the state is the sole employer, and so there is no motivation for personal gain. Why exercise one's mental powers when the lone beneficiary will be a parasitic ruling class which handles national property as their own but wastes it as if it belonged to someone else? It has been noted time and again by those who experienced the communist system firsthand that no consideration is given to the cost of projects, to poor quality production, inefficiency, and grossly underpaid workers. Whereas in nineteenth-century England a worker dissatisfied with his lot could turn around and sell his labor elsewhere, the communist society decrees that his labor must be sold under conditions beyond his control. This is because there is only one employer, the state, for whom the worker works—or he does not work at all.

Unlike free enterprise societies, where taxes are more hidden than overt, the Russian consumer has been forced to "save" in a very direct way: a sort of sales tax imposed on the basic cost of production. This tax represents what the West would call all income tax, corporate tax, sales tax, state tax, communal tax, and all gross profit, including cost of investment.

This is how the system works:

If the sum total of all types of overhead—cost of producing the means of production and consumption, and social benefits (e.g., education, health, etcetera)—is, say, 300 billion units, and the production of consumer goods and services is 100 billion units, then the sales tax amounts to 200 billion units, or, the difference between the two. Of course, the planners can switch these ratios around as they wish, having no consumer opinion to worry about. In any event, the consumer can only consume what he earns minus the amount of the sales tax. And he always consumes less than he earns. How much less is wholly dependent on worker productivity: The bureaucracy and the military will always have what they want from the overall national income, so if the worker wants more for himself he must produce more.

But with incentive totally missing, production has been declining in Russia and all communist societies, with the result that the masses are left with an increasingly smaller part of the productive pie. Hence, a worker must work infinitely longer than his counterpart in the West to purchase some item or commodity. With low worker wages the norm, service industries are geared almost exlusively to those who do have the where-withal to pay—the ruling class of bureaucracy and military.

Marxists inveigh against free enterprise societies because of the profits accruing to individuals and corporations, although the greatest part of those profits is reinvested in expanded production. In communist societies the incomes of the elite (the bureaucracy and the military) are twenty times and more those of the average skilled worker. Although this fact is kept carefully hidden from the masses, the privileges and benefits that accrue to the ruling class have the same function as capitalist profit used for personal purposes.

More Flaws in Marx's Thinking

In the natural sciences theories can be proved or disproved through observation, measurement, and/or experimentation. In economics, a man-made scientific discipline, it's sufficient to have enough people accept a theory as being true for it to become valid. Marx's theory of the proletariat pitted in mortal struggle with capitalists for control of the means of production is a case in point. Another instance of a priori thinking on the part of Marx is his "labor theory of value." In fact, his system of economics, sociology, and politics is based on this theoretical assumption. If the theory is false, it literally undermines the entire structure of Marx's thinking.

Labor, said Marx, echoing Adam Smith, is the source of a

nation's wealth. In Part III of *Capital,* in that section called "The Production of Absolute Surplus Value," Marx defined labor as follows:

> Labor is, in the first place, a process in which both man and Nature participate, and in which man of his own accord starts, regulates and controls the material reactions between himself and Nature. He opposes himself to Nature as one of her own forces, setting in motion arms and legs, head and hands, the natural forces of his body, in order to appropriate Nature's productions in a form adapted to his own wants. By thus acting on the external world and changing it, he at the same time changes his own nature. He develops his slumbering powers and compels them to act in obedience to his sway.

This give-and-take relationship between man and Nature that Marx saw was certainly true for primitive exchange economies. It was a relationship that produced a high level of empirical thinking, the kind that prompted Marx to write with confidence that "the value of each commodity is determined by the quantity of labor expended on and materialized in it by the working time necessary, under given condition, for its production." What could be simpler or more evident than noting that a baker needed a certain number of hours to bake bread, or a shoemaker a certain number of hours to make or repair shoes?

Further, it was the type of economy where, in Marx's view, labor was a purposeful activity. He wrote, "At the end of every labor process, we get a result that already existed in the imagination of the laborer at its commencement. . . . Besides the exertion of bodily organs, the workman's will will be steadily in consonance with his purpose." Is it any wonder that thinking as he did, Marx endowed the proletariat with the virtues and powers that would lead them to overthrow the capitalists, take over all means of production, and usher in a brave new world?

Here, then, according to Marx, was a working class busy creating not only value (wealth), but also more value than inherent in the commodities produced. This idea embodies the concept of surplus value, used to create profits which are then used as capital by the capitalists to hire more workers and acquire more means of production.

In retrospect, one can readily see the flaw in this type of thinking: Despite the fact that Marx had a full century to observe an economy in the process of integrative, organic growth as a result of man's mind utilizing applied science and organization, he continued to apply mechanistic thinking to the productive process. Marx broke the process down into individual components and analyzed the system from that viewpoint. He saw the human being as the helpless victim of natural laws, like bodies in space subject to gravitational pull or other cosmic laws. Like Smith and other classical economists, he gave no credence whatsoever to the human mind as an economic factor because thinking can never be quantified.

For Marx, the worker was exploited because he contributed far more to production than he received in wages. Such exploitation can be determined in an exchange economy, where the fruits of applied science are absent. But in an advanced technological society, the kind that evolved out of the Industrial Revolution, to speak of exploitation one must first know how much value a worker has contributed to the productive process. How does one understand Marx's labor theory of value when there is the use of tractors, fertilizers, laboratories, computers, university research, advertising, and promotion? Marx simply never envisioned such an economy. He faced a world of commodities and his interest was to determine the exchange value of these commodities.

But in an advanced economy there is no longer any relationship between the exchange values of different commodities, nor any "material reaction" between man and Nature. As a result of applied science, there is a different form of thinking, a higher level that involves the marshaling and organizing of forces not based on empirical thinking. In this type of society the determining factor in the cost of labor is the power relationship between organized labor and business, with allowance for the share demanded by government.

Today, "exchange value" of commodities that can determine price relationships and be measured by the amount of labor involved is a fiction. It had meaning in the time of Adam Smith, was obsolete by the time of Marx, and has no validity whatsoever in a modern advanced economy. Neither does Marx's distinction between "concrete" labor that creates "use value" (the labor of a shoemaker or carpenter, for example), and "abstract" labor, the labor that creates "exchange value."

At one point following the advent of the Industrial Revolution, the working class emerged as a recognizable social stratum ill-equipped to effect rapid industrialization. Marx seized upon that moment in time to construct a "natural scientific approach" (still practiced by Keynesian economists) that refused to allow for gradual evolutionary change in working conditions. He postulated that wages would rise only if profits fell, and that the division of labor, grinding ever finer in the productive process, would more and more reduce wages while profits rose. He could not envision a society where both wages and profits could rise simultaneously. Nor did he see that the division between manual and mental labor is the very basis of the history of civilization. It can be observed that the wealth of nations grows in direct proportion to the amount and success of mental labor applied. The greater the proportion and the higher the level of mental work, the greater the material wealth of the nation. Conversely, the greater the proportion of manual labor, the lower the wealth of the nation.

Marx proclaimed that revolution was the only way out of working class misery, refusing to concede that the underprivileged could be liberated through different methods, such as shortening the workday, easing the hardships of the labor process with the use of applied science, and increasing nominal and real wages. The idea of government tax monies and corporate profits being used to provide workers with various material benefits in a free enterprise society was wholly beyond his ken.

Marx's labor theory of value is false because it has no meaning in an advanced economy. He was right that physical labor is the source of wealth, but the qualification is that it is the source of wealth in a primitive economy only. In an advanced sociotechnological economy the source of wealth is brain work, man's ability to think that transforms natural forces into productive ones. The wealth is then the gain, where output is greater than input, because brainpower has shortened the working process while increasing output. The labor theory of value is a mere conceptual and speculative construction that has not been valid for more than two centuries. When this is realized, the entire theoretical structure of Marxism, which is based on the acceptance of the proletariat as the creator of a nation's wealth, falls apart.

Russia Expands Because of Domestic Economic Failure

The connection between the economy of a Marxist state like Russia and the global expansion of its military imperialism may not be readily apparent, but there is a very real connection indeed. It prompted Milovan Djilas, the Yugoslav Marxist turned critic of the system to write:

"Founded by force and violence, in constant conflict with its people, the Communist state, even if there are no external reasons, must be militaristic. The cult of force, especially military force, is nowhere so prevalent as in Communist countries. Militarism is the internal basic need of the new class; it is one of the forces which make possible the new class's existence, strength and privileges."

A communist ruling class, to protect its position and privileges, concentrates on building up those areas that will ensure its rule and retention of material benefits. There are two such areas—bureaucracy and the military. Needing the military to protect them from the people under their domination, the bureaucracy, i.e., the Communist Party, gives the military whatever they wish. In return the party receives their loyalty.

The military are the most pampered stratum in a communist society because only the threat of ruthless use of force keeps the people under communist domination from deposing their masters. In Russia, since the 1917 Revolution, the military has created a state within a state, a huge superstructure divorced from civilian society. The best technological minds of the country have been drafted by the military, and productivity is geared first and foremost to military needs.

Of Russia's Gross National Product, only what is left after the military and the bureaucracy take their share is allocated for civilian needs.

The problem that arises as a result of such blatant inequalities is that an apathetic, underpaid, overworked labor force operates on a low level of productivity. There is never enough of anything for the masses, but this is basically of no concern to the ruling class and the military. However, what is of concern to them is that Russia continues to fall further and further behind the West in technological development, and is unable to make adequate use of its own natural resources.

These economic shortcomings have prompted the Russians to formulate a foreign policy which might be described as "inverted colonialism." Whereas previous colonial powers sought to take control of foreign raw materials bases to supply their technological requirements, Russia seeks to harness the technological superiority of the West to its own stagnant economy. In their eyes, this is the sole raison d'être for détente, which permits Russia to purchase whatever it wishes in the West without foregoing the right to undermine the West via subversion and other weapons of the "ideological" struggle.

But there's more: There are geopolitical areas, such as the Horn of Africa, Iran, and the Middle East, which are of vital importance to the West by virtue of either geography or source of raw materials. Here the Russian—and Cuban—military are active to wrest control of the areas away from the West. For them to succeed would mean the very real possibility of future Russian political blackmail to ensure a continued flow of Western technology, expertise, and loans to Russia.

Ostensibly, it is the role of communism to free the proletariat from capitalist fetters; however, the free use of Russian and Cuban military forces in such areas as Angola, Mozambique, and Afghanistan shows that freedom of the proletariat had nothing to do with the use of communist military in those countries. None of the countries had a proletariat, and none were anywhere near a stage of social evolution that mandated a radical change in societal structure as postulated by Marx. He wrote, "No social order ever perishes before all the productive forces for which there is room in it have developed; and new, higher relations of production never appear before the material conditions of their existence have matured in the womb of the old society itself." What productive forces and what material conditions existed in Angola, Mozambique, or Afghanistan to warrant Russian and Cuban imperialist interference in those countries? The simple reason for such policies is the temptation to use a bloated military machine for aggrandizement purposes, a temptation that becomes more reckless as the West shows timidity and hesitation.

In the final analysis, the cause of Russian imperialist expansion is to be found in the dismal failure of communist economic policies. At home, only the military stands between the people and the despised ruling class, which manages all property and income in its own interest. Abroad, the military is used both as a vehicle for Russian aggrandizement and as a means of facilitating future Russian political blackmail.

THE STAGE IS SET FOR JOHN MAYNARD KEYNES

14

The early 1930s saw the Western world plunged into an economic crisis of the first magnitude. Suddenly, a major depression elevated unemployment to the status of a paramount political issue. Unemployment was no longer a mere economic statistic, but a factor that was shaking the democratic system of free enterprise down to its very foundations. By 1932 there were about 15 million unemployed in the United States, and a twenty percent unemployment rate in Europe. By 1933 the desperation of the unemployed swept the Nazis into power in Germany. Years earlier, in 1917, a different kind of economic crisis born of a disintegrating distribution and production system, had resulted in the imposition of a brutal communist dictatorship in Russia.

The same feeling of helplessness that today bedevils Western leaders faced with mounting inflation, gripped Western leaders more than four decades ago when unemployment threatened democracy. To do nothing—and there were many who, fiercely clinging to the laissez-faire approach of Adam Smith, advocated precisely that—was tantamount to inviting governmental take-over by totalitarianism. Whereas nazism was a factor only in Germany, and a relatively new one at that, the Marxist ideology had taken root in all continents.

A carefully orchestrated campaign of disinformation about

the true situation in Russia had been extraordinarily successful in hiding from the West the facts about the hunger, privation, slave labor camps, arbitrary executions, and paranoiac rule of the Communist Party in that country. Millions of people in the West, subjected to an incessant barrage of propaganda, came to believe that a "worker's paradise" of full employment and material abundance was possible. All that was required was the expropriation of all means of production by the proletariat, the fictitious (in any advanced society) amorphous social class. Ruling in the name of the proletariat would be a disciplined Communist Party.

There had been upturns and downturns—"cycles"—in the economies of the West from the time of the Industrial Revolution onward. The difference between the past and the early 1930s was that hardened, dedicated Marxist revolutionaries were now offering the frustrated, unhappy unemployed an alternative system of government and economy.

It could not be denied that totalitarianism, Stalin's Russia and Hitler's Germany, had indeed eliminated unemployment. They had done so through programs of planned government deficit spending. True, totalitarian solutions were effected at a terrible price—the total loss of personal freedoms, the reduction of human beings to cipher-status, aud the iron rule of a new class that set itself up as the final arbiter over the personal, political, and economic life of the nation—but, said the statists, keeping silent on all negative aspects, people *are* working. In the frenetic atmosphere of the times, hardly any attention was paid to the nature of employment under totalitarianism. In Nazi Germany production for war had soaked up the unemployed like a sponge. In Russia, millions were forced to work for no wages at all and others toiled for mere pittances, exhorted on the basis that a shining future awaited them once industrialization was complete. Workers had no right to change jobs or strike for better pay or safer working conditions. However, unaware of these heavy costs of employment, the thinking in the West was that work, any kind of work, for any kind of pay, was preferable to unemployment, with its erosion of personal dignity and the very real danger of physical starvation.

It was a time, in the West, to question the basic tenets of Adam Smith's theory of laissez-faire.

There had been criticism before of the asocial aspects of laissez-faire. England's Lord Lauderdale (1759–1839) had called for a greater emphasis on the accumulation and use of public wealth, rather than a hands-off approach to entrepreneurial capitalism. John Rae (1786–1873) was of the opinion that the state should intervene in the private sector on behalf of the public benefit; the Swiss, Jean Charles de Sismondi (1773–1846) advocated economic programs to promote general prosperity. In Germany, Friedrich List (1786–1846) criticized Smith for his overconcern with exchange value. The intent in an economy, he insisted, should be to expand the rate of production above the level of consumption, not just to equalize production and consumption. He also recommended a protective tariff during the early stages of a country's industrial development to ensure national self-sufficiency and prosperity. Gustav Schmoller (1838–1917) was hostile to the classical method of deducing economic laws, and two of his contemporaries, Karl Knies and Bruno Hildebrand, denied the existence of economic laws altogether.

Further criticism of classical economics was leveled by the Neoclassical School, whose greatest exponent was Alfred Marshall (1842–1924). This group attempted to bridge the discrepancies between classical theory and the reality of the marketplace. Whereas the classic economist approached the economy from the producer's point of view, the neoclassicists approached it from the consumer's standpoint. The result was a concept known as "marginal utility." It must have been in the air, because it was independently arrived at by Marshall in

England; W. S. Jevons (1835–82), another Englishman; Carl Menger (1840–1921), an Austrian; and Leon Walras (1842–1924), a Swiss.

The marginal utilitists noted that the classics had been unable to work out an acceptable theory of distribution and prices, and were unable to solve the puzzle of the relation of value in use and value in exchange. It simply didn't occur to them that the determination of prices is not a theoretical problem at all, that exchange value is a mere mental construct and doesn't exist. It may have existed in a primitive, pre-industrial economy, but has no validity in an advanced economy where creative human thinking, using applied science and sophisticated organizational techniques, have raised the productive process to the point where manual labor has become an inconsequential factor. Under such new conditions, any attempt to quantify or determine the contribution to end results by individual economic components is doomed to failure.

Like the classical and Marxist economists, the neoclassicists saw the consumer as an economic automaton, psychologically motivated in exact and quantifiable ways. An example of this type of thinking is found in the writings of Herman Gossen (1810–1858). He averred that in the process of consumption, every additional unit consumed accorded less satisfaction than the preceding unit; that is, consumption worked according to a law of diminishing returns.

With the Neoclassical School, economics wandered into strange byways. The sole concern was with theory, working with components as one works with mathematical formulae. In this type of discipline, there was no place whatsoever for Marxism, with its sociopolitical generalizations and philosophical *Weltanschauung.* Again, as had been the case with Smith and Marx, the human element—the recognition of the human mind as an economic factor capable of creating qualitative changes that could make obsolete economic "laws" and bring about entirely new socioeconomic conditions—was absent.

Certainly there was no preparation for the kind of situation that erupted in the early 1930s. Then a practical solution to unemployment in the West had to be found quickly if the free enterprise system and the democratic form of government with it were to be saved.

The stage was set for the acceptance of the ideas of Lord John Maynard Keynes (1883–1946), British peer, believer in democracy and free enterprise, and economist par excellence.

Keynes's Differences with Classical Economics

The ideas of economists and political philosophers, when they are right and when they are wrong, are more powerful than it is commonly understood. Indeed, the world is ruled by little else. Practical men, who believe themselves to be quite exempt from any intellectual influences, are usually slaves of some defunct economist. Madmen in authority, who hear voices in the air, are distilling their frenzy from some academic scribbler of a few years back.
—John Maynard Keynes (1936)

The 1930s were underway, there was a depression in the West, and the burning issue was high unemployment. The question Keynes asked himself was: Is it possible for democracy to achieve full employment without destroying the free enterprise system? His answer was, yes, if democracy uses government as a macroeconomic organ to introduce planned deficit spending. Although this was the approach taken by Stalin's Russia and by Hjalmer Schacht, Hitler's Minister of Economy, Keynes was strongly opposed to the politics of totalitarianism. He believed that government deficit spending could be applied within the framework of democracy without imperiling its existence.

In developing his theories, Keynes had one of two ways to go. He could question the basic tenet of classical economics, i.e., laissez-faire, with its postulates of the harmonizing effect of laws; the inherent predilection of demand matching supply; the iron law of wages (wages must always remain at subsistence levels because as wages rise the working force grows to the point of excess, whereupon wages fall and the working force decreases, ad infinitum), the law of diminishing returns (greater investments or an increased labor force does not automatically lead to greater output); and so forth. All these were supposed to result in a general market equilibrium (but didn't). Or he could try to save classical economics by finding some solutions peripheral to the problems that beset classical theory.

Keynes chose the latter route. Years later, in 1946, long after Keynesian economics had been accepted in the West, a last article by Keynes appeared posthumously in the *Economic Journal* stating why he had opted for adjustments in classical theories rather than scrap them in favor of a new economic approach. He wrote:

> *I find myself moved, not for the first time, to remind contemporary economists that the classical teaching embodied some permanent truths of great significance, which we are liable today to overlook because we associate them with other doctrines which we cannot now accept without qualification. There are in these matters deep undercurrents at work, natural forces, one can call them, or even the invisible hand, which are operating towards equilibrium. If it were not so, we could not have got on so well as we have for many decades past.*

What were the "permanent truths" of classical economics that Keynes accepted? Specifically, he had in mind the existence of laws by which the economy operates—the Newtonian mechanistic approach. Such "natural forces" tend toward equilibrium, in that the labor and capital markets are balanced by the interplay of supply and demand. That creates equilibrium, according to the classics, because whatever is produced will be consumed.

As a matter of fact, the classics tacitly accepted that society would be able to consume all it produced; it would have seemed absurd to them to think that production could remain unused or unusable. This was tacit in Say's law, which said that supply creates its own demand, that purchasing power grows out of production. If all productive resources are employed, and there is no unused wealth left to be allocated to production, there can be no place for involuntary unemployment: Everyone is busy working, producing what everyone will consume.

Classical analysis is both logical and consistent if one accepts the theory that all productive factors are continuously employed in the economic process. Jean Baptiste Say, in his principal work, *Traite d'Economie Politique* (1803) phrased it thus: "It is worthwhile to remark, that a product is no sooner created, than it, from that instant, affords a market for other products to the full extent of its own value."

Then why wasn't there full employment? Where did the "natural forces" that are supposed to lead to equilibrium go awry?

Classical analysis, in Keynes's view, had not taken note of certain factors. In his major work, *The General Theory of Employment, Interest and Money,* Keynes argued that "the postulates of the classical theory are applicable to a special case only and not to a general case. Moreover, the characteristics of the special case assumed by the classical theory happen not to be those of the economic society in which we actually live, with the result that its teaching is misleading and disastrous if we attempt to apply it to the facts of experience."

To what did Keynes object in classical economics?

For one, Keynes said that Say's law was wrong for the modern economy, that it is effective demand that creates production and not the other way around. Full employment, he maintained, could only be achieved when effective demand was sufficient to absorb all that had been produced; in short, purchasing power must be kept above production if production is to expand. If demand, translated into purchasing power, is less than the economy's productive output, unemployment must result. Because without sufficient consumer demand business will retrench, with attending layoffs and dismissals.

Another point where Keynes differed from the classics was in his view of the role of government in the economy. At the time of the classics, free competition was supposed to require the elimination of government from any role whatsoever in the economy. Laissez-faire was, after all, formulated in opposition to mercantilism, which identified the wealth of a nation with the wealth of the ruler, and which advocated and justified the interference of the ruler in the economy on the grounds that he was the owner of the means of production. The idea of free enterprise, on the other hand, emphasized the freedom of the producer and consumer. Without limiting this freedom, Keynes did, however, advocate bringing the government back into the economic picture as a macroeconomic organ to do what classical theory had never been able to do—solve the discrepancy between theory (equilibrium) and the reality of the marketplace. Although the use of government in the economy was a break with the past, there was nothing in the original concept of free enterprise as incorporated into the laissez-faire doctrine that contradicts the imperative of a macroeconomic organ.

Aside from the calamities that followed from Keynes's undeniably creative thinking, it is important to note that from the outset his mathematically oriented mind rarely transcended mechanistic thinking. Like Smith, Marx, and the Neoclassical School of economics, Keynes emphasized individual economic components—"employment," "savings," "investments," "effective demand," "multiplier effect," "interest"—isolating them and bringing them into a causal relationship with each other. Like his predecessors and contemporaries, Keynes viewed modern economy as a matter of simple mechanical interrelationships. Actually it is more akin to an interrelationship of organs within a life system.

Keynes: Employment More Important Than Production

Cognizant of the political implications of unemployment, Keynes believed that employment should take priority over production, that is, employment is more important than what is produced and in what quantities. Crucial to the survival of democracy, in his opinion, was how many people were involuntarily out of work, and not what was being produced or how much or how little. Full employment, he said, would increase purchasing power and in turn fuel production.

But what created unemployment in the first place?

One can follow Keynes's reasoning, leading up to the conclusion for which he is best remembered—advocacy of government deficit spending in times of high unemployment. Such spending was intended to create jobs regardless of what was produced, if anything.

To begin with, Keynes believed that the source of unemployment was excessive savings and insufficient consumption and investment.

People have a "propensity to consume," according to Keynes, which only takes part of their income, the rest going into savings. If the "propensity to consume" were one hundred percent, meaning that all income was spent and none saved, we would have full employment because then consumption would equal production. Under those circumstances, the assumptions of the classics, that supply creates its own demand, would be correct. However, people do save, and those savings, if not invested, are what create unemployment. The reasoning is that investment funds withheld from the market deny the productive sector the means to expand, modernize, and hire more labor.

The difference between what is spent and saved, said Keynes, shows up inevitably as unemployment.

What keeps an investor from investing?

Investors have "expectations," pointed out Keynes. In good times, investors are satisfied with the "marginal efficiency of capital," that is, the anticipated rate of return on investment. But if they are sufficiently disturbed by business conditions they won't invest. Maybe they fear a business downturn for whatever reason, or simply aren't satisfied with the rate of return being offered. Or maybe they are too uncertain about future interest rates, a possibility that led Keynes to advocate government control of interest rates and supply of money.

Certainly, applying Keynes's reasoning, once a business downturn did begin, there would be no incentive for an investor to invest in the face of rising unemployment bringing with it decreased consumer demand.

The sum and substance of Keynes's observations was that unemployment could not be solved by leaving it to the forces of supply and demand to harmonize the performance of the economy—Smith's "invisible hand." What was needed was a macroeconomic organ to solve what classical economics had been unable to solve—the problem of creating full employment without sacrificing the basics of the free enterprise system.

That macroeconomic organ, in Keynes's opinion, was government.

Deficit Spending and Other Keynesian Ideas

By now the Keynesian process is well known, even to laymen not aware of its origin. A democratic government, in times of excessive unemployment, deliberately incurs deficits. It spends more than it takes in from taxes, and uses this excess to institute programs and projects designed to create employment, regardless of what is done or produced. Once government deficit spending has done its job by creating demand through increased employment, and a business upturn begins, the government ceases its deficit spending and lets the free enterprise system function without interference. That is, until the next business downturn occurs, when government interference in the economy is repeated in the same way as before.

Of course, the above is gross simplification. But it is, basically, the heart of Keynesian economics—not as practiced by modern governments as we know, to our sorrow—but as orginally conceived by Keynes. His writings comprise some twenty-seven volumes, and one will find in them conflicting statements on any number of economic phenomena as well as terms and concepts which really never had any validity in the real world and were merely mental constructs.

One of Keynes's most cogent critics, economist Henry Hazlitt, asks us to recognize the "slipperiness, vagueness, and changeability of most of Keynes's basic terms and concepts, and his habit of begging the question by unproved mathematical equations and sheer assertion" (*The Failure of the New Economics,* 1959).

What Hazlitt had in mind, and what has disgruntled many an economist during the past decades, are the vague variables set up by Keynes to replace the perfect equilibrium posited by the classics. Some have already been mentioned: "propensity to consume," "marginal efficiency of capital," "effective demand," and "investor expectations."

The "propensity to consume", for example, presupposes an income of which some is spent and some saved. Actually, in today's economy, total income is insufficient to meet basic needs. The majority of people need to spend more and would do so if allowed to keep more of their income. Another Keynesian term that had a run of popularity was the "multiplier." According to it, every dollar of investment would have a multiplier effect on the economy of about three to one, that is, would increase the national income by that amount. The dubious logic is that the dollar spent would "make waves," resulting in more jobs being created and more income generated all around. The dubiety of the concept can be gauged by the following example:

The United States government decides to spend $50 billion over and above its income, that is, to show a $50-billion deficit. At the time the deficit spending gets underway there are some 8 million unemployed out of a working force of 93 million. Keynesian theory has it that the $50 billion deficit will, via the "multiplier" effect, generate some $150 billion in new income. Translated into increased employment, this would effectively wipe out unemployment completely. Well, the United States government has been running budget deficits of that size, and the unemployment statistics haven't budged. In 1976 there was a tremendous increase in consumer spending *plus* a government spending deficit of $60 billion, with no effect on the number of unemployed.

Take any or all of Keynes's concepts and terms, and they all add up to a static system involving causal relationships. It's like a physicist thinking in terms of the conversion of matter to energy. Add or subtract something *here,* and the impact must be felt *there.* Put an extra gallon of gas in the automobile gas tank and the car will go faster! From that kind of thinking it's only a step to conclude that if we want lesser inflation we must have higher unemployment, and that only higher inflation will bring down the rate of unemployment. This well-known concept is the Phillips Curve, one of dozens of theories by mathematically minded economists in recent years that somehow never work the way they are supposed to.

Keynes's theories abound in formulae which are basically meaningless if one regards an advanced, high-technology economy based on applied science as an organic-type entity. And in such an entity there is a constant shifting of interrelationships between economic factors which, in the final analysis, are determined by the way human beings think about them. It may be possible to measure in monetary terms such things as income, investment, and consumption, but to try to put individual hopes, fears, expectations, and general business sentiments into mathematical equations is both ludicrous and impossible. They simply don't lend themselves to being quantified.

All of Keynes's supply-and-demand curves and other mathematical approaches to economics are, in Henry Hazlitt's words, "merely analogies, metaphors, visual aids to thought, which should never be confused with realities." However, formulae become important when, like the a priori concepts of Karl Marx, they are taken seriously and applied to the real world. The formulae and esoteric terminology on which Keynes and his supporters and detractors lavished so much time have been relegated to curiosity topics. But Keynes's basic philosophy of government deficit spending, now expanded to massive government intervention in the economy, is a legacy from which the West must extricate itself if its economies are not to be destroyed.

Keynes's Simplistic Economic Cosmology

When Keynes pondered the problem of unemployment, he saw it as a statistical category and not as an economic factor operating within the framework of an organic society. Once one accepts that approach, it follows that unemployment will be treated as an isolated phenomenon, the same way Keynesians have historically treated money, credit, purchasing power, or any other economic component. It is the way of the value-free natural scientist who observes, measures, and quantifies without having to contend with human thinking, prejudices, and preferences. Keynes, applying such principles, concluded that income, consumption, and level of employment are related to each other in a simple pattern, and even came up with a mathematical formula expressing the relationship.

In Keynes's economic cosmology there was perfect and active competition: Wages could be determined based on labor involved; aggregate real income always increased when employment went up; aggregate consumption increased by a certain proportion when aggregate real income increased; the division between consumer consumption and savings could be mathematically determined; savings and investments were identical to each other; and the workings of the economy were so predictable that prices and wages always changed uniformly as a unit.

Keynes treated "labor" as a lumped total, as Marx had. Anyone aware of the diverse makeup of labor unions in the United States knows the fallacy of this approach. "Labor" does not set "its" wage rates; in an advanced economy, thousands of different wage rates are set every day.

Keynes was the first major economist to develop the idea of "aggregates," a concept unknown to classical theorists who dealt with microeconomic phenomena. He dealt with unemployment, investments, material income, etcetera as aggregates, turning them into macroeconomic organs, and thus replacing Smith's "invisible hand" with recognizable forms playing their part in the economic process.

The brilliance of this approach is undeniable, but equally undeniable are the dangers involved. To place aggregates in a simple causal relationship to each other in an advanced, organic-type society can only lead to formulations which are always in need of adjustment. Individual prices and wages move up and down constantly; investments are subject to a myriad of human emotions; government decisions and even lack of decisions play a vital part in determining consumer, producer, and investor climate; and international considerations are also involved. To postulate a "functional relationship" between "effective demand" and the volume of employment is to say nothing. To speak of a "socialization of investment" is to invite socialism and state planning, which Keynes emphatically didn't want, although he was willing to use socialist tools of government intervention to reform and preserve capitalism.

Hazlitt points out that Keynes wanted both freedom and

controls, "that is, he wanted government currency manipulation, exchange control, import quotas and prohibitions which are the very negation of free trade and a free economy." Such contradictions led Keynes to swing from free trade to hyperprotectionism and back again. In his *Treatise on Money* (1939) he gave definitions of saving and investment which he repudiated in his *General Theory* (1936), then tacitly adopted anyway.

Wanted—Full Employment

Keynes was motivated by the desire to create an economic climate that would ensure "full employment," a phrase whose meaning continues to baffle economists and politicians alike. Obviously, "full employment" cannot be taken literally. In an advanced society people are always on the move, changing jobs. Also, there are those who don't want to or don't have to work, as well as the inefficient no one wants, and the unemployable handicapped. But "full employment" is a catchy phrase with political overtones, especially in a world where totalitarian societies are forever trumpeting to workers, "See, everyone can be put to work! Only in the capitalist society is full employment impossible!"

There was a way to increase employment when the rate of unemployment was unacceptable, opined Keynes, and that was for labor (to Keynes labor always acted like a unified force) to accept lower wages. In Keynes's mathematical world, this would bring down the variable costs of production, causing prices to fall immediately and in full proportion to the fall of costs. On paper, this is logical thinking which can even be set down in a mathematical formula; but in practice Keynes knew that a direct reduction of wages would entail an impossible struggle with the labor unions, and was therefore not to be contemplated. What, then, to do when unemployment was high and it was necessary to raise prices so that wages wouldn't be greater than the productivity of workers seeking employment? Keynes's solution was: Lower the value of money and you automatically lower real wages. By increasing the money supply, reasoned Keynes, more money would be available for investment, leading to a fall in the rate of interest. This would increase the marginal efficiency of capital—the anticipated return of investment.

But, asks the skeptic, wouldn't this be inflationary, with labor unions insisting on higher wages to overtake the decreased value of money, which would be buying less and less? No, said Keynes, who fortunately for him was not alive in the inflationary world of the 1970s. Inflation is possible only when employment doesn't increase even when there is a rising consumer demand, with rising prices as a result. But under what conditions would employment not increase if consumer demand was growing? After all, if consumer demand was growing, more people should be hired to increase production to meet the demand, right? Not always, said Keynes. The trouble was, in his opinion, that people were saving too much, creating a shortage of investment funds and keeping production from growing. This belief, of course, was the base of Keynes's philosophy of how government deficit spending should make up the difference between what he thought investment should be and wasn't.

Commenting on Keynes's currency devaluation recommendation via increasing the money supply, Professor Jacob Viner, in the 1936 issue of the *Quarterly Journal of Economics* had this to say:

> *Keynes's reasoning points obviously to the superiority of inflationary remedies for unemployment over money-wage reductions. In a world organized in accordance with Keynes's specifications there would be a constant race between the printing press and the business agents of the trade unions, with the problem of unemployment largely solved if the printing press could maintain a constant lead and if only volume of employment irrespective of quality, is considered important.*

President Roosevelt Applies Keynes

Keynesian economics is a case where theory followed practice. The first definite and conscious application of Keynes's theories were made by President Franklin Delano Roosevelt in his New Deal, in 1933. To reduce unemployment, Roosevelt brought into being such programs as the Civilian Conservation Corps (CCC), a plan to employ more than two hundred and fifty thousand unemployed youths between eighteen and twenty-five in damming streams, seeding forests, and building dust storm barriers. He also created the National Industrial Recovery Act (NRA), which included a vast program of public works for the unemployed. Another agency, the Federal Emergency Relief Administration, was authorized to spend $500 million in direct aid to state and local relief agencies. The Works Progress Administration (WPA) was set up to provide work for artists.

By 1937, Roosevelt was signaling that he wanted to cut back on government intervention in the economy, but the economy was again beginning to slide, and again Keynesian economics prevailed. The governor of the Federal Reserve at the time, Marriner Eccles, claiming never to have heard of Keynes, urged Roosevelt to have the U.S. government act as a "compensatory agent in this economy; it must unbalance its budget during deflation and create surpluses in periods of great business activity." This statement is pure Keynes.

As a cure for unemployment, Roosevelt's application of Keynesian theories didn't work. During the ten-year period between 1931 and 1940 the average deficit for the U.S. government was $2.8 billion, which was 3.6 percent of the GNP of the period, and the average number of unemployed was 9.9 million, which constituted 18.6 percent of the total work force. Another Keynesian remedy for unemployment was low interest rates, which Keynes admitted could only be produced by increasing the money supply, a deliberately inflationary proposal. But statistics show that between 1929 and 1940 interest rates went down but unemployment increased.

In the seven-year period from 1934 through 1940, when the cheap money policy was pushed to an average infra-low rate below 1 percent (.77 of 1 percent) an average of more than seventeen in every one hundred persons in the labor force were unemployed. It took a second world war to pull the United States out of its economic doldrums. Interestingly, in retrospect, believers in Keynesian economics contend that unemployment was not cured because deficit spending under Roosevelt didn't go far enough, that it should have been greater.

Analyzing Keynesian Terms

In earlier years, as part of the comic section, many newspapers used to run a feature called "What's Wrong With This Picture?" The picture presented would have vital components missing or show erroneous ones or both. For example, someone might be wearing two right-hand gloves, or there might be a bird with only one wing, or a telephone might be missing a receiver.

In a strange way, Keynesian economics, as formulated by its founder, constitutes the same kind of picture amusement as that old newspaper feature. There are flaws, omissions, and contradictions galore.

One can begin anywhere—with Keynes's key terms, for example, like "income," "saving," and "investment." One finds Keynes defining each of these in terms of the other, like saying "white is the color produced by reflection of all the rays of the solar spectrum," and, "when all the rays of the solar spectrum are reflected the result is the color white." He explained an economic crisis as a "sudden collapse of the marginal efficiency of capital," which is like saying that when people are out of work, unemployment results. What Keynes called a "quantity of employment" and put into algebraic equations, turns out, on his own definition, to be not a quantity of employment but a quantity of money received by laborers who are employed.

He doggedly pursued attempts to quantify what cannot be quantified: the human element involved in such phenomena as social income, consumption, investment, and extent of employment. He postulated a precise, mechanical relationship between these phenomena in the manner of the natural sciences, forgetting, as did Smith and Marx before him, that there is such a thing as a creative human mind at work in the economic process.

Keynes's concern with the need of increasing investments leaves out of the picture the question, "Investments for what?" Keynes assumed that national income was nothing more than the sum total of all income, and had no relation whatsoever to what had been produced by this income. He looked at the economy from the standpoint of demand, and assumed that if demand was sufficient we would have full employment. This, as pointed out earlier, treats employment as a statistical political phenomenon and not as an economic one. Instead of being concerned with real productivity, Keynes was concerned with spending as an end in itself to produce employment.

Here is his famous example of this kind of thinking: "If the Treasury were to fill old bottles with banknotes, bury them at suitable depths in disused coal mines which are then filled up to the surface with town rubbish, and leave it to private enterprise on well-tried principles of *laissez faire* to dig up the notes again . . . there would be no more unemployment."

As economist Etienne Mantoux has commented, "A policy of combatting unemployment can always succeed, at least for a time, if one will *at all costs,* put people to work, without regard to the productivity of works undertaken." Or Hazlitt: "Nothing is easier to achieve than full employment, once it is divorced from the goal of full production and taken as an end in itself. Hitler provided full employment with a huge armament program. The war provided full employment for every nation involved. The slave labor in Russia had full employment . . . Coercion can always provide full employment."

What is missing from Keynes's ideas on investment is that there should be an end result to investment that is meaningful to economic growth, that is, investment should result in increased production. If it doesn't, then real income will tend to decrease. There would be income from the point of view of those workers being paid for *not* adding to national production. But from the point of view of the national economy their wages are not real income at all. Money has been paid out and nothing has come to the nation in return to add to its wealth. Keynesian thinking has been applied—employment for its own sake without regard for what, if anything, is being produced. The result is inflation, along with a decline in worker morale and the fostering of work alienation.

Nothing seemed more logical to Keynes than that increased employment would automatically lead to greater income and therefore more production. In modern societies, however, more production can result in decreased employment, and less production is possible with increased employment. The former statement is true wherever applied science and organization are utilized without regard to union "featherbedding." The latter is true in such instances, as for example, in communist societies, where relative full employment does not result in greater production. It still takes seven persons to do a job in the Russian agricultural system that can be done by one person in American agriculture.

People respond to incentives, and when these are absent, productivity is low. Also, and this is true in free enterprise societies as well, the hiring of thousands of bureaucrats to oversee nonproductive programs or simply to add to an already swollen bureaucracy, increases employment and thus consumer demand. Yet, it adds nothing to meaningful production and therefore does not contribute to the wealth of the nation.

Also missing from the Keynesian picture of the modern

economy is that in an advanced society unemployment is possible, even with demand. Consider a factory producing goods for which there is no effective demand although purchasing power exists. Or consider the effect of halting a government-funded military program. Thousands may be rendered unemployed, yet the incident would have nothing to do with demand or the lack of it. Or suppose there is an effective demand for a certain food product. The result might well be a price increase without an increase in the actual supply of the item. Business enterprises will often forego investment in favor of raising prices because of increased demand. Note that there is no increase in production at all, only higher prices. Recently, the price of automobiles went up even though there were thousands of unsold cars. Another possibility is increased income and demand oriented toward a sector of the economy not suffering from unemployment, hence there would be no effect on the rate of unemployment. There is, for example, a high incidence of unemployment among young blacks and the unskilled. Keynes's famous "multiplier" effect wouldn't even reach into this sector of the economy.

A Misguided Emphasis on Savings

Keynes attached considerable importance to savings. A few comments are in order.

The sum total of all deposits in all American financial institutions in 1975 came to over $746 billion. Of this sum, actual money, i.e., currency, was only $82 billion; the rest were credits created by the financial institutions. Unfortunately, money and credits have been lumped together. We now have terminology like M1, M2, M3, etcetera that doesn't distinguish between money and credit. Actually, the role of money, that is, currency, in the economy keeps diminishing year by year.

Borrowers pay interest for *credit,* not *money.* Money plays a role insofar as it becomes "reserve" when deposited into banks, and the relation between these deposits and credit issued is fixed by government.

To tie the issuance of credits in any way to the amount of deposits is not only archaic but even dangerous in an age when credits determine the strength of the economy. Credits are given in anticipation of their successful use: They are earmarked for specific purposes that are supposed to engender greater value than that of the credit given. If this objective is accomplished, the lender receives a return on his investment, the borrower makes a profit, and wealth is added to the nation. The particular credit transaction then disappears from the entry ledgers of both borrower and lender without a real dollar ever having entered the picture.

Actual money—currency—belongs in a different category. It has a physical existence and may be circulated. It may also be loaned and used as repayment, but on an infinitesimal scale as compared to the role of credit. Yet money and credit have been merged in economics under the heading "money supply," or, M1—currency plus deposits. Of what importance is money supply when the scope of credits is $3.5 trillion compared to the $96 billion of legal tender money extant? Legal tender money can actually be done without in our modern economy, but not credit.

Later, the full implication of a credit-based economy will be explored. At the moment it is enough to point out that credit has become the typical means of payment in an advanced society, while actual money has been pushed far into the background. We operate in a credit economy involving billions of book entries. They may be likened to a kind of vibration, changing in intensity from moment to moment as credits given and credits repaid increase or decrease. It is a sort of credit force-field with billions of debits changing to credits and back again to debits all the time.

In this context, the actual money supply is no longer an important indicator of anything. Statistically expressed deposits show only the "frame" of the debit-credit "film" process. Savings, as well as the rate of interest, two factors supposedly responsible for either equilibrium or unemployment in Keynesian economics, are strictly incidental phenomena in a mature economy. The important factor is to maintain the vibrational intensity of the credit-debit phenomenon, so to speak. Any unnecessary interference on the part of government with this wealth-producing process that slows it down or impedes its operation is contrary to the best interests of the nation. It prevents the creation of wealth, which is the yardstick for any modern economy.

Why Involuntary Unemployment?

Keynes averred that unemployment was the result of too much savings and insufficient consumption and investment. When one retraces economic history two centuries, that is, to the early years of the Industrial Revolution, a phenomenon is observed from which one can develop a more plausible theory about unemployment.

That phenomenon is the business cycle, something never explained by either the classics or Keynes. One can disregard Marx completely in this instance because he simply lumped such phenomena under the catchall heading of "capitalism" without bothering to explain it.

A business cycle comprises a downturn and upturn, each following the other at intervals. When the economy turns down, it is because production has outraced consumer purchasing power, and producers cut back and discharge or lay off workers. Eventually, depleted inventories necessitate resumed production, and the producer, satisfied that consumer purchasing power has been built up, makes the necessary investments and begins hiring more labor. The economic upturn begins.

Unemployment is the result of a process, not the cause.

The cause lies in an unrecognized fact: that at no time

during the past two hundred years has a macroeconomic organ existed to ensure a rough equilibrium between consumer purchasing power and rate of production. This is to say, there were never any means whereby the population was able to absorb the full amount of production, which was increasing geometrically thanks to a greater use of applied science and organization in the productive process. With wages low, consumer credit unknown, and transactions on a cash basis, the money economy was unprepared for the avalanche of goods that poured into it during the first decades of the twentieth century. When people could not purchase this ocean of goods, there was a sharp cutback in production with an attending rise in unemployment.

The crash of 1929 was the culmination of this process of production that could not be absorbed by existing wage rates.

By this time, too, a further serious problem had become a part of the economic scene: New workers were continuously entering the labor market, but productive efficiency, thanks to applied science, couldn't hire all the available people. Even when a business upturn began, there were always more unemployed, percentage-wise, than there had been before.

A saving feature for people, in the past, was that downturns brought price decreases. The reason was that there was a relatively free market in labor, and government taxes were at a minimum. With any sharp rise in unemployment, consumption fell drastically and prices came down. They were not held in place as they are today by high taxes, which take fifty cents of every dollar, and unyielding wages, which incorporate minimum hourly rates. Also, labor unions insist on increases to meet inflation, with no consideration for higher productivity. Keynes's belief that increased demand will increase production and thereby increase employment is seen to be very simplistic. There is a great demand for goods, but the lack of consumer purchasing power because of high taxes at all government levels, plus a continuous rise in prices, makes this demand go unfulfilled. Production thus does not increase. Another reason for this is that the private sector finds it increasingly difficult to borrow capital on advantageous terms because of restricting government monetary policies and the need for vast expenditures to meet government regulatory agency requirements.

The Good and Bad
of Keynesian Concepts

Despite its flaws, shortcomings, and contradictions—and they are many—there is no denying that the essential philosophy expounded in Keynes's major work, *The General Theory of Employment, Interest and Money,* which appeared in 1936, came at a time when the West was desperately groping for solutions to high unemployment.

As Garet Garrett, a contributor to Henry Hazlitt's book, *The Critics of Keynesian Economics,* has written:

"The moment of the book was most fortunate. For the planned society they were talking about the Socialists were desperately in need of a scientific formula. Government at the same time was in need of a rationalization for deficit spending. The idea of welfare government that had been rising both here and in Great Britain—here under the sign of the New Deal— was in trouble. It had no answer for those who kept asking, 'Where will the money come from?' It was true that government had got control of money as a social instrument and that the restraining tyranny of gold had been overthrown, but the fetish of solvency survived and threatened to frustrate great social intentions . . . the appearance of the Keynes theory was like an answer to prayer. Its feat was twofold. To the Socialist planners it offered a set of algebraic tools which, if used according to the manual of instructions, were guaranteed to produce full employment, economic equilibrium, and a redistribution of wealth with justice . . . And the same theory by virtue of its logical implications delivered welfare government from the threat of insolvency ... The balanced budget was a capitalist bogey. Deficit spending was not what it seemed. It was in fact *investment* and the use of it was to fill an investment void—a void created by the chronic and incorrigible propensity of people to save too much."

Keynes set the stage for today's massive interference of government in the economy. In his concern for democracy and the free enterprise system, he knew that high, sustained unemployment could destroy the system and bring on a total-itarian form of government, as already existed in Russia and Germany.

His prescription for full employment came down to gov-ernment deficit spending, low interest rates, and an increased money supply, all during times of business downturns.

Classical economists regarded employment as an economic category. Keynes elevated it to an end in itself, gave it highest priority, and a distinctly political coloring.

In his preoccupation with the problem of unemployment, Keynes didn't concern himself with such vital matters as the quality of life, economic security, the economic rights of individuals, or the standard of living. These are all major components of a modern economy which create important interrelationships which affect wages, costs, prices, and em-ployment. But Keynes concentrated exclusively on three com-ponents—employment, interest, and money.

He set in motion a process that never solved unemployment, but did add the phenomenon of inflation to the economy. Through government intervention new jobs and programs were created which had little or no relationship to real productivity.

In the interval, government has become the biggest spender and investor in the economy, as well as the biggest employer in the socioeconomic system. All economic considerations are subordinated to government spending, and a chain reaction has resulted: Spending reinforces government activities, taxes are raised to pay for the spending, which increases government activities.

Although there should be a permanent role for government in the economy—a subject which will be explored later—Keynes's view of government was that of an external factor artificially used for a limited time. He never saw government as an integral part of an organiclike economy, but as a temporary means to forcibly inject money into a sick economic body to prevent political collapse. Government was a doctor, ready to rush to the aid of a patient with a quick fix, and then withdraw until needed again.

Had Keynes lived, he would have seen a Western world confronted with a host of problems of which unemployment would be but one, and not the most important one at that. Today, there is inflation (which Keynes himself unwittingly introduced), tax inequities, urban problems, social welfare, education, energy, public health, ecology, housing, crime, etcetera. Each of these problems requires a macroeconomic organ to solve it, but they all have been deposited on the doorstep of government.

There is no denying that government is required to help with solutions, but the task at hand is to narrow the scope of government activity while expanding its responsibilities.

Thanks to Keynes, there is no longer any incentive for thrift. The knowledge that the dollar is becoming progressively less valuable has a shattering psychological effect on people. With the relentless rise of prices, and with workers being pushed into higher tax brackets whenever their income is increased, the concept of thrift loses all meaning. What is the sense of saving if an item costing one dollar today will cost fifteen or twenty cents more next year? The peoples of Britain and Sweden, well along the road of Keynesian economics, eschew thrift and simply let the government act as Big Brother to meet their needs for social security and welfare.

From advocacy of indiscriminate spending with its inflationary results, it is only a step to the advocacy of government planning. Indeed, some Keynesian economists, taking a leaf out of the Marxist manual, recommend precisely that. They preface their counsel with the qualification that they want nothing so far-reaching as what exists in communist societies, but that's like agreeing to become a little bit pregnant.

Keynes never transcended the classics: He simply treated symptoms instead of the cause.

Keynes bravely defended his views, which met with considerable opposition when first broached. He plaintively wrote, "The difficulty lies not with new ideas, but in escaping from the old ones, which ramify for those brought up as most of us have been, into every corner of our minds." Yet what Keynes proposed were mere modest reforms. Today, some four decades after his *General Theory of Employment,* in a vastly changed and much more sophisticated economy than the one that confronted him, we face the same difficulty in escaping from old ideas. Except now we must escape from Keynesian concepts, as disastrous for us as classical economics was for the 1930s.

PART THREE

Economic Sanity

Including
the ROMAN-LOEBL
Approach to Economics

Economic Sanity Needs a New Way of Thinking

15

> A political economy is not an ordered plan of wise men with computers. In reality, it is a complex amalgam of the attitudes and motivations of individuals, their willingness to work, their self-confidence, their belief in the future, their willingness to save and invest, their ability to cooperate with each other in joint enterprises, their creative impulses that produce technological and managerial innovation. The presence or absence of these qualities in political leadership, and thus the extent to which they are encouraged among the people, is the true essence of economic policymaking.
> —George and Joan Melloan, The Carter Economy

Viewed through a powerful telescope, a distant galaxy appears as a shimmering light. Its form is vague and detail is lost. One knows there are billions of suns, stars, and planets in that tiny corner of space, but even from within the galaxy all celestial bodies will be no more than tiny points of light separated by huge distances of darkness.

Today's American economy, the most complex, wealthiest, and most dynamic the world has ever known, resembles a galaxy in many respects. One can mentally envision it: a dynamo of humans and machines, of research and education, of billions of transactions, legal work, and government involvement on the local, state, and federal levels. But to live and work within the economy itself is to be exposed to details that never reflect the overall form. One simply notices things as they happen or as they are reported in the media. Like sun flares, there may be sudden crises—a major labor strike, a sudden spurt in food or fuel prices, an abrupt increase in taxes on salaries and wages—and the best an average individual can do is mentally piece together the general "tone" of the economy from all available signs.

Americans are only dimly aware of what is going on in the country economically. Individual attention is highly circumscribed. A worker thinks in terms of net pay after taxes, and what that money will buy; labor unions think in terms of membership benefits; businessmen are oriented toward costs and profits; bureaucrats concentrate on developing a power base; lawyers focus their attention on particular cases; presidential aides think in terms of ploys that will enhance the image of the chief executive; and legislators think in terms of pleasing their particular constituents first and the rest of the nation second.

All this is mechanical, discrete thinking.

The road to economic sanity begins with a new way of thinking about the economy. It is equivalent to reorienting one's thinking to the understanding that the world is round, not flat.

It is learning to think organically.

Consider:

If the banking system is not operating properly, the lines providing credit to business enterprises will break down. Business retrenchment and unemployment will result. If the education system is turning out functional illiterates, our young people who must one day run the country will lack proper qualifications. We will lack in research, innovation, and general brain work, our economy will suffer and our international position deteriorate. If labor unions get high wage increases without contributing to a rise in productivity, the result will be higher prices and workers thrown into higher tax brackets. If a business enterprise raises prices simply to show a higher profit to stockholders, again prices will rise. Labor will demand a greater share, and the government will automatically come in for its share. If the federal government saddles the private sector with huge costs for complying with regulatory demands, those costs will be passed along to consumers, which, like other factors mentioned above, will increase the rate of inflation. If the government vies with the private sector for credit capital, recklessly running up staggering deficits year after year, and these sums are used for nonproductive purposes, business enterprises will be starved for capital. There will be fewer jobs, less emphasis on research and development, and a tendency for companies to use whatever capital is available for short-term gains.

Inevitably, in all the above, the economy as a whole must suffer.

Not thinking organically, many Americans fail to realize that a breakdown of or undue emphasis on any single component of the economy at the expense of others may well have disastrous economic consequences.

In a totalitarian society, where directives are handed down from above and disobedience is punishable by prosecution or worse, the organic factors present in a free enterprise society are missing, and hence the dynamism. Where there is no personal incentive, and where the individual is regarded "merely as a means of production," to use the words of Pope John Paul II berating the Polish communist leadership, then there is low productivity, shoddy workmanship, inefficiency, and waste. The end result is massive apathy and indifference on the part of the people. Under totalitarianism, only the privileged classes of the military and the bureaucracy thrive because they have the power to appropriate for themselves the fruits of the economy.

The nature of totalitarianism tells us that the worst thing possible for the American economy is to impose arbitrary rules and regulations on it from a centralized bureaucracy. To place the economic destiny of the United States in the hands of those either indifferent or hostile to free enterprise dynamics is to court disaster. At best we would wind up with a dismal welfare state like Britain. At worst, we could one day find ourselves groaning under some form of totalitarian-type dictatorship.

Concomitant with an organic way of thinking about the economy is the need to remember that the economy was made for man, and not the other way around. We must subscribe with all our hearts and souls to the Judeo-Christian concept that the individual is infinitely more important than the state. The whole trend in modern history has been to denigrate the individual in favor of the state. The process is complete under Marxist totalitarianism, but the statists in the Free World have been relentlessly pressing in that direction. Their cry is for a "planned economy," showing an abysmal lack of faith in the ability of free human beings to solve their own problems given the opportunity to do so.

Let's consider a planned economy and why it doesn't work.

A Planned Economy Doesn't Work

People are inclined to think in terms of extremes. The moment the free enterprise system manifests shortcomings, voices calling for a planned economy, always there, become shriller and more insistent. By "planned economy" they mean total government control of the economy, the "totalitarian temptation," as French political writer Jean-François Revel aptly calls it. The siren song is that a planned economy is much neater than the fluid, competitive free enterprise system. Surely, say the planning advocates, central economic planning is infinitely preferable to the messy way of meeting supply and demand via millions of personal decisions. Forgotten or conveniently not mentioned are the end results of planned economies—the dismal productivity, the atrophy of initiative, the elimination of incentive, the apathy that turns into resignation as, more and more, government takes it upon itself to make every economic decision.

It is a remarkable phenomenon that even after more than sixty years of economic failure, the planned economy of Russia has not dampened the enthusiasm of those who believe that government knows best. Russia is unable to feed its people and must import expertise and technology from the West to keep its economy running, and still the advocates of "planned" economies refuse to draw the proper conclusions. Worse, they celebrate the victory of statism over free enterprise wherever it occurs, as though what has patently shown itself unworkable elsewhere will suddenly acquire a magical formula for success.

Those who call for a planned economy erroneously believe that an entire society can be run in the same way management runs a business enterprise. The guiding philosophy is completely different.

A business enterprise is primarily motivated to show a profit. To that end it plans its production in the light of projected demand, striving for efficiency and carefully watching costs. To help increase its share of the market, the company does market research, marketing, advertising, and promotion. It makes purchases of whatever it needs to function by soliciting competitive prices on the open market. It tries to anticipate consumer preferences for color, style, and whatever other elements help determine buying habits. The success or failure of the company plan is a matter of concern only to the management, employees, and stockholders, if any, of the particular enterprise.

In a planned economy, the planning body, i.e., the governing bureaucracy, controls the *entire* economy. It determines what to produce and in what quantity, allocates material, sets prices, and stipulates labor costs. It does this for all enterprises as if they were one single enterprise. The sole task of factory management is to fulfill the target figures set by the planning board. It is of no concern to management if more or fewer goods are produced than needed or if an enterprise shows profits or losses. Management fulfills its function once target quotas are met. Also, in a planned economy, the quantity produced is the criterion; quality is unimportant. Nor are consumer preferences considered; hence advertising and promotion are not required.

The inevitable consequence of such an approach is an extraordinary waste of material, labor, energy, and machinery as managers strive to do nothing more than "meet the plan."

It still would be an impossible situation if the bureaucrats trying to make all economic decisions for an entire economy were hardheaded, experienced businessmen. But they're not. Under communism they are party hacks. In a democracy that opts for a planned economy, the bureaucrats are mainly lawyers, academicians, and political appointees. The results are policies and programs based on the arbitrary bureaucratic conviction that government knows what is best for the people. It has happened in Britain and Sweden, and has been happening with a vengeance in the United States.

What Kind of Government Role in the Economy?

What kind of government do the American people want?

It seems strange to pose that question two hundred years after the answer was given via a revolt against British domination that produced a new nation. A government of the people, for the people, and by the people, in Lincoln's words, still sounds good. Politically speaking, we are still a democracy, one of the few left in a world where one country after another has slipped behind the curtain of totalitarianism. We have genuine elections, though not enough of us vote, and public opinion still manages to make itself heard when the issue becomes important enough. We don't live in fear of midnight knocks, with loved ones being

spirited off to concentration camps or psychiatric wards, there
to be reduced to human vegetables because of dissident political
views. We are free to practice our respective religions, to freely
assemble for discussion purposes, to move about the country
without internal passports or the mandatory requirement of
reporting our whereabouts to the local police. We can buy
books, newspapers, and magazines of conflicting viewpoints,
including those that espouse communist totalitarianism. We
criticize our elected officials without fear of arrest, and there
is still nothing to stop an enterprising individual from becoming
wealthy through his own efforts. All this is in the realm of
political democracy.

Our measure of economic democracy is something else
again.

The United States is a mixture. We certainly aren't the kind
of capitalist society Marx inveighed against, wherein high profits
for a wealthy few who owned all means of production were
achieved through the payment of subsistence wages to the
working force. We have small- and medium-sized companies
personally owned, and giant conglomerates owned in the main
by thousands of individual stockholders as well as by pension
trusts, themselves owned by thousands of stockholders. To
Marxists, who owns the means of production is all-important.
To a democracy like the United States, the important factor is
the wealth produced by the means of production and the
manner in which it radiates outward to benefit the maximum
number of people. We have referred to this kind of productive
wealth elsewhere as gain. Without such gain, which is the fruit
of applied science operating in conjunction with technology,
the United States would never have been able to achieve the
preeminent power it enjoys, and which is the envy of the entire
world.

That gain is now in danger of deterioration because we have
allowed a true Frankenstein monster to grow up in our midst—
a federal government that is busy spinning webs of rules,

regulations, and taxes that are gradually stifling initiative, destroying incentive, and pauperizing the middle classes who have historically been the backbone of the nation. The government must be made responsive to the wishes of the people. It must be their servant, not their master. This is the way our Founding Fathers intended it to be, and the way it should be.

Americans enjoy political but not economic democracy. The role of the federal government in the economy—its taxing and spending powers, its power to harass and intervene wherever and however it wishes—is one of exercising arbitrary prerogatives. The American people, though conscious of this legislative and bureaucratic arrogance, have ·no voice in such matters. Something happens to elected representatives when they come to Washington: They begin listening more to the persuasive voices of special interests than to what the American people as a whole are trying to tell them. In no time at all they are playing the same old game, taxing and spending and favoring certain groups over others.

The American people must be given their rightful authority to decide on the role they want the federal government to play in the nation's economy. And this role should be voted on after a period of open debate.

This means that the federal budget, and the substantial off-budget spending, must become election issues. Economic goals and programs—the orientation of the economy—must be determined democratically by ballot, not left to the alliance of legislators and special interests, nor to economists engaged in sterile theorizing.

Competing political parties should be required to submit to the people, as election issues, all major federal programs they favor, and their costs. The difference between party programs and costs would give the people a meaningful choice. The people should also be apprised of the cost of programs operated by the federal bureaucracy versus similar-type programs operated by the private sector.

Even while such debates are in progress, there is a way to reduce inflation and guarantee stable purchasing power. That way is to stabilize prices by stabilizing government expenditures and reducing them. The time is long overdue for reducing the scope of the federal budget. This is a major reason why there has been such a strong movement for a constitutional amendment, the case for which was succinctly put by Robert H. Bork, member of the National Tax Limitation Committee (*Wall Street Journal,* April 4, 1979): ". . . we must somehow stop the seemingly inexorable rise in the share of society's wealth claimed by the federal government, and so far nothing short of a constitutional limit has worked."

Curbing Federal Regulatory Agencies

The power of federal regulatory agencies must be curbed, and in some instances agencies must be phased out completely.

It is not so much a matter of the allocated budgets of regulatory agencies that should be a source of concern, although these budgets run into the billions of dollars themselves, but the costs incurred by business enterprises trying to meet regulatory demands. These costs run well over $100 billion annually.

In some instances, regulatory agencies are no longer needed once the public has been sufficiently sensitized to the problems the agency was created to solve. Examples are the Equal Employment Opportunity Commission (EEOC)—are there really so many insensitive companies discriminating on the basis of sex or color of skin as to warrant the continuation of the EEOC? —and the Occupational Safety and Health Administration (OSHA), which has authority over the health and safety of workers in virtually all private work places. It rode off in all directions at once since its formation in 1970 because it was never offered guidelines for selecting what it should inspect.

The Environmental Protection Agency (EPA), the most

costly regulatory agency to the private sector and therefore one greatly responsible for fueling inflation, should be severely restricted in its operations. It should handle only the most flagrant violations. It is, for example, destructive to economic expansion and the creation of new jobs when the steel industry is forced to spend $458 million (1978) out of a total of $3 billion for capital expenditures, for pollution control.

Agencies like the Federal Trade Commission (FTC) and the Securities and Exchange Commission (SEC) should be restricted to the duties for which they were originally intended, and nothing more. Congress' original purpose in creating the FTC was to administer the antitrust laws in a manner more subject to congressional control than the federal courts had seen fit to do when they interpreted the Sherman Act of 1890. To see how far the FTC has wandered, one has but to note that in 1978 the FTC published a report recommending a federal ban on TV advertising directed at children under eight. For such activities the FTC receives a budget of $64.7 million and employs 1,665 people, including 600 attorneys.

The SEC was brought into being following the crash of 1929. It was intended to protect investors from deceit and manipulation of stock prices, a worthy cause. By 1979 the agency had run amok. It was trying to regulate the structure of corporate boards, management compensation, questionable payments by U.S. corporations, and was examining accounting rules—all functions outside the sphere of the agency as defined at its inception.

In a category all by itself is the Department of Energy, which contributes nothing to the industry it was set up to control, and costs companies untold millions of dollars a year in paper work answering the agency's requests for information. Total deregulation of the energy industry is long overdue, and with it the phasing out of the Department of Energy. Nor is there any excuse for the creation of a Department of Education with an initial budget of over $14 billion.

A New
Concept: "Gain"

16

In the tapestry of history, stretching backward into unknown beginnings, who is to say what is truth and what is myth? One doesn't speak so much of events but of the ideas promulgated over the centuries and millennia, ideas by which men still live. Is it truth or myth that an "invisible hand" governs the rules of the marketplace and creates a rough equilibrium between all parties involved in the productive process? Adam Smith, philosopher and intellect, averred that it was truth. Is it truth or myth that there are historical laws at work which, operating through violence, give birth to successive socioeconomic systems? Karl Marx averred that it was truth. Is it truth or myth that government bureaucracy is a wiser and more capable force than the nation's citizenry to bring fiscal prosperity and social order into life? The statist, politician, and conventional economist aver that it is truth.

There is a myth still extant that should have been laid to rest long ago: that labor is the source of a nation's wealth. It is still accepted as gospel by Marxists. And labor leaders in capitalist-oriented nations still harbor that notion, though not with the same conviction and intensity that it is believed by the unsophisticated in Third World countries who cling to the myth of Marx's proletariat.

Consider:

Recently a television program looked into a Marxist-oriented black African country. In one of the factories taken over by the government from the white owners who had fled, workers were shown in earnest discussion. They were the "proletariat," encouraged by the new ruling class to believe that they could build a paradise for themselves now that their "exploiters" were gone. Factory production was at a standstill while everyone debated momentous questions: how much time to devote every day to the study of Marxist theory; how much deference one must show to supervising personnel; and how one could show solidarity with the "proletariat" in other countries. These were serious people, obviously brainwashed into believing that through their efforts and labor, their poor, backward society would soon flourish like a green bay tree.

The notion that labor is the source of wealth in a primitive, pre-industrial society only would have been met with indignation. The assertion that manual labor is the least important component in an advanced, technologically oriented society that's based on applied science and organizational techniques would have been vehemently denied. They understood only that for years they had worked in factories owned and operated by hated "capitalists," who paid them wages but appropriated the "profits" for themselves. No one but themselves, they were convinced, was responsible for turning out goods, i.e., creating wealth. Once they expropriated the means of production and banished the "capitalists," all "profits" would then accrue to themselves, the "people," the "laboring masses."

Simple economics for simple people.

What is the source of a nation's wealth?

It has been a long time since that question was last posed, about a century to be exact. Marx posed it and answered it in the same way Adam Smith did, with the one word "labor."

It is time to ask the question again. Two hundred years have passed since the Industrial Revolution. Empirical thinking has long since given way to applied science as the economic base of an advanced society. Under the old system, manual labor was indeed the source of wealth in an exchange-type economy. Commodities produced by labor were exchanged for other commodities also produced by labor. The process was simplicity itself: The more people worked, the more was produced.

It doesn't work that way and hasn't worked that way for a long time now.

There is nothing empirical about nuclear or computer technology, or automation. They are the reasons, and not increased labor, for the massive increases in production decade after decade. The ability to transform natural resources into productive use has become awesomely efficient thanks to the applications of higher levels of thinking where applied science creates "energy slaves," that is, where nature contributes its share of the productive process free of charge.

Involved in this process is a much greater output than there is input. The difference between the two is social "gain," a phenomenon that has remained hidden because it cannot be quantified and is therefore of no interest to conventional economists who deal in numbers and equations in the style of the natural scientists.

It is gain that is the true source of a nation's wealth.

Until the Industrial Revolution, gain was produced when a worker was able to produce more than he needed for his own maintenance. As man's intellectual abilities developed, the transformation process from natural resources to productive use became more effective. The development of primitive labor using primitive tools to the level reached by the time of Adam Smith was the result of learning from experience, that is, of empirical thinking. The Industrial Revolution with its integration of inventions, innovations, applied science, labor, and organization reflected a much higher level of thinking.

Output increased greatly over input. The result was gain.

The transformation process, by making use of natural forces, increases the difference between input and output, i.e., the gain is a function of the level of thinking applied to the productive process. The real source of gain is the result of this transformation process, and not because of the Marxist belief that labor power is a "source of not only value, but of more value than it has itself."

The word "gain" is not used as a synonym for profit, but as a difference between output and input with regard to the use of natural resources. Profit is an output-input relationship expressed in terms of cost.

By making use of natural wealth and forces, we literally make nature a partner in man's efforts to become independent of it. A windmill or water mill can be explained as the transformation of natural forces into "energy slaves." Other such examples are the steam engine, the hydro turbine, the steam turbine, the atomic reactor, and solar energy aggregates. The gain or benefit we receive through such transformation is the difference between our input and nature's output.

The more gain we achieve in the transformation process, the more wealth we create. The scope of the gain depends primarily on the natural environment. If there is no wind or river, there can be no windmill or water mill. If the land is impossibly rocky, there can be no agriculture. Given a certain natural environment, however, gain then depends on the intellectual level of thinking applied by man to the productive process.

Without nature's contribution, there would be no gain in the form of surplus product, and therefore no economic development. The higher the intellectual level upon which the productive process takes place, the greater the gain.

Profit can be quantified, gain cannot. It's not too difficult to determine profit and ascribe it to the productive process. Gain is something else again. In the pre-industrial economy it had no particular meaning at all. Most of the working population was on the farm, and most wealth was based on the contributions of these farm workers on a sort of forced-labor basis; that is, there was a simple exchange of labor for subsistence. The great majority of producers, farmers, and handicraftsmen, the three mainstays of primitive economy, didn't work for profit, but for exchange. This type of economy is inappropriate subject matter for economic theories in that no systematically organized body of knowledge can be derived from it that would serve as a base for economic theories. Only philosophers and theologians dealt with economic matters at all, and then from their own non-scientific point of view.

In the modern economy of an advanced society, the concept of gain is of decisive importance in understanding the economy.

Understandably, neither Quesnay, Smith, nor Marx, three giants of economic thinking, thought in terms of gain. They all posited the right questions: "What is the source of wealth?" and "How can it be optimized?" But their answers were fallacious because of two important factors: They were unable to think in any terms other than Newtonian mechanistic physics, and they were unable to conceive of a highly integrated, technologically oriented, organic economy in which applied science replaces manual labor as the primary means of creating wealth. None of those three economists, and no conventional economist to this day, have thought of gain as the single most important factor in economic development. All have thought of economics as the allocation of scarce resources. Conventional economics at the time of the horse and buggy would have given us graphs, "laws," and voluminous reports on what the government should do to conserve scarce resources, such as horses, wood, oats, etcetera. One could not expect an economist to concern himself with something not yet invented—the automobile, a product of creative minds. Yet the gain of the automobile age is undeniable, as is the gain of the oil age versus the coal age, and as is the gain of computers over the simple adding machine or earlier abacus.

The changes in the development of the properties of gain correspond to changes in the level of thinking applied to the transformation process in production. The scope of gain in pre-Industrial Revolution times was dependent on empirical thinking, that is, on experience gained in the working process. Gain was more or less restricted to individuals depending on what benefits they managed to accrue to themselves as a result of their own labors. A second stage of gain was ushered in with the Industrial Revolution, when the contributions of organizers, inventors, and entrepreneurs expanded the scope of gain greatly. Much more could be produced with far less manual labor, and the entire nation began to benefit progressively from the gain radiating through the economy. This kind of gain is still increasing in advanced societies although, as we shall see, certain dangers have arisen which threaten its unhindered continuation.

Who owns "gain"? Who appropriates it?

During the Industrial Revolution, gain materialized in the profit gleaned by the owner of the means of production. It wasn't dispersed throughout society. As a result, growing wealth was accompanied by great impoverishment. Marx and his followers studied that society and came to the conclusion that the owners of the means of production became wealthy through the exploitation of the workers. Actually, their source of wealth was the transformation of natural forces as a result of the application of a higher level of thinking. Of course, the objection that gain should have been shared and not simply appropriated by the owners of the means of production is a valid one; but it is not valid to say that workers produced more and that the surplus was the result of their work. The surplus—gain—was really the result of a higher level of thinking on which the new productive process took place. It was the result of the organizer, innovator, inventor, and the integration of applied science into the economic process.

If we compare the gain in production based on mere empirical thinking and manual labor with the gain just described, we would see only a basically quantitative difference. The same products were produced, the same labor employed, but more was produced by applying less strain and more skill.

The real source of gain, therefore, during the Industrial Revolution, was the transformation process, and not the labor power which Marx believed was a "source not only of value, but of more value than it has itself." Marx's belief has validity only in an economy where manual labor is the primary productive force, and value can still be discerned and quantified in terms of work done versus reward received.

Is it possible that in an age of scientific and technological progress, gain can still be appropriated by the owners of the means of production? Perhaps the best way to answer this question is to compare gain during the age of manual labor and empirical thinking with gain in the age of scientific thinking.

A farmer constructed a water mill to use the power of the flow of water to grind his grain. By so doing he transformed a natural force into a productive one and put an "energy slave" to work for him.

The gain, i.e., benefit, of the water mill belonged to its owner, the farmer. He could give away his ownership or share it, or give away his gain or share it. He could permit his neighbors to use the water mill free of charge, or he could charge for the benefit. In the latter case, he sold or exchanged the gain, and so turned it into profit.

Now transform the power of the flow of water into "energy slaves," not by empirical thinking, but by the use of applied science. Take a water turbine and, with its help, run a generator. The owners of the water turbine and generator could not, of course, manufacture these machines in the same way the farmer produced a water mill. Scientists, designers, and researchers are needed. Various industries like mining, machine tool, chemical, electronics, and so on have to be developed; also banking and a viable transportation system. Indirectly, the educational system, administration, legislatures, etcetera will also be involved.

The water turbine and generator are thus national products in the sense that all parts of the nation must integrate their efforts to build such transformers of natural resources and turn them to productive use.

Not only are the water turbine and generator the products, in a real sense, of the entire nation, but they cannot be run like the farmer operated his water mill. There must be a team of collaborators with special skills and knowledge; electricity has to be distributed, and a complex administrative apparatus must be put to work. Without such components, the transformation process would cease to function.

The effect of the transformation process depends upon the intellectual level on which the construction of the transformation aggregate has been based. The result of everyone's efforts will be that millions of "energy slaves" will be put to work on behalf of the nation. The water mill was an "energy slave," but it benefited only the farmer and those with whom he shared the energy, or to whom it was sold. The electrical energy produced by modern "energy slaves" such as the water turbine and generator is, on the other hand, of benefit to everyone in heating, lighting, production, transportation, and television—in short, for all industry and households.

Millions benefit from this kind of gain, in a thousand different ways. Such gain is hardly expressible in monetary units. To be without electricity, for example, is to become sharply aware that the gain from the use of electricity is by far greater than the profit derived from the use of the water turbine or its asset value.

In the United States, billions of horsepowers and kilowatts are at the disposal of the American people. There are over 100 million personal passenger cars, nearly every household has a television set as well as more than one radio set; and the Gross National Product is two trillion dollars. America has produced far more than could have been produced by manual labor working around the clock. As a matter of fact, most of the commodities and services produced could never have been produced at all without applied science. If one imagines a developed economy without that part of production made possible by applied science, one would see a majority of that nation starving to death. Hardly a quarter of the people would survive, and they would live on a level similar to undeveloped countries. Thanks to gain, both profits and the standard of living have increased, a situation inconceivable to Marx, who postulated that wages must fall when profits rise, and wages rise only when profits fall.

Modern gain, as opposed to gain of pre-Industrial Revolution times, belongs to the nation as a whole. It is, by its very nature, social. Unfortunately, since people, as a rule, don't think in those terms, this social property is not properly protected. Only tangible means of production are protected, hard assets that can be entered onto balance sheets of corporations. This classical concept of ownership is no longer sufficient. What must be faced is the realization that we create products and processes that embody the effort of the entire nation, even of past generations, and that the gain belongs to everyone.

Who in his right mind would insist that electricity, or the fruits of computer technology, for example, should accrue only to a select group? Who would say that an excellent educational system, training minds that will in time add immeasurably to a nation's wealth, should be reserved for an elite? Gain is also present in a democratic system of government that permits utilization of brainpower and imagination, because the human mind works best under conditions of freedom. The cultural level of a people, achieved during a historical process, is gain for the nation. The network of roads and highways that accompanies a modern automobile industry is gain.

If we use electricity, we think in terms of the price of its units. We are convinced that we pay not only cost of production, but profit as well, and that all the gain is appropriated by the owner, whoever that may be.

If we buy a TV set, we think only in terms of cost. It doesn't seem reasonable to figure the gain we would have lost had we been forced to see live whatever cultural, sports, or other events we watch. Nor do we think of the gain in getting news quickly, as quickly as only diplomats once could.

If we purchase a pair of shoes we never give thought to the fact that without the gain of applied science, we would have to work some sixty hours to earn as much as was needed to buy the shoes. Our gain in such a purchase is more than what was once a full week's work. The owner of a shoe factory may tack a profit onto every pair of shoes sold, but this profit will be the equivalent of less than one hour's wage for the shoe worker. The consumer of the shoes will derive a much greater gain.

Dr. Eugen Loebl, world renowned economist, has coined the phrase, "lucroactivity of science" to connote the social character of gain that benefits everyone. The objective of lucroactivity of science is to optimize gain and cut down on its losses.

If economists—classicists, Marxists, and Keynesians alike— had realized the importance of creative thinking as an economic factor and had projected it into economics, they would have realized the role played by gain. But they never did and still don't.

Since gain is the result of the integrated effort of the entire nation, it belongs to all the people and should be protected no less than any national treasure. In effect, the nation needs a macroeconomic organ to protect gain because it is essentially social property. In gain we face a kind of joint tenancy. We owe a debt to former generations who made certain types of gain possible for us, and we have a responsibility to future generations to make sure that they will not only inherit the gain which was in part a legacy of the past to us, but will also inherit whatever additions our present efforts are obligated to engender.

Who or what will protect the assets of such a joint tenancy? Who or what will protect the social ownership of gain?

We cannot properly give an answer to that question until one thing is made clear: The major concern of an advanced society should not be oriented toward ownership of the means of production, but toward what those means of production accomplish and for whom. We cannot leave it to the private sector to protect gain because the private sector doesn't take the ownership of gain into consideration. It is concerned with hard assets, material production, and return on capital. Workers, on the other hand, are concerned with their wages. They don't even think of gain in their capacity as consumers.

There is no question but that an important responsibility of government must be the protection of the nation's gain. However, this by no means automatically implies government interference with the economy or the life of the nation in a manner that reduces gain, as is currently the case in the American economy. Government, by applying impeding tactics, can easily diminish gain. When government makes it difficult for a conscientious business or industry to function at optimal efficiency, lower its prices to consumers and replace obsolete equipment by saddling the enterprise with unnecessary, costly paper work or using a regulatory agency to litigate and harass, then government is diminishing gain and must be called to account.

Undue interference by government in the economy, resulting in a diminishing of gain, cannot be dealt with as an abstract principle. It is as pertinent as a corporation's decision of what to do with assets. Once government is given the responsibility of protecting a nation's gain and developing policies that will extend its benefits, then government must be monitored by the people. It must be shown that government interference is, when exercised, necessary to the optimizing of gain. Where unnecessary, such interference must be eliminated.

The entire concept of social gain is applicable only to a mature economy, one based on applied science. In the early stages of the Industrial Revolution the ownership of the means of production and the ownership of gain were practically identical inasmuch as gain was the reward to those who owned the means of production. In an advanced society, as noted, a joint tenancy of gain has developed. The nation as a whole has invested in itself over a period of time, and the results of this investment—ranging from quality education to a socioeconomic infrastructure to legislation based on respect for the individual— must be protected.

This protection must also be extended to such factors as environment and natural resources, but again in a manner that doesn't diminish gain via unnecessary rules, regulations, and laws.

The establishment of guidelines for the protection of social gain means, to begin with, the recognition of the economy as a gigantic transformer: nature's input plus man's creative thinking resulting in output greater than input. It means a recognition of the economy as not merely a relationship between aggregates and not a predetermined and inevitable process, but a fluid interrelationship determined by man's mind. The ultimate criterion is: Is the nation's gain being increased or diminished? It is a criterion that is applicable in all fields—production, education, culture. If there is involuntary unemployment and/ or inflation, then gain is being diminished. A labor leader who pushes for increased wages for his constituents without making provision for increased productivity is diminishing gain. A producer who arbitrarily raises prices to show greater profits rather than seek more efficient ways of production to bring prices down is diminishing gain. An administration that creates a new multi-billion-dollar agency that simply sets up a new bureaucracy to harass the private sector is diminishing gain. A Congress that passes laws that benefit certain interests at the expense of the national interest is diminishing gain. Any government interference with education that lowers educational standards, for whatever reason, diminishes gain—a loss that will be felt by the nation in succeeding generations. A system of internal security that doesn't properly protect the nation from terrorism or subversion diminishes gain in that the society may one day come apart, creating fear and panic in the populace. And because peace of mind is part of a nation's gain, an inadequate military force also diminishes gain, as does any defense budget that tolerates waste and inefficiency.

It will not do to regard the many components that go into an advanced economy as individual entities and determine the loss or increase of gain in terms of each component isolated from the others. An advanced economy is a living organism in which different subsystems exist, each one vital and unable to exist by itself outside the system. Each one has a particular role to play, but all interpenetrate each other and depend upon each other. Oftentimes, a tightrope must be walked to ensure that gain in one area does not result in disruption or debilitation in another area. This is the responsibility of the macroeconomic organ assigned to protect gain—government; but in all instances there must not be a diminishing of gain.

Does government planning, as defined by statists, play any role in this protection of gain? No. Not plans, but goals, should be the objective in a free society. Obviously, goals should include such things as employment for all who want to work, a stable currency, preservation of environment, and the fostering of culture. The guideline is gain—its increase for the benefit of the entire nation. The role of government as the macroeconomic organ responsible for protecting social gain can be defined;

today, government has set itself up as an antagonist to all other sectors of society—to the private sector, to consumers, to labor, to education, to culture. It operates as an outside force with a hostile bureaucracy whose sole raison d'être is to expand its powers regardless of its accomplishments.

The continuation of such a situation is intolerable.

GOVERNMENT
LENDING,
NOT SPENDING

17

Most people, economists and laypersons alike, think of the United States as a money economy; in actual fact, the single most important fact about the U.S. economy is that it is a credit economy.

If noted economists like Walter W. Heller, Milton Friedman, and Paul Samuelson show little or no sign that they grasp the full significance of that fact, one can hardly expect the American people to understand it.

In the days of Adam Smith, two centuries ago, the economy was one of exchange, and money was literally a commodity to be exchanged like any other. Coins of gold or silver were used because they were a more convenient means of exchange than, say, cabbages or lamb's wool.

Although Smith was for a laissez-faire economy, decrying the kind of government interference in the economy that had marked the mercantilist system, he had no objection to government being responsible for money. In effect, money was a component of the economy that Smith believed should be protected by government.

The problem at the time was to supply the economy with money that had a stable purchasing power. Smith even envisaged corn as a better means of exchange, believing that the value of corn was more stable than the value of gold. When gold and silver did become money, it became the duty of the government to make sure that people were not cheated with coins containing less gold or silver than the determined nominal value. This led to a state monopoly in producing coins. Unfortunately, it opened the door to state monetary tampering. Whenever the state was in need of money, it cheated the public by adding cheap metals to gold, thus gaining extra gold for itself.

Nevertheless, it was the better of two evils. It would have been a disaster if just anyone could mint coins. When paper money came into existence at a more developed stage of the economy, banks were permitted to print it, but the money was backed by gold. Once paper money was no longer backed by gold, it was mandatory that government should monopolize the printing of money. Without this monopoly the economy simply could not have functioned.

As the Industrial Revolution spread, the means of production and the production of raw materials rapidly developed. Trade advanced in both scope and volume, and barter became inconvenient and inefficient. No longer were commodities— either goods or coins of precious metal—exchanged; rather, they were bought and sold. Thus, money evolved from an optional means of exchange into a regular means of payment.

Whether the means of payment was gold- or silver-backed money made no real difference: Even if the form of money remained the same, its function had changed along with the needs of producers and consumers.

Once money became an acknowledged means of payment, a virtual Pandora's box was opened in terms of potential monetary manipulation.

Different moves at different times by the federal government tried to keep pace with the problem of money management and supply. In 1863, under the Lincoln administration, the National Banking Act was passed, authorizing the formation of local private banking associations under federal authority, and giving them the power to issue notes on the basis of U.S. bonds up to ninety percent of their par values. On May 30, 1908, the Aldrich-Vreeland Emergency Currency Act became effective. By this law, any ten national banks having equity funds of at least $5 million could organize themselves into an association with power of note issue, using as collateral state, municipal, or corporation bonds, as well as commercial paper.

Around this time the clamor on the part of the banking institutions became great for the establishment of a central bank of issue like the Bank of England. Contemplated was a federally established but privately controlled institution whose notes would be legal tender and obligations of the government, with commercial paper or government securities as reserve collateral, to be used for the creation of credit.

In 1913, after three banking debacles—in 1873, 1893, and 1907—resulting from crass monetary manipulation, the government took action and passed the Federal Reserve Act.

The Federal Reserve, or FED, as it is called, is a government agency and not a commercial banking system. It has the power to increase or decrease the "money supply," a term that in recent years has lost most of the original meaning initially ascribed to it, as we shall see. The FED exercises its power by manipulating the supply of bank reserves, which are the share of deposits that commercial banks belonging to the FED system (membership is not mandatory) are required to keep on hand or at other FED banks.

In effect, the FED determines what percentage of a bank's holdings must be retained as reserves. In this way it wields an awesome power, arbitrarily exercised because the FED is, after all, an arm of the administration in power. This means that FED decisions are strongly influenced by political considerations.

Let's say that the FED, for whatever reason, decides that

credit—for it is credit we are really talking about and not legal tender money—is too easy to come by. The FED orders a hike in the percentage of bank reserves. Stipulate ten percent. That means that for every $1 million the bank gets in new deposits, it must keep $100,000 in reserve, and has $900,000 to lend out to individuals, businesses, or government agencies via purchase of their securities.

If banks have a large amount of money to lend, that is, credits to extend, interest rates normally come down. Borrowing becomes easier and business expands. Conversely, if the FED reduces the credit supply by decreeing higher reserves, interest rates rise as borrowing becomes more difficult and more expensive. Business either contracts or stagnates, lacking capital to expand.

Conventional economists aver that the rate of growth of the money supply is of paramount importance. If it's excessive, they say, the result is clearly inflationary because there is then too much "money" chasing too few goods and services. To the average citizen, this conjures up a picture of hundreds of millions of dollars being released into the economy via government printing presses. The procedure is actually different.

When the FED wants to give the banks the wherewithal for substantial lending, it purchases U.S. Treasury securities on the open market. The FED itself controls the prices of these securities through an entity called the Federal Open Market Committee.

Purchases of securities are paid for with checks drawn on the FED. These checks are deposited into the bank accounts of those from whom the FED has bought the securities, and that portion over and above the reserve requirement becomes available for lending. If, on the other hand, the FED sells U.S. Treasury securities, payments made to it by the purchasers siphon funds out of banks, reducing the availability of credits open for lending. Those who suffer most when this contraction occurs are the nation's small businesses, who are cramped for capital even in boom times. Large corporations always have priority for credit at the banks and can better afford to pay high interest charges.

A disturbing element to the monetarists, whose attention is fixed on the nation's money supply, is that there is a multiplication factor involved when the FED increases the lending power of banks.

Say that the FED "open market" purchases $1 million in Treasury bills from a dealer. It pays by check, drawn on itself. The purchasing bank gets $1 million in new deposits, sets aside the required reserve—say, ten percent—and lends the rest. The borrower of the $900,000 puts that loan into another bank, which sets aside a reserve of $90,000 and lends $810,000. This process of keeping and lending continues until all $1 million of the FED's original purchase price is held by banks as reserves. By that time, the lending capacity—"money supply" to the monetarists—has been increased immeasurably. The monetarists would keep the growth of the money supply at a uniform six or seven percent annually.

As it happens, "money supply" doesn't mean what it sounds like at all; in fact, no one is certain any longer what it means. Originally, the main concern was an M1, i.e., the total amount of cash and demand deposits extant. Now, the inclination is to concentrate more on M2, which is M1 plus long-term deposits. Whichever definition fits, the "money supply" has been falling, which should please the monetarists. Alas, they are confused because, thanks to the ingenuity of the free enterprise system, banking innovations and sophisticated cash management techniques have been springing up that render obsolete the conventional interpretation of money supply. There are now automatic transfer services, which allow nonbusiness customers to hold a substantial proportion of their transaction balances in interest-bearing accounts rather than in demand deposit balances; negotiated order of withdrawal accounts (checkable savings deposits held in some thrift institutions); money market funds, which offer a highly liquid, high-yielding asset; and repurchase agreements, available to corporations, which come into existence when an income-producing security like a Treasury Bill is sold from a bank's own portfolio to a customer and repurchased a day or two later at a lower prespecified price.

Confusing, to say the least!

Concentrating on the "money supply" is like going to Las Vegas and concentrating on the piano player in the lounge when all the action is at the tables. Economically, the action is in the availability and use of credit because, as specified, the United States is a credit economy.

Credit was created when the necessity arose for a means of bridging or prolonging the production-consumption cycle. Raw materials were being processed and goods produced where payments were not immediate. Consumers paid cash, but producers needed a monetary device that would afford them the opportunity of bridging the gap between the time of production or processing and the time of payment. Credit came into being, and for a long time it meant deferred payment, repayable at an agreed-upon time in cash money.

As society has grown and changed, so has the function of credit. Look at credit as it exists today: We receive wages, salaries, interest, and dividends by check, and pay most of our bills by check or credit card. Checks, like credit cards, are a form of credit. Similarly, we pay for shares of stock by check and when they are sold receive payment by check. Shares are also a form of credit. Companies buy other companies with shares—more credit transactions. An individual may repay his debts in cash, but the economy as a whole repays its debts via book entries. The government repays its debts by issuing new bonds or similar type IOUs, all of which represent new debt. Actually, it isn't even possible to repay in cash, as far as government is concerned.

A company with a line of credit from a bank possesses

capital. A company pinched for credits is actually pinched for capital. Thus, capital insufficiency is actually a matter of insufficient credits.

Today's shortage of capital is caused by a lack of credits.

It cannot be stressed enough that credit is a device developed by business in the free enterprise system to facilitate short-term and long-term transactions. A mature economy needs capital, a great deal of it. It can't be gold because there isn't enough to go around and also because it is a commodity useful only in an exchange-type economy. It can't be currency—legal tender cash—for a variety of reasons: The idea of transacting substantial business deals using actual currency is ludicrous and unworkable; beyond that, the idea of every business enterprise having to petition the government to run off the trillions of dollars required to carry on the nation's business, since government alone is authorized to print money, is in the realm of insanity.

Because the United States is a credit economy, legal tender plays an insignificant role in it. If necessary, we could do without it, but we can't do without credit. Without it, the U.S. economy would come to a standstill.

The fact is that the sum total of U.S. credits is estimated at about $3.5 trillion, created by some 20 billion book entries annually. In contrast, cash money, the total U.S. currency in circulation, comes to a mere $96 billion.

Where does the $3.5 trillion figure come from? First, we have corporate debt of about $1 trillion. Then comes Treasury, federal agencies, and state and local government debt—another $1.250 trillion. Installment debt is about $300 billion, and residential mortgages are about $750 billion. Total credits: $3.5 trillion.

Conventional economists speak of money and credits as though they were one, ignoring the basic difference between them as means of payment. Modern credit is a creation of the free enterprise system and plays a specific role: It is given for the express purpose of producing a greater output than the value of the credit input. It is earmarked for specific purposes—working capital, asset purchase—unlike cash money, which can be used for any purpose whatsoever. Credit extended to the private sector creates real wealth in the form of goods and services, whereas credit taken by the government is used for nonproductive spending. Which brings us to an important point:

It is not only the amount of credit available that matters but for what purpose the credit is used.

A farmer knows that it is not only the quantity of rain that falls during a year that is a decisive factor in determining the size and quality of a harvest; what is also decisive is *when* and *where* the rain falls, and the productive work required to reap the harvest.

What is clear to any farmer should have its counterpart of clarity to economists contemplating the credit situation, but it doesn't. Our conventional economists worry about the money supply, telling us that the greater the money supply the greater the inflationary pressures. Their concern should be with the credit supply and *how* and *where* it is used.

To loosen or tighten the money supply (Milton Friedman argues that money is too tight and Arthur Okun says it isn't tight enough) without taking into consideration the use to which credit is put is to becloud the issue and sow confusion. The possibility of the government invoking the Credit Control Act of 1969, which gives the president the authority to permit the Federal Reserve at its discretion to do anything necessary to restrain credit is something that must be avoided at all costs. It would be the final step in untoward government interference with the one monetary tool that has made America the economic power it is. Yet Arthur Okun, a respected economist, believes that "it's time to bring credit availability back into the act along with interest rates." Here is yet another example of an economist who doesn't grasp the significance of the difference between credits and money supply. Still another is Henry Kaufman, a general partner in the Salomon Brothers investment firm, who has declared that "if we could control debt expansion we could control inflation." What he really should be saying is that if we could control nonproductive government debt expansion we could control inflation.

It must be drummed into our economists that in a credit economy such as we have in the United States, debits change to credits and back to debits with great speed. These transactions are in the form of billions of book entries, nothing more, and have absolutely nothing to do with the money supply, which is really an insignificant factor. As noted, corporate credits are earmarked for specific purposes, and when these purposes are fulfilled, the debit is taken off the books until the borrower replaces it with a new debit. To the lender, the sole importance of the process is that the productive output be greater than the credit input. Sufficient credit will never cause inflation so long as it is used for increased production. The credit supply could literally be endless, provided that it was extended for productive purposes. There would be no inflation because real wealth was being created. It is when credit is used for nonproductive purposes that we get inflation. It's true that government will always require a budget for nonproductive purposes, but that budget should come from a responsible tax system (see chapter 18, "Toward a New System of Taxation").

The monetarists clamor for a tight money supply, but the present inflation occurred despite it. This is because they had their eye on the piano player and not on the gaming tables. Even *Business Week* speaks of a "tower of debt" without analyzing the significance of who owes how much. There is no denying that the U.S. debt structure has exploded during the four-year period 1975 to 1979, but any effort to tabulate the "tower of debt," which are credits, is meaningless. Credit is like a vibrating force-field, and we should be concerned when the rate of vibration slows, because it indicates that wealth is not being created. Also, corporate debt, which has risen thirty-six percent since 1975 to more than $1 trillion, is not the same as U.S. government debt (including the Treasury and federal agencies), which has risen forty-seven percent to $825 billion during the same four years. Nor is it the same as state and local government debt, which has increased thirty-three percent to $295 billion. Corporate debt is healthy because we can assume that even when plans don't work out, the intent is to create wealth. The same can't be said for federal, state, and local debt. Residential mortgage debt has climbed during 1975 to 1979 fifty-four percent to $750 billion, and this, too, is healthy, because houses are wealth—tangible assets. Consumer installment debt, up forty-nine percent to $300 billion, is mainly a buying spree in reaction to fears of continuing and spiraling inflation.

Again, the real cause for concern when examining the nation's "tower of debt" is federal borrowing. Treasury borrowing went from $3.5 billion in 1970 to over $45 billion in 1978, while federal agencies went from $10 billion to $36 billion. To finance 1978's federal deficit of $51 billion and part of the $40 billion deficit predicted for fiscal 1979, the Treasury borrowed close to $33 billion in net new cash during the second half of 1978.

Out of some $380 billion in credit extended in 1978, the federal government and its agencies took twenty-two percent, or more than $80 billion, and used it almost entirely for nonproductive purposes. Those seeking a basic cause of inflation need look no further.

Under its "spending" policies, the U.S. government, as we know, devises and subsidizes a wide variety of nonproductive programs. No return on the vast federal outlay is possible because no real wealth is being created. The more the government spends, the higher the prices, which in turn lead to wage increases, which lead to higher prices, etcetera. This is the inflationary spiral in which we are caught. Having no better ideas, the federal government fights inflation by increasing the rate of interest and decreasing the money supply. The result is greater unemployment.

Sensibly, credits should be used to make full use of the vast productive potential in the nation. The important factor in granting credits to anyone is that credit input will equal a greater output. Naturally, there is a risk that this might not happen, but American banking institutions make thousands of decisions daily regarding the credit-worthiness of loan applicants.

The replacement of the government "spending" policy with one of "lending" would literally unlock the national productive potential. Under the lending concept, the government would offer credits to the banking system free of charge in order to supply the economy with as much credit as is needed. The proviso is that the credit would be used for productive purposes and would be repaid.

As a matter of procedure, government lending could be accomplished by the issuance of debt instruments. These would not be for sale in the money markets in competition with the productive sector, but for deposit in the FED as credit entries, deposits on which no interest would be paid. The FED, in turn, would open credit lines to member banks, and because these particular government debt instruments would carry no interest charges, none would be imposed on member banks by the FED.

The credits, or capital, thus created would be loaned to business enterprises by the banks according to strictly commercial criteria.

In other words, what is advocated is a policy of government lending carried out on a strictly commercial basis through strictly commercial channels.

The rate of interest charged to the borrower would be calculated to cover the bank's overhead, risk, and profit— nothing more. As a result, the cost of credit to the borrower should be reduced to around five or six points, perhaps less.

Mortgage rates would be around three or four percent, with other rates in line with the credit rating of the borrower.

Under no circumstances would the government extend credits directly to corporations, nor could it decide who would be given credit, or the rate of interest charged. Once the government deposited its certificates with the FED, it would have fulfilled its economic responsibilities.

With such a policy operative on every level of government, it follows that the federal, state, and local governments would no longer compete with the private sector in the capital market, via the sale of paper. The FED's "open market" operations would become past history. Government bonds would slowly disappear from the market, as would new bonds. Government bonds would no longer offer high yields and would not be sold on the open market.

Offering sufficient credits to the private sector would become an absolute obligation of the federal government via the FED. The stimulus to business growth would be enormous: There would be ample credits at a greatly reduced cost of capital. With business borrowing via credits, taxes and prices would not increase, since credit would be granted only under the usual commercial condition that the borrower must produce more than one dollar for every dollar borrowed.

Such a policy links economic stimulus to fiscal responsibility. More investments could be made, more technology and innovations developed, competition would intensify, and prices would decline.

Lest the lending approach seem too revolutionary or theoretical, it is necessary to underscore the fact that the capability is already built into the FED and the banking system. Thus, no new bureaucracy is required to make the changeover from government spending to lending. The principal novelty is simply in perceiving government lending as preferable to government spending, otherwise the approach remains mainly a matter of book entries.

One can anticipate a question posed by conventional economists: Where is the banking system going to find the deposits to support lines of credit to satisfy the requirements of capital-hungry companies?

Lets talk about deposits: They are a creation of the banking system. If the reserve requirement was, say, twenty percent, five dollars would be created for each dollar actually on deposit in any one bank. Of course, reserve requirements are adjustable. In the 1920s the reserve ratio was 1:10, so that for each dollar on deposit in a bank ten dollars was created by the system.

Under such a system, the banking system and the economy as a whole have been made dependent on the rate of savings. Unbelievably, credits, to date, are created as a multiple of bank deposits on the basis of an arbitrary formula called "reserve requirements."

There is no need for reserve requirements.

This by now obsolete system came into being at a time when people deposited gold into banks for safekeeping. Inasmuch as there was a possibility that the depositer might want to withdraw some of his gold at any time, the bank prudently kept around fifty percent of its deposits in reserve, and made loans on the overage.

But—one must emphasize it tirelessly—we are now in a credit economy in which, with small exception, all transactions are by check and book entries. Even consumer installment credit, a matter of some $300 billion, are not cash transactions, but check and book entry recordings. Yet we continue to hang on to the outmoded nineteenth-century concept of "reserve requirements."

What does the government do with its insistence on maintaining reserve requirements save make it that much more difficult for the private sector to obtain credit?

The nonsense of reserve requirements has already been recognized internationally with the existence of some $800 billion Eurodollars, which *Business Week* (August 21, 1978) describes as "a vast, integrated global money and capital system almost totally outside all government regulations, that can send billions of Eurodollars, Euromarks and other 'stateless' currencies hurtling around the world 24 hours a day. Stateless money is deposited and lent through banks in the Euromarkets with absolutely no bureaucratic interference. These banks hold no required reserves against deposits in case of a crisis in the future. And they have no insurance on deposits to push up costs." There is literally no limit to the amount of credit that can be created from Eurodollars.

What are possible objections to the concept of government lending?

One is that simply offering credit to business enterprises doesn't guarantee that the credit supply will be used. After all, credit is available for housing, but many who need housing don't take out mortgages to build. The answer to this objection is that humans are, after all, human: They have fears as well as desires and needs. And one fear is that the cost of borrowing is such that the borrower may not be able to meet that expense in an economy that is gripped by inflation and where the breadwinner may suddenly be out of a job.

Another objection is that government lending would fuel productivity and create an economy functioning at peak activity. Wouldn't that be inflationary?

The answer is: not necessarily. Yes, *the creation of a large amount of credit could be inflationary if used unproductively by government and inefficiently by business.* To use credits to further swell an already bloated federal bureaucracy would certainly fuel inflation, as would the use of credits to create nonproductive jobs. Similarly, the use of credits by the private sector to maintain an inefficient operation or turn out shoddy products would also make no sense. Any commercial lending institution should and would be hesitant to provide a credit line to a company obviously unfit. Since the government would not make credits available directly to business, but through the commercial banking system, it would devolve upon the latter, as it does now, to make prudent loans that have a reasonable chance of being repaid.

It is vitally important *where,* to *whom,* and for *what purpose* credit is extended.

There are three areas where the concept of government lending can be introduced immediately for dramatically positive results. These are small enterprises, housing, and energy.

There are some 13 million small enterprises in the country. Were it not for them, there would be no competitive market, only huge corporations bureaucratically hidebound and far less responsible and adaptable to public needs than smaller firms.

In a report on "Technology, Economic Growth and International Competitiveness" prepared for the United States Congressional Joint Economic Committee, Professor Robert Gilpin stated:

> *Defense of bigness was challenged by Jewkes and collaborators in a very detailed study of the sources of invention. Jewkes was able to show that individuals and small firms in competitive industry had a higher propensity to invent than large firms. In contrast to the rugged individualism and daring of the private entrepreneur, large corporations tend to be overly conservative. The scale of the organization itself makes the coupling of new knowledge and market demand difficult. In a number of areas—especially scientific instruments, machinery and electronics—(the small firms) tend to predominate as inventors. Frequently the small firm makes important innovations which are then picked up and marketed by large firms. This has been the case of computers and electronic data processing. When large-scale capital investments are required, however, small-scale firms tend to be at a disadvantage. Yet the large firms may use these resources to suppress innovations and prevent the entry into the market of small firms with radical innovations.*

Small enterprises provide about fifty-five percent of all private employment, forty-eight percent of all business output, fifty percent of all business activity, and forty-three percent of the Gross National Product.

In the past years these firms have been languishing for lack of capital, and many have been forced into mergers or bankruptcy. The facts speak for themselves: in 1969 $1.1 billion in new capital was invested in young companies. By 1974 that investment had fallen to $16 million. In 1972 there were 418 underwritings for companies having a net worth of less than $5 million. In 1975 there were four such underwritings. In 1969 the Tax Act increased the penalties on capital gains, driving potential investors away from small company financings. The Tax Reform Act of 1976 compounded the damage.

Small companies have historically been the creators and training grounds for most new jobs. A Commerce Department report on new technical enterprises shows that young high-technology companies, between 1969 and 1974, reported an average sales growth of 42.5 percent and an employment growth of 40.7 percent. The average for mature companies was an 11.4 percent sales growth and a six-tenths of one percent employment growth. During 1969 to 1974 six established companies with combined sales of $36 billion in 1974 experienced a net gain of twenty-five thousand jobs, whereas five young high-technology companies with combined sales of $857 million had a net increase in employment of almost thirty-five thousand jobs.

To encourage expansion, the elimination of corporation taxes for small enterprises is recommended (as indeed, it is for all corporations). In addition, the government should earmark credits for small businesses via the commercial banking system. The cost to the companies should simply be the handling cost to banks plus a nominal profit. There should be no interest charges.

It cannot be emphasized enough that the sole criterion for the extension of government-guaranteed credits should be a greater output than input. American commercial lending institutions are historically trained to evaluate every loan application on its own merit, and this system shouldn't change. If a small enterprise can show that the infusion of credits is a reasonable commercial risk, it should receive those credits.

It should be kept in mind that inflation does not result from the productive, profitable use of credits; it results only from the nonproductive use of credits, driving up prices as more money chases after the same, or less, amount of goods and services.

The earmarking of unlimited amount government-backed credits for small enterprises, at the prescribed cost—no interest but simply a lending bank's overhead, risk, and profit margin— would generate thousands of new jobs, cutting down on unemployment payments and stimulating economic growth. Credits to the small companies would create the kind of competition to the giant corporations that keeps the "sap" of the free enterprise system flowing.

Unlimited government-backed credits should also be made available to the housing construction industry, and to mortgagees.

Homes are a part of a nation's wealth, tangible assets that can be bought and sold over and over, not like throw-away items with built-in obsolescence. Homes are also a part of a nation's gain in that few things contribute more to individual and family well-being and satisfaction with democracy than home ownership.

The government, through its fiscal policies, has acted as an impediment to home purchasing. High rates of interest to potential mortgagees and to the housing construction industry have kept people from buying or building homes. It is a tribute to the ingenuity of the free enterprise system that it is still able to come up with ways of meeting peoples' desperate need to own their own homes—at least as long as the federal bureaucracy doesn't interfere.

A recent development is the creation of tax-free bonds to purchase homes. Basically, the process involves the sale of bonds by local governments on which interest is exempt from federal income tax and, in certain instances, state tax as well. Proceeds are turned over to local lenders, and the funds are loaned on mortgages to people buying homes. What makes such borrowings attractive, especially in times of high interest, is that the tax-free aspect of the money permits mortgage rates up to two and a half percentage points below those of generally available mortgages. Such financings cost the localities involved next to nothing. Thrift institutions take care of servicing the loans in return for their portion of the monthly payments, which means that the locality doesn't have to stand behind the bonds. The overall results are most gratifying: Run-down downtown neighborhoods are rehabilitated, the flight to the suburbs is slowed, both buyers and sellers of homes are pleased, and local taxpayers aren't hit with expenses.

The explosive growth of mortgage revenue bonds issued by municipalities—from $137 million in July of 1978 to $1.4 billion a scant eight months later, testifies to the deep hunger of Americans for their own homes.

Is the federal government happy with this growth? Not at all. Tax-free bonds means there is no taxable interest and hence no revenue to the federal government. The Department of Housing and Urban Development (HUD), as jealous of its prerogatives as any federal regulatory agency, is unhappy that others—savings and loan institutions—decide who is to be beneficiary of low-interest mortgages. HUD also resents the loan of such funds to middle-class families, preferring that the money goes to low income groups via local housing agencies.

President Carter has called for legislation to restrict the benefits of this type of financing to low and moderate income families, and Henry Reuss, chairman of the House Banking Committee, wants such loans curtailed.

Such public measures of desperation as described above

would not be necessary under a policy of government lending. Akin to the case of small enterprises, government-backed credits would permit mortgages of three or four percent. A proviso could be that the mortgage applicant be in a lower or middle income range, thus restricting the advantage of low cost mortgages to those who need them most.

There is so much that can be accomplished in the field of energy via a policy of government lending that common sense and the urgency of the situation demand an immediate beginning.

In the chapter titled "Toward a New System of Taxation" it is recommended that corporate taxation be done away with because it is an impediment to economic growth. Certainly, all companies engaged in energy—be they in oil, gas, coal, or solar—should, beginning at once, no longer have to pay federal income taxes. It's time to stop treating industry with the kind of suspicion one reserves for a house guest who looks as though he might make off with the family silver. How quickly it's forgotten that the energy industry, until the federal government and the OPEC countries interfered, gave the American people the most efficient system of energy at the lowest costs in the world.

It has already been determined by a special study what the oil industry, for example, will require in capital expenditures over the next few years. Surely it's in the national interest to make all necessary capital (credits) available to the industry at the lowest possible cost? Unfortunately, the Carter Administration has consistently shown a greater concern with oil company profits than with developing new sources of energy. There is a perversity in this attitude, a carry-over from other administrations as well, that must stop.

In making unlimited credits available to the energy industry at low cost, the objectives would be manifold: finding and developing new domestic sources of oil and gas, funding research and development of new energy sources, stimulating solar energy development, and so forth.

Thus would the government help, not hinder the energy industry. Concomitant with such steps, and in line with recommendations made elsewhere in this book, there should be a drastic reduction of regulatory impositions on the energy industry. It's costly, exasperating, frustrating, and hopelessly ineffectual in solving our energy problems.

There are many other areas where ample credit would be economically fruitful. For example, if earmarked credits were available to reduce the cost of installing energy-saving, raw material-saving, or nonpolluting equipment, it would serve the national interest in terms of environmental protection and conservation of resources. Our concern, besides economic growth, should also be the protection of national gain. We could have a higher Gross National Product, but more pollution, waste, shoddy goods and services—a lower quality of life in general. On the other hand, by directing the flow of inexpensive credits to finance activities beneficial to the nation, rather than expanding bureaucratic regulations, we could channel the self-interest of individual business enterprises into the mainstream of the national interest.

In another area, plans could be worked out for using the credit lending concept at the city and state levels to, say, employ unused labor capacity.

As long as we accept the right of the government and its agency, the Federal Reserve System, to determine the price the private sector must pay for its credits, we are severely crimping—and will sooner or later eliminate—the most important area of the free enterprise system: the capital market.

A policy of government lending would greatly bring down the size and scope of the federal budget. Fiscally irresponsible government programs could be eliminated with concomitant reductions in a swollen bureaucracy if the private sector were given the tools—ample credits—to create real economic growth. It must be emphasized and reemphasized: Capital becomes capital only through productive and efficient economic performance. Any amount of credit granted is justifiable as long as it is tied to prudent economic use.

Toward a New System of Taxation

18

In feudal times a collector was dispatched by the lord of the manor to collect taxes. Amounts owed were arbitrarily decided, and woe betide those who wouldn't or couldn't pay.

Is there a familiar sound to this bit of past history? Today, it's Congress that arbitrarily decides how much taxes every American and business enterprise must pay, and the collector is the Internal Revenue Service. The IRS employs over 200,000 people who, in turn, keep some 2 million others busy doing paper work for the agency. These include accountants, tax lawyers, and hundreds of thousands of corporate employees. The cost of the man-hours spent by those striving to satisfy IRS demands for information—not to mention the cost of the paper itself—runs into the billions of dollars.

The American system of taxation has its roots in the Middle Ages. It's a system based on the philosophy that government has the right to spend as it deems necessary, and the citizenry must passively pay for all such expenditures. It's a tax system taken over from the times when a ruler, needing money for the maintenance and growth of personal power and glory, taxed his subjects so that he could indulge himself. Times changed, democracy came into being, free enterprise changed the structure of the economy, but the United States still has the same philosophy of taxation. It is cumbersome, obsolete, inefficient, and irrational—and no one questions it.

Consider this scenario: It is 1776 and the American people have formed the United States of America. Representatives are chosen to form the new government. A Bill of Rights is drawn up specifying that the government will protect human rights, that it will be the servant of the people and not its master. To ensure the success of that objective, an internal system of checks and balances operating on the administrative, legislative, and judicial levels is set up.

A government must have duties and responsibilities, and these are carefully defined by the people. They include such federal powers as taxing for federal purposes; borrowing on the nation's credit; regulating foreign and interstate commerce; providing currency and coinage; conducting foreign relations and making treaties; providing an army and navy; establishing and maintaining a postal service; protecting patents and copyrights; regulating weights and measures; admitting new states; and a mandate to "make all laws which shall be necessary and proper" for the execution of all powers vested in the U.S. government.

So far all is in accord with historical fact. To carry out its obligations a government must have funds—a budget.

Consider the following hypothetical situation:

Assume the Gross National Product of 1776 to be, say, $100 million. This is the value of all goods and services produced annually, against which there is an equal amount of money in the hands of the people with which to buy those goods and services. Prices are stable because there is no excess of money in circulation over and above the value of goods and services produced. Thus, there is no inflation.

The government is asked to come up with a budget to cover the cost of all obligations imposed on it by the people. The sum of $10 million is specified.

This cost, everyone knows, will be nonproductive in that

it will not contribute to real economic wealth. It will go primarily to government employees and to government contractors and their employees.

One of the prerogatives accorded the 1776 government is to create money; however, to create $10 million which will not be matched by an equivalent amount of goods and services would be inflationary. The reason is that there would be more money in circulation than there were goods and services. The dollar would be worth only 90 cents because there would be $1.10 for every $1.00 worth of goods and services. Prices would rise. Workers would demand higher wages to offset the higher prices, and business enterprises would raise prices to meet higher labor costs. An inflationary spiral originating from excess currency created by the government would be set in motion.

Obviously, an intolerable situation and one to be avoided.

Two important decisions are made.

The first is that, barring any extraordinary conditions which must be submitted to the people for judgment, the federal government must live within its determined budget, just like any family or business enterprise. The second decision is that the government budget will be raised via a single tax levied at the retail level on every product sold. Should the economy grow, the tax percentage would decline. Thus, if the Gross National Product rises to $200 million, double the 1776 GNP, and the government budget is still $100 million, the tax levied will be reduced to five percent, instead of the ten percent originally imposed.

Should the GNP go below $100 million, an additional percentage will be added to the one tax imposed to ensure the government of its budget.

A modest Internal Revenue System is set up to monitor tax revenues.

That's the way it should have happened, but didn't.

The American people are well aware of the inequities and

complexities of the federal income tax system. It has come to a point where every rule and regulation has spawned twenty subrulings and regulations, each one a statistical maze that requires the work of an accountant and attorney to decipher. And even these experts are not always sure of themselves.

Efforts have been made from time to time to simplify tax forms, but somehow the complexities remain and in many instances grow worse. Again, as in the case of corporate taxes, the people have no way of knowing precisely where their money is going, although they do know that the bulk of it goes for nonproductive purposes.

Before even making a recommendation regarding personal income taxes, an important point must be made.

The average person tends to think of the government as needing money to pay its bills. This isn't so. The government pays the nation's bills, since the government meets its responsibilities through the money it receives from the people. The distinction may seem insignificant, but it isn't. By thinking of government as paying its own bills, we automatically classify government as a separate entity with the right to determine how much and where it spends. But according to the democratic philosophy upon which the United States is founded, it should be the people who spend via the government. It should be the people who decide which needs are to be met through the government and in what proportions—how much should be spent on defense, welfare, education, transportation, research and development, etcetera (if indeed the people want the government involved in all the aforementioned areas). The government should serve as a cashier. It is a dictatorial government that spends as it wishes and forces the people to pay for its expenditures.

How extensive are our democratic rights if we have no say in how a federal budget is being spent? This is not economic democracy.

Any new tax system must be one that takes into account

the need for the American people to know precisely how much they are paying in taxes and where those taxes are going. It is not economic democracy when we have to guess that about fifty cents of every dollar goes for overt and hidden taxes, nor is it economic democracy when this vast sum flows into a common "budget," at which point legislators take over and decide all by themselves how to allocate the funds. We all know too well the narrow, parochial interests that influence many legislators and cause them to allocate funds in ways that don't serve the national interest at all.

To whom does the nation's income belong? The conventional answer by individuals and business enterprises is: "To us—after taxes." This kind of thinking is right in line with that of legislators like Ed Muskie, Senate budget chief, who seeks to preserve the rising tax trend. But other, more enlightened legislators, understand very well the issue at stake. Congressman Jack Kemp (Republican, New York) has argued that it is inherent in the Declaration of Independence and the Constitution that all the income belongs to the people. "Since, by this view," he says, "government is the servant and not the master, the people's income is their own; that portion which they wish to provide to government to carry out responsibilities agreed to in the constitutional framework, and nothing more, is government revenue."

Of course, that isn't the way it is. Under our tax system, there is absolutely no limit to the amount of money the government can take in as revenue. As a matter of fact, the government spends far more than it takes in, the current deficit officially estimated to be running at about $50 billion. Even this staggering figure is regarded as too low by Leonard Santow, senior vice-president of the J. Henry Schroder Bank and Trust Company, who believes that the government deficit in fiscal 1979 will be closer to $66 billion. One hears the argument that the government "needs" the money to channel into the many areas that are the beneficiaries of this largesse. Yet one searches the Declaration of Independence and the Constitution in vain for any justification of the nature and amount of current government spending. It would be bad enough if the federal government spent right up to the hilt of its revenues, but it consistently goes beyond that by billions of dollars. Also, because of the complex system of overt and hidden taxes imposed at the federal, state, and local levels, the American people have no way of knowing how much taxes they are actually paying. It has been estimated that a full fifty cents of every dollar goes for taxes.

In 1978 Americans worked 153 days out of the year just to pay taxes.

On the federal level all taxes flow into a general budget, and are allocated in the main for nonproductive programs. The public doesn't even know how their money is being spent, and if it were known, the people would have no voice in the matter. Yet why shouldn't the nation have the right to decide directly on the principal items in a proposed budget? Fifty years ago, when the government budget was two percent of the GNP, it didn't matter that much. Then, total budget outlays were $3.127 billion while the GNP was $150 billion. Now, although the GNP has grown only nine times what it was a half century ago, the federal government budget outlays are *133 times as great!*

With workers being pushed into higher tax brackets every time they receive a wage increase, and with Social Security taxes slated to rise annually, Americans may one day find themselves reacting much as the people of Sweden are reacting today. Sweden has the highest tax rate in the Western world. Because of that, Swedes consider it senseless to work harder or longer, and they show their discontent by taking more leisure time. From 1950 to 1977 public sector spending in Sweden rose from twenty-four percent to sixty-four percent of the GNP, and the income transfer system went wild. As an example, a married breadwinner with a wife not working and with four children to support who earned $4,600 in 1978, after taxes and adding transfers netted $14,117. A similar family with the breadwinner earning $23,000 is left with the same $14,117.

Melvyn B. Krauss, writing in the *Wall Street Journal* of February 1, 1979, points out that because of this tax system: "The average annual working time for men in manufacturing industries has decreased 24 percent from 1960 to 1978. In this same period, absenteeism was up 63 percent and overtime was down 70 percent." Gunnar Myrdal, Nobel prize winner and the one most responsible for the drafting of the Swedish Welfare State, finally got around to admitting in a recent article that "For the majority of people . . . a high and progressively increasing marginal tax rate must decrease the willingness to work more than necessary." And he added, "Of all the deficiencies in our income tax system, for me the most serious is that the laws directly invite us to tax evasion and tax cheating."

A barter system is growing in Sweden because of the high taxes. A housepainter offers to paint a dentist's house if the dentist will fix his teeth. Taxes are avoided and everyone is happy.

How far is the United States behind Sweden? Estimates range from three to ten years.

In the United States there are a host of reasons for the continuous rise in prices, but several of the most important ones are easily identifiable. Corporate prices automatically include provision for taxes, whether or not the company proves to be profitable. When taxes go up, and this has been the history of one administration after another, prices inevitably follow. Also, companies find it increasingly expensive to comply with government regulatory agencies that not only demand information but costly changes in productive methods. The cost of the information and the changes in production show up in higher prices.

It is impossible to itemize all the ways in which business enterprises suffer as a result of perverse government tax policies, but a few notable examples are in order. For one, tax-free depreciation allowances to companies are too little to meet the rising costs of replacing plants and equipment. This is a form of overtaxation that is dangerous in the long run to the viability of the economy. Also, and anachronistically, the greater the efficiency of a company, the greater its taxes. An inefficient company, on the other hand—that is, one that incurs losses— pays no taxes, even though the amount of anticipated taxes is a component of the company's product prices. Thus, the inefficient company cashes the taxes paid by the consumer which are included in the firm's prices. In effect, the inefficient company receives a premium for being less efficient than the profitable company.

Other taxes act as a damper on business expansion. There is a double taxation on dividends, levied once as corporate income and again as dividend income to shareholders. Capital gains taxes blunt the incentive to use excess capital to create new businesses and more jobs. The policy of taxing corporate earnings twice if distributed prompted Frederick W. Hickman, Assistant Secretary of the Treasury for Tax Policy from 1972 to 1975 to say, in the *Wall Street Journal* of September 25, 1975: "It inhibits investments in corporate form, discriminates against low bracket investors, encourages high debt-equity ratios, traps income in entities where it may not be put to optimum use and encourages corporate mergers and acquisitions which would be otherwise undesirable."

Depreciation methods also result in unfair corporate taxation. Martin Feldstein, president of the National Bureau of Economic Research, writing in the *Wall Street Journal,* stated:

> In 1977, the historic cost method of tax depreciation caused corporate depreciation to be understated by more than $30 billion. This understatement increased corporate tax liabilities by $15 billion, a 25 percent increase in corporate taxes.

This extra inflation tax reduced net profits by 28 percent of the total 1977 net profits of $53 billion. This is the single most important adverse effect of inflation on capital formation ... If historic cost depreciation is continued, taxpaying bondholders will receive little or no after-tax income.

Every incoming administration, aware of public dissatisfaction with the tax system, makes its share of promises regarding tax reform. President Carter was elected on his concern over rising public debt, government spending and chronic inflation, interconnected factors upon which impact can be made only via a thoroughly overhauled tax system. Carter promised meaningful tax changes and relief for the American people, but his initial recommendation, a $50 tax rebate, had no relation whatsoever to any of the hard-core economic problems facing the nation. The idea surfaced briefly and was mercifully forgotten. However, what did occur fueled inflation. It could be called the Carter fiscal explosion, involving $100 billion in new spending in just two fiscal years and a $125 billion increase in the federal debt.

A table based on Federal Budget statements for the years 1976 through 1979 is most revealing. It shows the following: The actual federal deficit in fiscal year 1978 was over $73 billion, some $17 billion more than the original Ford budget; the 1979 fiscal deficit looks to be at least $55 billion, which is $32 billion more than Ford projected for 1979; the 1980 projected deficit, even with large cuts, will be $45 billion worse than the Ford-planned $2 billion surplus; the total federal debt in 1980 is going to be $90 billion higher than the Ford projections called for; the 1979 budget deficit would have been $20 billion higher, had it not been for an inflation-windfall in income tax revenues and a $15 billion increase in Social Security taxes.

The Carter spending budget for fiscal 1979 is expected to be very close to $550 billion. President Carter discreetly makes no mention of approximately $14 billion in off-budget items, which creates a much higher deficit than he admits. In addition, Carter has given the country a Social Security program resulting in the biggest peacetime tax increase in United States history— $227 billion over the next decade. His energy proposals—one must make it very clear that there is no federal energy program, only disjointed proposals—contain potential tax increases that have been estimated at a low of $50 billion a year to a high of $300 billion.

In 1977, economist Walter Heller estimated that the 1979 federal tax bill for Americans would be about $40 billion higher than in 1977, mainly as a result of higher Social Security rates and inflation.

The Democrat-dominated Congress has made a big point about the $18.7 billion tax cut voted in October 1978, but this cut in no way offsets higher Social Security levies and higher personal tax rates arising from inflation. When one considers the $8.5 billion increase in the Social Security payroll tax, and combines it with the conservatively estimated $13.5 billion boost as inflation pushes Americans into higher tax brackets, we don't come up with a tax cut at all, but rather with a net tax increase of about $3.3 billion! By 1983 the new tax bill will provide about $30 billion in annual tax "relief," but the Social Security tax increases and inflation-induced increases by then will total some $94 billion.

A simple example will illustrate the hocus-pocus of tax reduction promises. A breadwinner earns $20,000 in 1979. Congress says that his taxes will be $167 less than those paid in 1978; but Social Security tax increases will be $82 and inflation will add another $97 for a total of $179. Suddenly, there is no real tax reduction, but an increase of $12.

Robert M. Bleiberg had this to say in *Barrons*, November 6, 1978:

> Congress, so an overwhelming weight of evidence now suggests, time and again has passed measures that it neither understood, weighed or even necessarily had a chance to

read. As a consequence, in recent years, it has spent an incredible amount of time clarifying, rewriting and more often than not, wholly undoing its own handiwork . . . Not surprisingly, U.S. tax laws have been a succession of financial and economic disasters. They have inevitably favored consumption over saving and investment, undermined incentive and discouraged growth.

Of course, the federal government is not the only culprit in the tax gouging of Americans. Total federal taxes in 1977 were $346,318 million, up 71.7 percent from five years earlier. But there were also state taxes, totaling $101,026 million, up 68.7 percent from five years earlier; and local taxes, totaling $67,557 million, up 55.5 percent from five years earlier. All told, federal, state, and local taxes increased 67.8 percent between 1972 and 1977.

Statistics compiled by the Organization for Economic Co-operation and Development (OECD) indicate that all taxes—federal, state, and local—currently amount to about 30.3 percent of U.S. total domestic production.

These are the days when the cry for a balanced budget is heard in the land. The cry has the ring of fiscal responsibility. But consider: A budget can be balanced in one of two ways—by reducing government expenditures so that they don't exceed government income via the existing tax structure; or by counting on the tax structure to generate higher government revenues so that even with anticipated future increases in government spending, outgo will not exceed income.

To show how it works, start with the supposition of a 1980 federal budget deficit of $50 billion. Actually, Carter has been talking about a $29 billion deficit for 1980, but this is totally misleading because he makes no mention of the huge additional deficit contained in off-budget accounts, primarily engendered by the Federal Financing Bank. At any rate, federal spending growth for 1980 is anticipated at 7.9 percent. The 1979 Carter budget projects contemplated increases in federal tax receipts of 13.4 percent in 1979, 10.3 percent in 1980, and 14.5 percent in 1981. On this basis, Carter can talk about a $1.2 billion deficit in 1981. *But that deficit is without any federal reductions in spending—the deficit reduction comes only from a major increase in tax collections!*

An editorial in the *Wall Street Journal* (January 23, 1979) said:

> One searches in vain in the Carter budget for genuinely significant proposals for spending cuts. The great sprawl of federal agencies and programs is largely untouched. One of the government's biggest money wasters, the Department of Housing and Urban Development, shows up with an 18 percent spending increase. The government's biggest department, HEW, comes up with a 10 percent increase, putting its total spending at just under $200 billion ... The 1980 budget is a statement by the administration that it intends to continue to do business the way the federal government has done business for years.

Two tax proposals already in use in other countries, and about which one may expect to hear more of in the United States, are VAT (Value Added Tax) and Tax Indexing.

VAT is a tax on consumption rather than income. It is a sales tax that is levied at each stage of production and distribution, i.e., on the prices charged on sales, minus the costs paid for goods and services. Like all taxes, the consumer ultimately pays the entire tax burden, but at each point along the way to the final sale the tax is carefully hidden in the product price. VAT is widely used in Europe where, historically, tax collection has always been difficult and complex compared to the American system. With VAT, European governments don't have to rely on the honesty of business enterprises to file annual tax statements. Unfortunately, VAT is highly conducive to inflation: By the time the final consumer price is reached, the taxes that have been added along the way are truly awesome.

The use of VAT in the United States would solve no problems and simply add to the woes of the people. For one, VAT would hit hardest at the people who could afford it least, adding immeasurably to the cost of goods and services most used by the poor and middle class. For another, VAT does nothing about the real problem of taxation in the United States, since it is an open-end system that supplies the federal bureaucracy with unlimited funds for arbitrary allocation.

Tax Indexing involves the automatic adjustment of the tax rate in line with inflation. Thus, for example, the annual income of a breadwinner would not by itself determine the tax rate: It would be adjusted according to the rate of inflation for the particular year, as reflected in the Consumer Price Index. If the CPI went up by ten percent, and the breadwinner's income for that year went up by five percent, then there would be a five-percent allowance in his or her income tax. If the CPI went up by ten percent but the breadwinner's income remained as was, the income tax allowance would be ten percent.

Tax Indexing was first advocated in the United States by economist Milton Friedman, in 1978. It is already in use in Brazil, Israel, the Netherlands, Argentina, Denmark, France, and Luxembourg. Also, Canada has been indexing personal income taxes since 1973.

The Carter administration has been vehemently opposed to Tax Indexing because under it the federal government is deprived of revenues necessary for new programs. As a matter of fact, during 1975 to 1978, the Canadian government was unable to introduce any new programs because of reduced revenues caused by Tax Indexing. The American tax system benefits hugely from inflation. Every time prices rise by 1 percent, the government collects 1.4 percent more in taxes. The Congressional Budget Office has estimated that federal tax collections will increase by $215.5 billion between 1979 and 1983 if the current rate of inflation continues. As Senator Gary Hart (Democrat, Colorado) puts it, "Without ever passing a tax increase, the government reaps a windfall each year at the taxpayer's expense."

As in the case of VAT, there is no pressure upon the federal government to reduce its spending via Tax Indexing. True, government revenues would be reduced, but that could simply mean that federal deficits would be greater, as though there had been a reduction in the tax rate. Perhaps the average breadwinner would not feel the effects of inflation as harshly, but the high rate of inflation would still be there, and the federal government would remain the same engine for inflation it is today.

Clearly, what is needed is a fiscal policy that takes a completely new approach to the size and scope of the federal budget, and the manner in which it is to be financed.

No modern economy can function without government. What is at issue is the role of government in the economy (which will be explored later on) and the funding of the federal budget.

Assume a federal budget of $400 billion, for argument's sake. How is it to be raised?

To begin with, one must keep in mind that a modern economy has no need of tax revenues to finance the federal budget. This is a difficult concept for the average person to grasp, thinking as one does in terms of government using actual money to pay the nation's bills. One must set aside this idea and think in different terms: *All the government has to be concerned with is that purchasing power is not in excess of the value of goods and services produced.*

Keeping the above in mind, it is recommended that the expensive, inefficient, and irrational federal income tax be eliminated and replaced by a single "skimming" sales tax paid on all products sold.

The tax would be levied at the final point of sale of a product, that is, at the retail level. There would be no tax levied on unsold products.

Even if the "skimming" tax came to the same fifty cents of every dollar now taken by the sum total of all direct and indirect taxes levied—and it shouldn't because of the enormous savings in bureaucratic expense—the advantages of the new system over the old would be enormous.

The American people, for the first time in our nation's history, would know precisely how much money they would be paying in taxes.

Any increase in the federal budget would be reflected in an increase in the rate of skimming, thereby alerting the American people to possibly unwarranted new federal expenditures. The government would have to justify its higher budget or risk electorate wrath.

No tax loopholes would be possible, as is true under the present system.

The cost of maintaining the Internal Revenue Service would be drastically reduced.

No longer would revenues raised from conventionally levied taxes flow directly into a general budget used to pay all government expenses, much of which offers little or no economic benefits to lower income groups.

An adequate portion of the skimming tax would provide the government with its legitimate expenses, including defense, international affairs, law enforcement, special programs like space flights and the development of new sources of energy, etcetera. An additional portion could be set aside for special contingencies.

The skimming tax could be graduated to serve socially beneficial purposes. For example, those goods that make up the "basket" of low income consumers could be skimmed at a lower rate while luxury goods included in the "basket" of high income consumers could be skimmed at a much higher rate. Clothing and food, of paramount concern to low income consumers, would have a lower or even negative skimming rate of taxation. The real purchasing power of the dollar would thus be made higher for low income groups. They could buy far more than they do now. The wealthy, on the other hand, might be less inclined to pay the higher skimming tax on products which only they can afford, such as expensive cars, jewelry, and furs.

The skimming tax could be used to encourage recycling, antipollution measures, conservation of raw materials, and the development of new energy sources. For example, goods made from recycled material could be taxed at a lower skimming rate, while cars with low gas mileage could be taxed at a higher rate. A high skimming tax could be imposed on products detrimental to health, like cigarettes and alcohol.

The rate of skimming could be used to give a much needed shot in the arm to the nation's small- and medium-sized businesses, which number about 13 million and employ fifty-five percent of the private work force. These firms, continuously struggling to hold their own against the giants, could be provided with special incentives by lowering the skimming tax on the goods and services they offer. Such benefit, along with the recommended elimination of corporate taxes extended to all businesses, would go far toward strengthening the competitive position of the small- and medium-sized businesses, which have all been destroyed by present government policy.

The skimming tax could be used to achieve socioeconomic goals which the nation, expressing itself through its elected representatives, would deem important.

By skimming, we could achieve a redistribution of income without directly interfering with the economy or the price structure of production and distribution. Only in peripheral spending, where goods and services leave the realm of production and distribution and enter the realm of households, would skimming appear in the form of a sales tax.

If the budget were to become an election issue, it's logical that the structure of the rate of skimming would also become an election issue. Every American would be concerned with basic problems: How big is the rate of skimming, and how is it structured? For the first time, people in a democratic country would have a say in economic issues which have a direct impact on their standard of living and on the redistribution of their income. This would be real economic democracy.

The rate of skimming depends on two factors: the scope of government outlay, and the growth of the Gross National Product. Obviously, if no attempt is made to curb government expenditure, the rate of skimming, no matter how it is applied, must be high and will go even higher as the government's appetite for spending increases. Concomitantly, if through a lower rate of productivity the Gross National Product declines, again the rate of skimming will have to be high. This is because, given a federal budget accepted by the people, sufficient purchasing power has to be skimmed from consumer income to coincide with the value of the goods and services available.

The rationale of a skimming tax is to skim off surplus purchasing power. As the GNP grows, the skimming tax would continually decline, so long as government expenditures grew more slowly than the growth of the GNP.

It should not be forgotten that the amount of money raised via a skimming tax is simply a device used by government to prevent inflation. That is, the government doesn't actually take the money generated from skimming; it simply makes certain that enough superfluous funds are skimmed off the economy so that there isn't more purchasing power than there are goods and services produced by the private sector. If there was, we would have a rate of inflation in direct proportion to the excess of purchasing power over the GNP.

Also, it should be remembered that government payment for the cost of programs entrusted to it requires no actual money, even though the government has the right to print enough money to satisfy its needs. In the American economy, payments are simply reflected by book entries. It's enough to issue certificates, bonds, or other IOUs. As a practical matter, the Federal Reserve Board would not sell the bonds on the open market, but simply open accounts controlled by the Treasury, in private banks, by depositing checks drawn on the United States government. The Treasury could then use checks drawn on these accounts to pay any expenses that fall within the framework of the federal budget.

A final use of a skimming tax could be to provide much needed expansion capital. This could be done by decreeing a lower rate of skimming generally, which would leave additional funds for expansion. This would result in greater productivity, more jobs, and real economic growth. Compare this with the present policy of greater government deficit spending to "stimulate" the economy via nonproductive programs and the general waste of taxpayer money in areas that contribute nothing to real national wealth.

Revamping the entire American tax system is a long-range project. A more immediate possibility, and one that would do much to encourage economic expansion and the creation of new jobs is the elimination of corporate taxes, the most counterproductive tax ever enacted.

It has already been shown that the more efficient a corporation, the more taxes it pays and, conversely, the less efficient a corporation, the less tax it pays. It is also a fact that in the final analysis the consumer pays all taxes, including corporate ones, because all taxes are included in product prices.

The abolition of corporate taxes combined with the introduction of a national profit-sharing plan, as recommended elsewhere in this book, would be the nation's reward to those who increase the nation's wealth.

The objective in any modern economy is to encourage production; the government should not act as an antistimulus. Yet corporate taxes prevent corporations from using much needed capital for expansion, creating new jobs, replenishing inventory and equipment, and so forth. What's worse, the corporate taxes paid are used to fund nonproductive programs so dear to a politician's heart. And on top of everything, the corporations, desperate for capital, are forced to compete with the federal government in the capital marketplace.

That is economic insanity.

Nor should it be forgotten that with the abolition of corporate taxes, the price of goods would be lessened by the amount of taxes presently calculated in the price. Considering the amount of corporate taxes paid in 1978, and the sum total of consumer goods and services—approximately $1 trillion— the resulting price of goods would be lowered by about four percent.

The creation of new jobs alone, resulting from such a change, would act as an enormous fillip to the economy. The reduction in the rate of unemployment would decrease the payment of unemployment benefits and, more important, give the newly employed a sense of pride and achievement. After all, who, with any self-respect, wants to be the recipient of handouts, be they welfare or unemployment checks?

REDISTRIBUTING THE WEALTH

19

The Social Share

There is nothing wrong with the principle that those who are well-off should contribute to those who are economically unable to fend for themselves. However, like the tax system itself, the scope and methods used by the federal government to effect income redistribution from the productive to the nonproductive sectors of society leave much to be desired.

As noted earlier, there has been a virtual explosion of income transfer programs by the federal government, reaching a dollar value of $250 billion by 1977. This means that for every dollar collected by the federal government in tax receipts, 69 cents is given out in either direct or indirect benefits.

All these funds come out of the pockets of consumers because all taxes are built into the price of goods and services. The irrationality of the system is evident in that even welfare recipients and the unemployed, in their role as consumers, contribute to the very benefits they receive by paying the hidden taxes included in the price of goods. Remember, all revenue from taxation flows directly into a general government budget which is used to pay all government expenses. What kind of economic democracy is it that pours every tax dollar into a general budget which is at the mercy of bureaucrats who decide how to allocate and how much? The beneficiaries of income redistribution go into the marketplace as consumers and pay prices for goods and services which include the $250 billion in taxes used by the federal government for income redistribution.

Funds which should have been earmarked specifically for income transfer beneficiaries are lost in the budget grab-bag.

Suppose no income tax whatsoever existed, but the American people expressed a willingness to aid the indigent and any others genuinely in need of economic assistance. To begin with, common sense dictates that any funds going to such people should not be taken from those whose incomes are marginal to their own needs. A breadwinner with a family of four to support and an income of, say, fifteen thousand dollars a year should not be required to pay taxes specifically earmarked to help those unable to help themselves. Under the present system, not only are all income classes forced to contribute in their role as consumers, but even the recipients of income transfers contribute.

Obviously, real distribution of income must involve *direct transfer* of income. This calls for a system of direct contribution into a special fund, not into the general budget. This fund has nothing to do with the federal budget for meeting its obligations in defense, law enforcement, etcetera.

Lets call it a "social share."

It would be paid as a tax only by those earning in excess of a predetermined amount, and would be progressive.

Unlike conventional taxes, the social share would not be subject to deductions or credits. Thus, there would be no loopholes. Also, there would be no need to involve an already bloated bureaucracy to oversee income transfer programs. Revenues for the social share would be utilized by the state, whose employees are better equipped than those in the federal bureaucracy to judge the needs of a state's residents. The social share would subsidize private institutions that provided free or low-cost services to those needing economic help. This would eliminate the high administrative cost of providing similar services through public agencies.

Taxpayers contributing to the social share would have the satisfaction of knowing exactly how their money was being used, and that it was not financing a massive federal bureaucracy.

The social share would flow to its beneficiaries in the fields of health care, education, public assistance, and so on. There are more than enough private institutions that could handle the flow of direct and indirect benefits. The individual states would simply fix their needed amount of the social share, aid in its distribution, and formulate the rules and guidelines under which it would be used. An important election issue on the state level would be the determination of the structure and purpose of the social share.

The $250 billion that is annually going for income redistribution must be withdrawn from the federal income tax system and replaced with a progressive social share tax applicable above a determined income level. Then with the income transfer budget itself in the hands of nongovernmental organizations and institutions, a long step will have been taken to reduce the federal budget and at the same time genuinely help the economically underprivileged.

Profit Sharing—An Essential Macroeconomic Organ

It's logical to assume that if an economy, through the use of applied science, increases its rate of production, the rate of consumption will rise proportionately.

Logical, but it didn't happen that way.

The problem of bringing consumption into line with production is still an unresolved one in the American economy.

Time and again production has raced far ahead of public ability to consume. In the past the problem was exacerbated by the fact that income was unevenly divided in the country. There was a large number of poor and unemployed who had little or nothing, and a broad mass of wage earners whose income was never enough to absorb the Niagara of goods produced. Boom and bust cycles became progressively shorter, with the bust periods increasingly more severe. While at the same time, production, with technological improvements as the deciding factor, required less time to reach the previous rate of production after every recession.

In the 1930s came the recognition of unemployment as a political factor, and the U.S. government set out to increase employment via deficit spending. Of course, that really didn't cure the malaise of the economy. It simply made the economic situation more tolerable for those who otherwise would have had little hope of getting by. What government should have done but didn't was set up a macroeconomic organ, self-sustaining, that would have allowed consumption to keep pace with production. Instead, government deficit spending, pumping nonproductive funds into the economy, simply became an end in itself. For it to stop would mean depriving its beneficiaries of income, which would have a contracting effect on the economy. In the absence of any better ideas, it was the only policy to follow if political upheaval—the kind that brought communism to power in Russia and nazism in Germany—was to be avoided. And it expanded in scope and volume as politicians discovered the vote-getting powers of deficit spending programs.

While the U.S. government was busy applying Keynesian economic thinking to the economy, the American labor union movement was busy establishing itself as a force in the nation.

And while repudiating Marx, the labor movement played the Marxist game by accepting one of its basic tenets, the antagonism between capital and labor, the theory of the trade-off between profit and wages. The prevailing notion was that any improvement in the standard of living of workers could be achieved only by wresting high profits away from the owners of the means of production.

But even as debilitating labor strikes were wracking the economy, a remarkable phenomenon was observed: The fight for higher wages, shorter working hours, and more humane working conditions was running parallel with economic growth.

Had higher profits and wages resulted only from increased prices, real increases in rewards for all would not have occurred. The struggle for increased wages in the nineteenth century would not have generated pressure for increased productivity if, at that time, it had been possible to raise prices as well as wages. However, the economic system was based on the gold standard, which resulted in a relatively stable price level reflecting the price of gold (or silver). Without this condition of stability, neither *real* wages nor *real* profits could have increased. Nor could *real* accumulation have increased, which is an essential for further investment and increased productivity. The pressure for higher wages would also never have materialized.

It was a vindication of economist Eugen Loebl, who had declared that the essence of economic development since the Industrial Revolution was the application of a higher intellectual level to the economy. This application, through the use of greater technology in production, would increase a nation's wealth along with wages and profits. Marxists said it was impossible, that the higher the profits the lower the rewards for labor, and the other way around. But when wages and profits rose together, it proved Marx's theory of impoverishment, and particularly his labor theory of value and theory of surplus value, was based on fallacious assumptions. The standard of living *could* rise without reduction in profits.

Despite conflict, the underlying movement toward the development of technology, better management, etcetera has been the expression of a common cause between labor and capital in the United States. This common cause has resulted in greater efficiency which has increased the national "pie," providing bigger shares for everyone.

It has been a masked but very real process of profit sharing.

The time is long overdue for the creation of a macroeconomic organ that will ensure the American people of a steady increase in their standard of living without their having to resort to crippling labor strikes or political activism.

It should be accepted from an ethical and not only an economic point of view that all those who, directly or indirectly, contribute to an increase in the nation's wealth should be entitled to a respective share in that wealth. Allowance should be made for the needy, the indigent sick, and the aged, but, as we have seen, in a manner markedly different from the current method of budget allocation.

The solution to consumption keeping pace with production is a national policy of profit sharing.

Profit sharing as a way of rewarding an employee for services rendered over and above salary is not a new concept. It has been applied in tens of thousands of business enterprises with results ranging from good to poor. It was initiated as a management tool to achieve higher productivity and give workers a sense of participation in the success of their company. However, its use has really been nothing more than a managerial gimmick, a voluntary gesture by employers.

It might have been widely adopted by American industry had it not been for the following factors:

1. Debilitating corporate taxes at various levels of government.
2. Demands for higher wages growing out of strong inflationary trends set in motion and fueled by federal government policies.
3. The enormous cost imposed on the private sector by demands for information and compliance with federal regulatory laws.

Because those negative factors are still with us, they have

led to a drastic reduction in productivity, a trend that must be reduced if the nation's economic strength is to be maintained.

The time is propitious to establish profit sharing as a basic element in the American economy.

We're dealing with the matter of consumption keeping pace with production. Further on, we'll deal with the role of government in this situation. Right now, it's important to note some basics:

An increase in production without a corresponding increase in purchasing power leads to economic disruption. The idea of the country being flooded with goods while income remains low or concentrated in too few hands, is irrational. However, any increase in consumption, which is the result of more money being pumped into the economy by the government without any increase in productive efficiency, is inflationary. If people are consuming more but producing less, prices will rise as surely as night follows day. Inflation also results when wages are increased without increased productivity, and even when wages remain stable but productivity decreases. Finally, inflation rages when government spends without economic justification.

All these factors must be considered in setting up a national profit sharing plan.

There is no material wealth except that which nature offers us and which can be transformed into useful wealth by our creative ability and labor. The United States has developed a mature economy that acts as gigantic transformer of natural forces and natural wealth into productive forces and wealth for human use.

This transformer has two components that constitute one entity—the economy. The first is the transformer itself, the means of production in its broadest sense, i.e., capital. The second is labor, both manual and mental, which created the transformer and maintains it.

The conflict between labor and capital (whoever may be the owner of the means of production) is not inherent in the capitalist system, but arises from a misinterpretation and misunderstanding of the essence of such an economy, the Industrial Revolution, and our own mature economy. Fortunately, the unconscious and unintentional cooperation between labor and capital has been instrumental in creating economic progress. This cooperation must be made conscious and intentional.

To do that, the first requisite is to create conditions for a stable purchasing power. *Only under the conditions of stable prices will pressure for higher wages result in increased productivity and greater efficiency.*

The second requisite is that the results of increased productivity must be shared with all those who contribute to it. Since, in practice, the most reliable measure of increased productivity is profit, profit sharing must become the sole and definitive source of increased wages.

The problem of inflation-unemployment must be solved on two levels. The first is the level of the individual enterprise. This is where profit sharing will, in fact, occur. Here, profit sharing is a microeconomic tool and is to be realized through agreement between workers and owners/management in a single business enterprise. But profit sharing also affects workers in other areas because wage increases are always projected into prices. Ultimately, any price increase will backlash and affect even the workers who received the original wage increase. In cases such as strikes by teachers, police, sanitation workers, and health care personnel, a large part of the population is affected and a conflict situation arises between the respective labor union and the nation at large.

Nationwide profit sharing would affect the workings of the whole economic system because it is based on the conviction that rewards must be linked to an increase in productivity. There is no other way to increase *real* income, *real* rewards, than by increasing productivity, as realized in profits. Unless this principle is accepted, stable currency—a primary concern of the economy and a requisite to the elimination of inflation—can't be achieved.

Profit sharing would be a clear-cut indication that employee contributions are appreciated. It would also put pressure on management to improve its performance. In such instance, employees and shareholders would be the ones applying the pressure.

The market doesn't always function as it should, and the pressure of the marketplace is not always enough to force improvement in economic performance. But with employees, management, and shareholders reinforcing each other, we would have an intensive pressure directed toward better economic performance. Labor unions would be expected to concentrate on the issue of efficiency as the only way to help their membership in its dual function as producers and consumers. It makes no sense to push for increased wages for union members only to have them pay for the increased wages as consumers. Presently, wage increases are largely the result of worker militancy and not of higher productivity. Inconsistencies in rewards for work rendered without regard to quality, combined with a currency gradually losing its purchasing power, is not conducive to high worker morale.

Sadly, workers have shown little interest in the efficiency of an enterprise. Profit sharing should correct that.

The present system fails to recognize that the essence of the economy is a network of thinking human beings who create wealth. Instead, the system is based on the assumption of conflict between labor and capital, thus creating conditions detrimental to the common good and to the nation as a whole.

The role of government must be to create preconditions for nationwide profit sharing in a way that doesn't interfere with private enterprise.

As it stands now, the government fiscal policies justify government expenditures and rewards for both labor and business enterprises regardless of any increase in productivity. Nominal profits and nominal wages increase, but real profits and real wages decline, as does the quality of life.

Only through a stable price system can increased wages become real increases, and this must be the responsibility of the federal government.

The government must curtail its interference with the economy while accepting the responsibility for creating a climate for the achievement of optimum economic performance. In the context of the introduction of profit sharing, government budgetary expenses must first be reduced and then stabilized at the reduced level. This would create the condition for stable prices.

There are three basic components of price: Taxes account for roughly fifty percent of the cost of consumer goods; salaries and wages account for about forty percent; and the remaining ten percent is profit.

The task for labor and business enterprise is to create a united front to force the stabilization of government expenditures and to pressure government to reduce those expenditures. As a beginning, pressure must be put upon government to eliminate corporate taxation. It is the most counterproductive tax ever brought into being. Corporate taxation means taking money from efficient corporations—those that show profits— and providing indirect government subsidies for the inefficient companies that show losses, by absolving them of the need to pay taxes. In effect, inefficiency is rewarded.

Exemption from corporate taxes would be dependent on the introduction of profit sharing. However, if any enterprise or whole industry was unwilling to introduce profit sharing, there should be no recourse to legislative force. Profit sharing must become accepted because of its own inherent qualities.

The abolition of corporate taxes and the introduction of nationwide profit sharing would contribute to the stability of purchasing power. This is because profit sharing would be tied to increased productivity but not to any increase in prices. Companies would be freed from the uncertainties of unstable prices, allowing management to arrive at economic decisions based on rational assumptions.

Furthermore, the nation's foreign trade would benefit, inasmuch as stable prices would greatly increase competition in the world market.

The general rules governing profit sharing must be mutually agreed upon by labor, capital, and government, but some suggestions are in order. Only profits not derived from price increases should be exempt from corporate taxation. Corporate reserves, particularly for further investment, must be allocated before there can be any profit sharing. Prior commitments may vary, nevertheless a minimum must be agreed upon in order to be eligible for tax exemption.

Rewards for increased productivity accruing to workers should not be taxed, although government might want to channel profit shares toward certain goals in the interest of solving overall economic problems. For example, the rate of taxation could be reduced on profit shares invested in certain industries of national importance. Thus, investment in certain enterprises could be made attractive, although never compulsory. Also, individual enterprises could offer their employees advantageous terms to reinvest their shares in their own company. In this way the enterprise could accumulate more capital and the employees would develop a greater interest in their own firm. Such a program would be strictly voluntary. This sort of reinvestment program could also be established for whole branches of related enterprises rather than for individual companies only.

One of the most important consequences of profit sharing relates to an essential and major factor in any economy: the socioeconomic and political climate. With profit sharing, the working population as a whole would feel like active participants in the economy and be willing to take on greater responsibilities.

A company and its employees may agree on different forms of profit sharing. Profits could be paid directly to employees annually or semiannually, in cash or stocks. Shares might be deferred until retirement, or paid into a special pension fund. If national interests prevailed, investments might be limited to companies in this country alone. In the case of investment, less or no income at all might be paid out from the profit shares.

A first step would be to establish profit sharing within the present corporate tax structure. Each enterprise would inform its employees of the increase in their share if corporate taxes were abolished. The enterprise and the labor unions would unite and demand say, a twenty percent minimum reduction of corporate taxes for all corporations that introduce profit sharing.

Unless this first step were taken, profit sharing might not be attractive enough to initiate a sociopolitical movement. Without such a movement, real change leading to full employment and a stable currency could hardly take place.

Profit sharing can and should be introduced in nonprofit institutions. In its 1977 annual report, the Federal Reserve Bank of New York reported that managerial innovations led to a greater than ten percent increase in productivity for measurable activities such as check processing and currency handling, while the increase in total expenditures was held to four percent and the work force was reduced by more than six percent.

Profit sharing is not merely a question of wages, but is a projection of the Judeo-Christian philosophy. Even as man has been given creative ability to master nature, so has he been entrusted with ethical responsibility to use his creativity in the spirit of love for his fellow man. We must, therefore, create a socioeconomic environment and system in which profit is the measure of the contribution to the wealth of the nation, and in which profits are shared by all who contribute to its creation.

THIRD-WORLD
ECONOMICS
20

The United States economy is unique in history in its ability to have given Americans the highest standard of living ever enjoyed by any people anywhere. Predictably, such an economy has been the envy of the rest of the world. How to achieve what the Americans achieved? The Marxists thought they had the answer: nationalization in the name of the "people." That would, they believed, harness the fruits of science and technology for everyone. People would be happy to work long hours for low pay to build "socialism." This approach wholly negates the value of the individual and makes economic progress subject to bureaucratic planning. And bureaucrats, no matter what their political affiliations, are not particularly known for their business sense. However, the main reason for the stagnation of Marxist economies is that they give short shrift to aspiring, enterprising individuals who, in free societies, are responsible for creating wealth through their brainpower. Its enough for Marxists that directives are blindly obeyed, even though the results are low productivity, job dissatisfaction, and shoddy merchandise.

Underdeveloped, or Third World countries that succumbed to Marxist blandishments or outright conquest have seen their economies run downhill, but have been unable to make necessary changes because of the ruling totalitarian ideology. Other

Third World countries, more fortunate in that they can experiment and adjust, have developed hybrid economic forms without quite knowing what they're doing. One country may allow small-scale entrepreneurial activity, highly taxed, but no individual or corporate ownership of medium- or large-sized businesses. Another country may permit freedom of operation to foreign multinationals with the bulk of profits going to the state. Then there are countries that have good resources, but a woefully weak administrative infrastructure. Deeply suspicious of foreign domination, they prefer to languish in economic lethargy and periodically apply to the United Nations for "loans."

It took two centuries for the dynamism, intellect, and business acumen of the American system to bear fruit. There is no overnight road to a high standard of living buttressed by an intelligent, well-trained, disciplined administrative infrastructure for any people. A high standard of living can come faster if a country has a commodity greatly in demand by others, like Saudi Arabia with its oil. But should anything happen to disrupt the flow of that commodity, the basic primitiveness of the people quickly becomes apparent and the economy soon stagnates.

The American economy achieved what it did through a combination of human, geographical, and political factors. It was doubly blessed by the fact that government interference in the economy was minimal as long as it was. When bureaucracy coupled with mechanistic thinking began to assert itself more and more, productivity fell, apathy grew, inflation rose, and the standard of living began to decline. There is a lesson here for Third World countries, but it isn't one that states the best economy is the one where government interference is least. What the role of government in an economy should be depends on many factors, but the important thing is that government should help, not hinder. In Japan the government helps the business sector develop markets on the correct assumption that this adds to the wealth (gain) of the nation; in the United States the federal government has become the single greatest impediment to business development and expansion. Obviously, every country must determine what steps its government should take to aid the economy.

The rock-bottom base for economic thinking, applicable to both advanced and underdeveloped countries, should be the Judeo-Christian concept of the value of the individual. This should take precedence over industrialization, growth of the Gross National Product, and the profit motive. Even with the best of intentions, any system that negates human initiative and aspirations, and disregards traditions and cultural heritage in favor of increasing the GNP must in time become a bureaucratic, dehumanized thing. This happens when the economy is perceived as a system of economic aggregates and not of human beings. The highest value in this system is to produce more goods with a lower input, with the result of maximum profits. Whether the profits accrue to the individual, corporation, or state depends on the prevalent political system, but the end inhumane result is the same under any system, except that it is more pronounced where totalitarian rule puts the individual at the complete mercy of the state.

The tragedy of many Third World countries—and of Iran— is that they chose to go the route of an increased GNP without regard for the cultural, social, and spiritual continuum of their respective societies. The elite benefit, but a spiritual and moral vacuum is created that breeds enormous frustration in the masses. This doesn't mean that industrialization shouldn't be pursued, just not as the all-important end in itself.

The Indian economy is an example of what the aforementioned type of fallacious economic thinking can cause.

After thirty years of industrialization, only some 60 or 70 million people out of a total of 650 million in India have adequate purchasing power. Uncounted millions have died of starvation, and hundreds of millions live below poverty level.

The social fabric of the country is disrupted, and the nation has become effectively divided into two different type economies. The Stalinist concept of planned development of heavy industry—to the virtual exclusion of other considerations—plus the Keynesian concept of government interference and spending has for decades absorbed the best brains of the country. Agriculture and the small peasant have been shamefully neglected in the pursuit of a dehumanizing industrialization.

Many Indians blame the first Prime Minister of free India, Jawaharlal Nehru, for the predicament India finds itself in today. They harken back to India's most revered personage, Gandhi, who admonished that agriculture and village industry should be India's number one priority. He believed that this emphasis would bring about a higher standard of living for the masses and a self-reliant society. However, Nehru, Gandhi's successor, believed differently. He was enamored of the Marxist-Stalinist approach that decreed the speedy development of heavy industry. In January 1956 he made the following statement before the Indian National Development Council:

> In the meeting of the Standing Committee, greater stress was laid on the heavy machine-making industry being encouraged, as it was said to be the basis of industrial growth. If you do not do that, then naturally industrial growth is delayed. There is one approach which has sometimes been put forward: that you should build up your consumer goods industries and gradually save money thereby, and build up something else, thereby getting some more employment. That, I believe, from the point of view of planning is a discarded theory completely. Of course, it does some good here and there; I would not enter into the details but this approach is not a planned approach at all. If you want India to industrialize and to go ahead, as we must, as is essential, then you must industrialize and not potter about with old little factories producing hair oil and the like—it is totally immaterial what the things are, whether they are small or big consumer articles. You must go to the root and the base and build up the structure of industrial growth. Therefore,

*it is the heavy industries that count; nothing else counts,
excepting as a balancing factor, which is, of course, important. We want planning for heavy machine-making industries and heavy industries, we want industries that will make
heavy machines and we should set about them as rapidly
as possible because it takes time.*

In April 1956 the government laid down by way of a formal
resolution, known as the Industrial Policy Resolution, that in
order to realize the objective of "a socialistic pattern of society,"
it was essential to accelerate the rate of economic growth, speed
up industrialization, particularly develop heavy and machine-
making industries, expand the "public sector," and build up a
large and growing cooperative sector. The resolution was
embodied in the second five-year plan.

Jawaharlal Nehru made his position very clear in his speech
delivered at the meeting of the All-India Congress Committee
held in Chandigarh on September 28, 1959. He said: "The
primary thing about an integrated plan was production and not
employment. Employment was important, but it was utterly
unimportant in the context of production. It followed production and not preceded production. And production would only
go up by better techniques which mean modern methods."

In the long run, it was assumed by Nehru and his advisers,
the rate of industrialization and growth of national economy
would depend on the increasing production of coal, electricity,
iron and steel, heavy machinery, heavy chemicals, and heavy
industries generally, which would increase the capacity for
capital formation. It was conceded that heavy industries required
large amounts of capital and a long gestation period; but, the
argument ran, without them India would continue importing
not only producer goods, but even essential consumer goods
which would hamper accumulation of capital within the country.
The heavy industries must, therefore, be expanded speedily.
That is why all the five-year plans, except the first, were based
on the premise that heavy industry was fundamental to rapid

growth, that its expansion largely determined the pace at which the economy could become self-reliant and self-generating, and that it would in turn stimulate the growth of medium- and small-scale industry, producing its components and utilizing its products, and thus ultimately provide a larger employment potential. The strategy governing planning was to industrialize the country quickly, and that meant the basic heavy industries being given priority.

The Industrial Policy Resolution of the Indian government accepted in April 1956 aimed at the realization of a "socialist pattern of society." Under the resolution, it was essential to accelerate the rate of economic growth, speed up industrialization, develop heavy and machine tool industry, and expand the public sector. This resolution was embodied in the second five-year plan.

Nehru's philosophy, and for that matter, the Indian government's economic philosophy, are actually the application of the Stalinist concept to India. The real issue is, whether this concept is at all rational and can achieve real economic growth, and whether it is applicable to the specific conditions existing in India.

Forced industrialization for post-revolution Russia had been a political imperative, surrounded as it was by a hostile world. Also, heavy industry had to be developed for military considerations as well. Since there was no free market and all means of production were owned by the state, the state was entrusted to run the economy, which could only be done via detailed planning. Nehru never accepted the totalitarian aspects of Stalinism, but did accept certain of its economic policies, specifically those having to do with massive industrialization no matter what the cost in human misery and societal disruptions.

Fortunately, the enormous concentration of economic and political power that existed in Russia didn't take place in India. A strong private enterprise system existed in India, and still exists. But this inadvertently created a problem for state planners like Nehru, who were confronted with a lack of enforcement powers that is an essential part of centralized planning. The private enterprise sector in India has historically operated as an infrastructure within a planned economy, based on the philosophy that the government is an operative economic body as well as being a policy-making body.

As it does in the United States, in India the power of the government greatly affects the private sector. The monetary system, including the banking system, is nationalized, and this limits freedom of enterprise. Only large corporations that have the power to influence government are able to create some limited freedom of enterprise.

In effect, what transpired in India is that the economy managed to combine negative aspects of both Marxist and free enterprise economics, with disastrous results. Even if Indian economists had chosen one system to the complete exclusion of the other, the absence of the guiding motivation of respect for human values within the economic framework would have effected the scope of the economic disaster that occurred, but not the disaster itself.

The remarkable phenomenon is that in the realm of politics, India has applied the most humane philosophy to its people—the Gandhian one that puts man at the center of all considerations. Amazingly, the followers of Gandhi never projected their leader's philosophy into the economic sphere. Gandhi's humanism was able to mobilize a whole nation to fight for its freedom and human dignity, but then came the economic planners and the state became all-powerful. The planners were faced with the question of what value should determine economic priorities. Should it be simple economic growth based on maximizing the input-output ratio or should the primary concern be with human beings? To choose the first alternative is to opt for massive and rapid industrialization. The fact that tens of millions of people would starve or live in abject poverty, as was the case in Russia, would simply be a price paid for this policy.

On the other hand, if the basic needs of India's masses were the central consideration, then different priorities were in order. Economic tools were called for that would eliminate poverty, hunger and unemployment but maintain human dignity and freedom.

The combination of Stalinist and Keynesian concepts led India far astray. A process of economic dehumanization was instituted.

Had Indian economists begun with humane considerations, they would have first concentrated on improving the standard of living of the rural population. India was, at the time it gained its freedom from the British, primarily an agricultural country. The objective should have been to create independent small farms, to support village industry, to educate farmers, and to create economic institutions like farmer's banks. The hundreds of millions of Indian peasants should have been mobilized to improve the standards of agricultural production. The role of the government should have been to supply the peasants with inexpensive commercial credits and to provide scientific aid in irrigation methods. The profit derived from this approach would not be something measured in currency, but in "gain," the tangible benefits derived by society as a whole. Farmers might not have made a profit, but they wouldn't starve. Village industry would become a part of an exchange economy. Whatever part of the crop could be sold at any profit at all would serve to purchase industrial products and thus help that sector of the market.

Even such problems as India's abnormal population growth could have been better handled had a more humane viewpoint dominated.

It must be remembered that voluntary population control requires, above all, a certain level of intellect. In its absence, and where unemployment and harsh poverty are the rule, a large family is a form of security against the batterings of economic hardships. Parents will need many children to help support them in their old age. The recognition of these circumstances should have fostered creative approaches to the problem. But all that happened was that hundreds of millions of people in this unfortunate state were simply neglected. Industrialization was all that mattered, and a better life for all was supposed to flow therefrom. A people who lose faith in their system automatically turn to whatever else is available. We may accuse Marxism of capitalizing on a deplorable situation and prove that its system is infinitely worse, but that doesn't deter people dissatisfied with their lot from listening to the blandishments of totalitarians. They may even vote these enemies of civilization into power through sheer rage and frustration with their system of government, not realizing that they are trading a mild form of dehumanization for a much more virulent one.

The problem of humanizing the Indian economy is even more urgent now than it was thirty years ago, and far more difficult considering how far India has strayed into statism. There are now actually three different economies existing side by side in India. There is a fairly modern state-owned heavy industry with a state-owned banking system, both subject to central planning. Second, there is private industry that operates within the framework of a government-run economy. Freedom in this sector is limited by a licensing system subject to severe government regulations. The third economy is agricultural, and embraces the overwhelming majority of working people. Here is where one finds the extraordinary poverty, unemployment, and misery in India. Agriculture is not properly integrated into the economy: It is a sort of pariah that is tolerated, nothing more.

In Europe, the concept of free enterprise has generally meant freedom from medieval restrictions on business, and it came into being when agricultural production was in the process of being superceded by industrial production. In India, the concept of free enterprise, i.e., the philosophy of laissez-faire, can be introduced with great potential into the agricultural sector of the economy, which includes some seventy percent of the population. The agricultural system would be based on small enterprises where the worker owns his own parcel of land. It is true that small agricultural enterprises, generally speaking, cannot apply modern agrotechniques and that production per capita is far lower than the kind of huge agricultural units that exist in the United States. But this is only one criterion. For countries like India the limiting factor is land, and consequently labor-intensive agriculture is the most important issue. Production per acre and not per capita is the decisive problem.

Products of modern agrochemistry and agrobiology, like fertilizers and seeds, and also technology like irrigation can be used in small farms as well. It is also possible to make use of certain types of agrotechnology like tractors, combines, etcetera on the basis of free cooperatives, where whole villages or a group of villagers would own or hire modern technology.

According to Charan Singh (*India's Economic Policy: The Gandhian Blueprint*, Vicas Publishing House, Ltd., New Delhi) "the ceiling on present possession of land should be imposed at a level not more than 27.5 acres per adult workers (including wife and minor children) and the area thus available is to be distributed to those who possess less than 2.5 acres" . . . "floor is laid at 2.5 acres and is not to be reduced below 2.5 acres." Actually, even within the limits set by Charan Singh, the concept of small enterprise could be even more narrow. The proportion doesn't have to be 1.1 (2.5 to 27.5) but rather 1.2, or, 2.5 acres to 5 acres, even if the maximum is set at 27.5 acres. This means that under the present conditions the main concern must be with those who are within the limit of 2.5 to 5 acres.

The following guidelines could prove immensely useful in determining agricultural policy for India:

Peasants will own the land on which they work, and this land will range in size from 2.5 to 5 acres.

These peasants will represent free enterprise in the classical sense of the term. They will pay no taxes and will not be subject to any rules or regulations, either from the local or central government.

They will be entitled to inexpensive credits at two or three percent interest with which to buy seed, fertilizer, tools, and participate in the cost of irrigation. They will be entitled to repay loans with their own products.

Kisan (peasant) banks should be established, banks that will lend exclusively to small peasant landowners. These banks could service one or more village groups. Besides being lenders, the banks would also act as economic advisers to the peasantry. It would be the duty of government to deposit its IOUs in the central bank, which would then extend credit to the Kisan banks for loans to peasants.

Small village industries would, like the peasants, be free from any taxes, and not be subject to government regulatory interference.

Of great importance is not to view the village economy as a mere economic phenomenon, but as a human problem, one in which consideration must be given to such human factors as habits and custom, initiative, and self-reliance.

Once a humane approach is taken, the types of solutions to questions will be predicated on concern for humans first, and growth of the GNP only incidentally. Typical questions might be: How should the system of peasant banks be established? What should be their structure? What should be the relationship of the central government to the banks? How should village industry be organized? How should a movement supporting village industry be organized? What should the role of cooperatives be? How are an exchange and regular village market to be organized? How should agricultural sales in the existing markets be organized?

The Indian example is the kind of thinking that can and

must be applied to every underdeveloped economy, taking into account the specifics of each country. The imperative is to begin with the Judeo-Christian regard for the individual and work outward from that. For underdeveloped countries to saddle themselves either with Marxist economics or Western Keynesian concepts would be to become the prisoners of dehumanized totalitarianism, in the former instance, and dehumanized economic thinking with built-in inflation, in the latter. Neither way is acceptable in a world that cries out for economic stability and security with no sacrifice of human rights.

EPILOGUE

As political systems throughout the centuries have discovered, one of the most potent forces in society is bureaucratic inertia. Once bureaucracy starts out to implement the policies of the government in power, the whole apparatus acquires a life of its own. In a democracy like that of the United States, this means that presidents and administrations come and go but the bureaucracy remains and relentlessly keeps expanding. The president proposes, the Congress enacts, and then the bureaucracy takes over, and woe betide the enterprise or individual who tries to buck the system.

Concepts presented in this book do buck the system, and one may expect hostility or, just as bad, indifference. When bureaucratic jobs and pet programs are at stake, such reactions are inevitable.

Only an aroused public, forcing issues by exercising economic democracy, can bring about needed changes. It was true in California, where it took Howard Jarvis and Proposition 13 to shake the state government out of its taxing habits; and it will be true if and when the American people act to make the federal government heed their wishes.

Americans want an end to inflation. They want stable prices, an equitable tax system, the halt of bureaucratic harassment, and the right to determine what the role of government in the economy should be.

The ways to meet these goals are outlined in this book. Some concepts, like a new system of taxation, are long-range projects; others can be implemented immediately. These are:

The introduction of a system of government lending—the extending of government-backed credit via the commercial banking system. A beginning could be made with small business enterprises, and the housing construction and energy industries.

The elimination of federal corporate taxes, concomitant with incentives for corporations to institute profit sharing plans based on increased employee productivity.

Pressure on the government to eliminate and/or cut back on regulatory agencies, roll back minimum wage laws, and place a moratorium on social programs. Many subsidies could be eliminated or reduced, many "temporary" programs stopped that no longer serve their original purpose, and many programs eliminated that have no current useful purpose.

All the above steps would effectively contribute to price stabilization, and result in an immediate reduction of the federal budget.

The main programs of the federal budget, as well as off-budget programs, should be made election issues.

A longer-range project involves the replacement of the present federal income tax system with a single skimming tax imposed at the final product point of sale, with skimming rates dependent on the nature of the product.

The skimming tax, as well as the concept of the social share, should also be election issues.

Given the determination of the American people to make the federal government their servant, economic democracy can become reality.

Economic democracy leads to sanity. The other road, the one we are currently traveling, leads to collapse.

INDEX

334

Equal Employment Opportunity
Commission (EEOC), 14, 17–18,
31–33, 249
Euromarkets, Eurodollars, 278
Evolution of Economic Thought, The
(Oser), 160
Exchange economy, 119–121, 125, 181,
204, 205, 214, 252, 255, 265–266,
271, 326

Failure of the New Economics, The
(Hazlitt), 221
Faraday, Michael, 139
Fascism, 173
Fate, Greek idea, and modern science,
137
Federal Energy Administration (FEA),
61, 62–63, 64
Federal Financing Bank, 42–43, 297
Federal Home Loan Bank Board, 34
Federal National Mortgage Association,
42
Federal Open Market Committee, 268
Federal Power Commission (FPC), 58,
61, 64
Federal Register, 115
Federal Reserve (FED), 267–269, 272,
275, 276, 284
Federal Reserve Bank of New York,
318
Federal Reserve Board, 42, 110, 304
Federal Trade Commission (FTC), 14,
18–19, 24, 28–30, 250
Feldstein, Martin, 294–295
Feuerbach, Ludwig, 176–177
Food and Drug Administration, 24
Food stamps, 47
Ford Foundation Energy Policy Project,
75
Ford, Gerald Rudolph; Ford
administration, 13, 62, 99, 295
Ford, Henry, 14–21
Fortune, 42, 54, 65, 111, 131
Free competition, 118–121
Free society, 3, 115–116, 119–122
Friedman, Milton, 65, 109, 112, 113,
115–128, 265, 272, 299
and monetary policy, 125–128
fallacies of, 118–125

Gain, 247, 251–264, 326
and profit, 254–255, 257, 259, 260
protection of, 259–262, 264, 284
scope and properties, 256–260
source of nation's wealth, 252–253,
255
Galbraith, John Kenneth, 99, 101,
128–130
Galileo Galilei, 137
Gandhi, Mohandas K., 322, 325
Garfinkel, Irwin, 48
Garrett, Garet, 235
Gas, natural, 58–59, 60–61, 64, 65

Gasoline, 27–28, 58, 67, 69, 70, 71
General Motors Corporation, 22
General Systems theory, 141
Gilpin, Robert, 279
Giscard d'Estaing, Valéry, 4
God and creation, 138, 148, 160, 166
Gold standard, 128, 235, 266, 311
Gossen, Herman, 133, 214
Gournay, Sieur de, 149
Government, economic role of, 3, 105,
107, 111, 112, 115, 128–130, 131,
159, 237, 300, 312
and protection of gain, 261–264
and varying factors, 320–321
as servant, not master, 246–249
borrowing, 274
Friedman's view, 115–128
redistribution of income, 315–316
regulatory demands, 11, 110
spending, 6–8, 9, 13, 41, 50, 82,
94, 102, 107, 108, 112, 114,
115, 128–129, 248, 249, 274,
291, 295, 297–298, 300, 303,
310, 313
(*See also* Bureaucracy; Energy
problem; Keynes; Lending;
Mercantilism; Planned
economy; Regulatory agencies;
Transfer payments)
Gramm, W. Philip, 59–60, 61, 69,
79–80
Gross National Product, 8, 10, 43, 50,
83, 85, 86, 193, 259, 284
and human questions, 321, 329
and small enterprises, 280
and taxes, 288, 289, 292, 303
Russian, 208
Guzzardi, Walter, 111

Haldane, Richard Burdon, 159
Hart, Gary, 299–300
Hazlitt, Henry, on Keynes, 221, 223,
224–225, 229–230, 235
Health Maintenance Organizations
(HMOs), 95
Health plan, national, 13, 81–96
alternatives, 94–95
and hospital costs, 87–89
cost, 81–82, 91, 92
examples in other countries, 84–86
Hegel, Georg Wilhelm Friedrich,
175–177, 179
Heisenberg, Werner, 140
Heller, Walter W., 99, 108, 113–115,
265, 296
Hertz, Heinrich R., 139
Hesse, Don, 22
Hickman, Frederick W., 294
Hildebrand, Bruno, 213
Hitler, Adolf, 142, 212, 215, 229
Hobbes, Thomas, 137
Holism, 141, 174
Hoover, Herbert, 38

335

Horney, Karen: *Neurosis and Human Growth,* 186
Hospital Association of New York State, 88
House Banking Committee, 282
House Energy and Power Subcommittee, 77
Housing, 281–283, 332
Hudson Institute, 49, 50
Human Events, 61, 63, 69, 79–80

Income transfer payments (*see* Transfer payments)
Indeterminacy, 140
India's Economic Policy (Singh), 328
Individual, value of, 321, 330
Industrial Revolution, 134, 135, 142, 144, 147, 151–157, 161, 162, 167, 169–170, 181–183, 184, 190, 197, 201, 205, 206, 212, 233, 252, 253, 256–257, 259, 262, 266, 311, 314
an intellectual revolution, 152, 155–156
Inflation, 3, 4, 5–11, 44, 78, 88–89, 93, 96, 108, 110–113, 131, 211, 226, 230, 234, 237, 243, 249, 262, 273, 274, 281, 288–289, 295, 296, 298–300, 303, 330
and bureaucracy, 39–44
and government lending, 278–279
and price and wage controls, 98, 101–102
and regulatory agencies, 24, 27, 33, 35
and unemployment, 48–49, 55, 107, 112, 114, 136, 222, 314–315
and welfare, 45–46, 52–53, 55
causes, 313
Heller's view, 113–115
review of data, 9–11
Institute for Research on Poverty, 48
Institute for Socioeconomic Studies, 10, 46
Institute for the Study of the USSR (Munich), 187
Integration, productive, 166, 180–181
Interest rates, 268, 272, 275
Internal Revenue Service (IRS), 287, 301
Inventory of Federal Income Transfer Programs, An, 46
Investment, inadequate, 3, 8, 23, 219–220, 226, 229, 230, 233, 236

Jackson, Andrew, 38
Jarvis, Howard, 331
Jensen, Michael C., 130
Jevons, William Stanley, 214
John Paul II, Pope, 243
Johnson, David R., 23
Johnson, Lyndon Baines; Johnson administration, 38, 87, 108
Jones, Mary Gardiner, 29
Jones, Sidney, 42

Journal of the Institute for Socioeconomic Studies, 89
Judeo-Christian philosophy, 138, 141–142, 170, 318, 321

Kahn, A. E., 75
Kaufman, Henry, 4, 272–273
Kautsky, Karl, 178
Kemp, Jack E., 109, 291
Kemp-Roth bill, 109
Kennedy, Edward, his health plan, 81, 82, 84, 89, 92–93
Kennedy, John F.; Kennedy administration, 108
Kepler, Johannes, 148
Keynes, John Maynard; Keynesian economy, 6, 39, 40, 53, 99, 105, 112–116, 126, 128, 130–132, 136, 148, 151–152, 157, 181, 206, 215–238, 260, 330
aggregates, 224
and classical economists, 215–218
and debasement of currency, 7–8, 111, 226, 236
and deficit spending, 219, 220–223, 226, 228, 236, 237, 322
and full employment, 225–226
emphasis on savings, 231–233, 236
employment and production, 219–220, 233–235
fallacies, 112
flaws and contradictions, 228–231, 235
good and bad features, 236–238
Roosevelt's application, 227–228
simplistic, 223–225, 234
slippery and vague, 220–221
writings:
General Theory, 217, 225, 235, 238
Treatise on Money, 225
Kisan banks, 329
Knies, Karl, 133, 213
Knudsen, Christian, 64
Kolyma—the Arctic Death Camps (Conquest), 198
Krauss, Melvyn B., 49, 293
Kripke, Homer, 33
Kuhn, Alfred, 141

Labor and wealth, 251–253
Labor costs, 116–117
Labor Department, 32, 33
Labor for Welfare Reform, 48
Labor, mental and manual, 206–207
Labor unions, 116–117, 121, 224, 225, 226, 234, 242, 315, 318
strikes, 314
Laffer, Arthur B.; Laffer Curve, 109–110
Laissez-faire, 149, 170, 218, 229, 327–328
(*See also* Smith, Adam)
Laplace, Pierre Simon de, 138